LIBRARY OF HEBREW BIBLE/ OLD TESTAMENT STUDIES

650

Formerly Journal for the Study of the Old Testament Supplement Series

T&T CLARK · LIBRARY OF BIBLICAL STUDIES ·

SOTS AT 100

Centennial Essays of the Society for Old Testament Study

Edited by
John Jarick

t&tclark
LONDON • NEW YORK • OXFORD • NEW DELHI • SYDNEY

T&T CLARK
Bloomsbury Publishing Plc
50 Bedford Square, London, WC1B 3DP, UK
1385 Broadway, New York, NY 10018, USA

BLOOMSBURY, T&T CLARK and the T&T Clark logo are
trademarks of Bloomsbury Publishing Plc

First published in Great Britain 2017
Paperback edition first published 2018

Cover design: Irene Martinez Costa
Cover image: Detail from Corpus Christi College MS 10, fol. 2r

A catalogue record for this book is available from the British Library.

Library of Congress Cataloging-in-Publication Data
Names: Jarick, John, editor.
Title: SOTS at 100 : centennial essays of the Society for Old Testament Study / edited by John Jarick.
Other titles: SOTS at one hundred
Description: New York : Bloomsbury T&T Clark, 2017. | Series: The library of Hebrew Bible/Old Testament studies ; volume 650 | Includes bibliographical references and index.
Identifiers: LCCN 2016050076 (print) | LCCN 2016050846 (ebook) | ISBN 9780567673640 (hb : alk. paper) | ISBN 9780567673657 (epdf)
Subjects: LCSH: Society for Old Testament Study–History.
Classification: LCC BS411 .S68 2017 (print) | LCC BS411 (ebook) | DDC 221.06/01–dc23
LC record available at https://lccn.loc.gov/2016050076

ISBN: HB: 978-0-5676-7364-0
PB: 978-0-5676-8357-1
ePDF: 978-0-5676-7365-7

Series: Library of Hebrew Bible/Old Testament Studies, volume 650

Typeset by Forthcoming Publications (www.forthpub.com)

CONTENTS

PREFACE

The Society for Old Testament Study was inaugurated in London on 3rd January 1917, and accordingly celebrates its Centenary in 2017. For one hundred years now it has been exercising its role—in the words of its Statement of Aims—as 'a learned society of professional scholars and others committed to the study of the Old Testament' which 'sees its task as serving the varying needs [of its membership] for support of their scholarly activities in Old Testament studies' and 'as having special responsibility for promoting Old Testament studies in the United Kingdom and the Republic of Ireland' through such activities as 'organizing meetings, commissioning and promoting publications, …and representing scholars of the Old Testament on other academic bodies'.

The present volume marks the occasion of the Centenary of SOTS by looking back over these first hundred years of activities and developments, taking stock of various aspects of the Society at this point in time, and looking forward to further developments in the field of Old Testament/ Hebrew Bible studies.

The contributors to this collection of centennial essays have all been long-serving officers of the Society, who between them constitute some sixty years of service to SOTS (or indeed seventy years, if the additional years on the committee as president-elect and past-president are included in the cases of the five presidential individuals among them): an unbroken sequence of Secretaries of the Society—David Clines (Secretary 1977–82 [and later 'Foreign Secretary' 2005–12]), Adrian Curtis (1983–88), Paul Joyce (1989–94), Katharine Dell (1995–2000), and John Jarick (2000–2009)—plus Ronald Clements (who served as 'Foreign Secretary' 1974–81) and Eryl Davies (who has served as the Society's Archivist since 2012).

Each of these essayists has brought a particular focus to their considerations of the Society's first hundred years and beyond: the antecedents of the 1917 foundation of SOTS in the case of the opening essay by Ronald Clements, the unfolding history of SOTS from then until now in the major narrative undertaken by Eryl Davies, a record of the Society's meetings and officers and sundry activities in the timeline compiled by John Jarick, a consideration of trends in Old Testament studies as seen (under the scrutiny of David Clines) in the papers that have been read at meetings and (under the scrutiny of Adrian Curtis) in the Society's publications over the years, a consideration of aspects of the guild of Old Testament scholars as seen (under the scrutiny of Katharine Dell) in membership statistics and surveys, and finally some considerations of the prospects for the future of the Society itself and of the study of the Old Testament/Hebrew Bible more broadly in the concluding essay by Paul Joyce.

I am grateful to each of the contributors for their excellent work on this range of celebrative topics. I also wish to thank the Library of Hebrew Bible/Old Testament Studies for agreeing to publish the volume, and the various staff at Bloomsbury who have been involved in its production, especially the production editor (and SOTS member) Duncan Burns for his splendid work on the project.

When SOTS 'came of age' in 1938 and celebrated twenty-one years of its existence, its 'Senior Secretary' Theodore Robinson wrote (in an Appendix to the volume *Record and Revelation: Essays on the Old Testament by Members of the Society for Old Testament Study*, edited by Wheeler Robinson) the following words which surely resonate again as the Society now celebrates one hundred years: 'The Society for Old Testament Study can look back on a history of steady progress and of successful activity in many directions. It has done its work quietly, and without ostentation, but it has unremittingly pursued its object in the promotion of Old Testament studies. While the present volume of essays represents its general work and interests, and commemorates twenty-one years [or as we can now say in this new volume: one hundred years] of development and achievement, it should serve also as an earnest of yet greater prosperity and usefulness for many years to come.'

John Jarick

CONTRIBUTORS

Ronald E. Clements, Emeritus Samuel Davidson Professor of Old Testament at King's College London; 'Foreign Secretary' of SOTS 1974–81 and President in 1985.

David J.A. Clines, Emeritus Professor of Biblical Studies at the University of Sheffield; Secretary of SOTS 1977–82, President in 1996, and 'Foreign Secretary' 2005–12.

Adrian Curtis, formerly Senior Lecturer in Hebrew Bible Studies at the University of Manchester; Secretary of SOTS 1983–88 and President in 2016.

Eryl W. Davies, Professor and Head of the School of Philosophy and Religion at Bangor University; Archivist of SOTS since 2012 and President in 2013.

Katharine J. Dell, Reader in Old Testament Literature and Theology at the University of Cambridge, and Fellow of St Catharine's College; Secretary of SOTS 1995–2000.

John Jarick, Lecturer in Old Testament at Regent's Park and Mansfield Colleges, Oxford; Secretary of SOTS 2000–2009 and *Book List* Editor from 2017.

Paul M. Joyce, Samuel Davidson Professor of Old Testament/Hebrew Bible at King's College London; Secretary of SOTS 1989–94 and President for the centennial year of 2017.

Abbreviations

ACATE	Association of Centres of Advanced Theological Education
BAJS	British Association for Jewish Studies
BBC	British Broadcasting Corporation
BHS	*Biblia Hebraica Stuttgartensia*
BZAW	Beihefte zur *Zeitschrift für die alttestamentliche Wissenschaft*
EC	Epworth Commentaries
HB	Hebrew Bible
ICC	International Critical Commentary
IOSOT	International Organization for the Study of the Old Testament
JEH	*Journal of Ecclesiastical History*
JBL	*Journal of Biblical Literature*
JSOT	*Journal for the Study of the Old Testament*
JSOTSup	*Journal for the Study of the Old Testament* Supplement Series
JTS	*Journal of Theological Studies*
LHBOTS	Library of Hebrew Bible/Old Testament Studies
NCBC	New Century Bible Commentary
NEB	New English Bible
OT	Old Testament
OTW	Oudtestamentisch Werkgezelschap
SBL	Society of Biblical Literature
SCM	Student Christian Movement
SOAS	School of Oriental and African Studies
SOTS	Society for Old Testament Study
SPCK	Society for Promoting Christian Knowledge
TBC	Torch Bible Commentaries
VT	*Vetus Testamentum*
YMCA	Young Men's Christian Association
ZAW	*Zeitschrift für die alttestamentliche Wissenschaft*

The Origins of the Society for Old Testament Study: Cultural, Political and Religious Antecedents

Ronald E. Clements

The Society for Old Testament Study met for the first time in the hostel of King's College London in January 1917, following a resolution and circular letter to potential members agreed by a small group of scholars meeting in the rooms of Canon R.H. Kennett in Queens' College, Cambridge in the summer of 1916. This meeting was itself a response to a suggestion put forward earlier by a group of examiners for the University of Wales meeting earlier in that year. The origins of a need for a society of persons meeting to discuss a common interest in the study of the Old Testament can be traced back more than a century earlier to the Napoleonic invasion of Egypt in 1798.[1] This military venture had far-reaching cultural ambitions and ultimately led to the renewal of western European access to Egypt and the Eastern Mediterranean—territories which were at that time under the control of the Ottoman Empire. The consequent political arrangements provided British and American access to the lands of the Bible which opened a path for research in the region and the beginning of archaeological excavation there. This renewed interest in the lands of the Middle East was linked to reawakened interest in Christian missions to Jews and the possibility of Jewish resettlement in their ancestral homeland.

1. *The Cultural Background in Great Britain*

By 1917 these developments were already past history, but they marked the beginning of greatly increased interest in Christian concern with the Old Testament. The freer access into Ottoman (Muslim) territory opened

1. Cf. Juan Cole, *Napoleon's Egypt: Invading the Middle East* (New York and Basingstoke: Palgrave Macmillan, 2007).

the path to fresh information about the manner of life of the peoples of the Bible and the geography of the region which fitted well with the emphasis on historical issues encouraged by the European Enlightenment. The uniqueness of the Bible as a divinely revealed rule-book for a Christian society came under intense criticism in the wake of the French Revolution, when belief in the divine origin of the moral foundations of social order took centre stage.

Taken together these critical interests generated a cluster of academic reasons why Christian commitment to the Old Testament came under strong critical scrutiny throughout the nineteenth century to an extent that had no real precedent. The authorship of key biblical books ascribed to traditional figures such as Moses, David and Solomon no longer appeared certain, or even credible. In what way was the Bible unique? A range of new questions called out for answers and the gap between the insights and conclusions of church-based scholars and those of an increasingly well-informed secular readership widened. To add to the confusion new discoveries of the earth's geology cast serious doubt on biblically based calculations about the age of the earth. Fossils were testimony to an age that preceded by millennia the biblical reports of creation a mere few thousand years BCE.

Moreover, at a popular level, the Old Testament figured prominently in one of the great success stories in the social history of the nineteenth century. This was the Sunday School movement that had begun in the 1780s as a predominantly lay enterprise to provide free education for poorer children in the basic skills of reading and writing on the day of the week which tradition had declared to be distinct and 'holy'.[2] By the middle of the next century Nonconformist churches in particular had eagerly embraced this movement, seeking to strengthen its religious character by introducing a firm moral emphasis. This used the Bible as a textbook illustrating responsible citizenship and sought to lift the spiritual horizons of young people to embrace the ideals of a worldwide Christian mission. To achieve these ends a variety of schemes and teaching guides focused on the Bible which soon gained precedence over older forms of catechetical teaching. This enabled Sunday Schools to emphasize personal character formation and moral responsibility; teachers were often themselves young persons, brought up through the schools with little, if any, special training for their new role. A simple technique of allegorizing morally difficult stories was enough to satisfy these broad aims. Biblical personalities were presented as virtuous heroes and leaders.

2. P.B. Cliff, *The Rise and Development of the Sunday School Movement in England, 1780–1980* (Redhill, Surrey: National Christian Education Council, 1986).

In consequence many well-meaning teachers devised their own ways of interpreting difficult texts. This was particularly the case where warfare and violence were concerned.

Overall, Sunday Schools were not concerned with biblical scholarship, or with explaining the gulf which separated humanity's violent past from the modern era—a feature encouraged by the foreshortened perspective on the length of humankind's life on earth which the biblical chronology offered. Sunday Schools had greater appeal for Nonconformist churches rather than the established national Church of England, but taken together they aimed to promote the ideal of Great Britain as a 'Christian' nation, embracing biblical values. The notion of biblical Israel as the prototype of a divinely governed nation, rather than a church, was widely adopted. To this extent 'nation', rather than 'church', was placed at the centre of the divine governance of the world and the Old Testament readily encouraged this perspective.

When the 1902 national Education Act decreed that all national schools should include some element of religious teaching, it ran into strong opposition from Nonconformist sections of the Church.[3] As a result the pattern established in the Sunday Schools of interpreting the Bible as a guide to good citizenship appeared the most satisfactory basis for doing so without favouring any one Church group. In their separate identities the various church denominations were feeling increasingly embarrassed by their divisions; a renewed focus on the Bible in preference to specific ecclesiastical doctrines presented a welcome path towards greater unity and mutual understanding. Overall the Old Testament was a highly popular resource for merging the ideals of 'nation' and 'church'—an issue which national conscription brought to the forefront in 1916.

In 1907 the concern to improve the effectiveness of contemporary Sunday School teaching by encouraging elementary knowledge of biblical criticism led two leading Nonconformist scholars—Alfred Garvie, the Congregational Principal of Hackney College, London, and the Primitive Methodist Arthur Peake—to convene a small committee for the purpose of planning a revised Sunday School curriculum which would improve the range of handbooks and notes offering guidance for teachers developed during the late nineteenth century. In 1904 the St Paul's Summer School was introduced during the summer vacation period in Oxford and Cambridge to offer up-to-date lectures on biblical subjects for teachers of religion. This grew to become the Vacation Term for Biblical Study, and King's College London introduced a similar scheme.

3. Marjorie Cruickshank, *Church and State in English Education, 1870 to the Present Day* (London: Macmillan, 1963).

These moves were in place by 1916, in spite of the disruption caused by the war. Nevertheless, from another direction the new situation increased the urgency for reform, so it is not surprising that the proposal to establish a society devoted to the study and teaching of the Old Testament should have come in 1917 from a group of university and college examiners meeting in Wales. These were T. Witton Davies of University College Bangor, William H. Bennett of Hackney College, London and Theodore H. Robinson of University College Cardiff. Their proposal was taken up by a larger group later in that summer when they met in the Queens' College, Cambridge rooms of Canon R.H. Kennett, the university's Regius Professor of Hebrew. Kennett invited interested scholars to attend a meeting in the following January in King's College London which was attended by fourteen persons. This assembly passed a resolution affirming the formation of the society and outlining its rules and constitution. The first President was William Bennett of Manchester, the first Secretary Theodore H. Robinson of Cardiff assisted by a small administrative Committee. The Society's aim was to provide lectures on Old Testament subjects at conferences, followed by discussion on contemporary research. Alongside these activities it would promote publications regarding current work and went so far as to express a hope for a new translation of the Old Testament. Membership was by election, with the primary qualification a competent knowledge of Hebrew with no additional confessional, professional or gender restriction. It was hoped to attract a wide membership of interested people. Lay persons as well as clergy were eligible, so as to include teachers and those with only a personal interest in the subject. The Society's rules reflected the desire to form a wide-ranging membership of persons interested in the Old Testament, whether for personal, professional or academic reasons. There was, in particular, a need to remove suspicion and hostility about the nature of biblical criticism, which had been received unfavourably in some religious circles. From their publications and the lectures offered it is evident that many of those who sponsored the formation of the Society regarded the new biblical criticism as a valuable advance for educational and religious purposes and an opportunity to allay needless fears.

With publications in the field of Old Testament studies appearing with surprising frequency, and a range of theories about the history and authorship of its writings often calling for complex literary and linguistic expertise, the need for a forum of information exchange was obvious. The 'Bible-awareness' of the Victorian age had left a legacy of public interest which stretched between hostility towards any form of biblical 'criticism' and belief that the Old Testament was no longer relevant to Christians since it was the obsolete 'Jewish Bible'. The original proposals for the Revised Version translation of 1881/85 had at first considered leaving this part of the Bible unchanged.

The national Education Act of 1902 reawakened the rivalry between the established Church of England and Nonconformists which the national religious census of 1851 had brought to the fore. Where the former saw the new requirements for religious education as an opportunity to affirm the essential Christian character of the nation, the latter distrusted it as 'Popery on the rates'! It revived tensions which had built up between the Established Church and Nonconformity at a time when the latter communities were at their peak of popularity. These tensions appeared all the more regrettable when Nonconformity was so obviously disunited by the division into separate denominations. The Quaker, Unitarian, Methodist, Baptist and Congregational labels were an embarrassment, and various proposals to lessen their impact were interrupted by the outbreak of war. By 1917 the proposals for a biblical basis for a national religious education programme were still waiting to be fully implemented. They highlighted the necessity for greater provision for the training of teachers in biblical subjects. It is apparent from a review of church practices and the general outlook of various interested parties that the Old Testament figured more prominently in the preaching and teaching of Nonconformists than of the Established Church. This shows up in the wide range of publications on critical biblical subjects that appeared after the 1860s. Subsequent popular anxieties led to calls for a specifically 'Anglican' (i.e. 'national') approach to such questions. The image of the Old Testament prophets as protesters and challengers of injustice opposing a complacent and comfortable establishment had particular contemporary appeal to many Nonconformists. Although this was an over-simplified reading of the Old Testament prophets, it was nevertheless essential to remove the impression that 'biblical criticism' was simply a new Nonconformist version of attempts to challenge the Established Church.

The need to modernise and improve the general understanding of the Bible among teachers of religion in the national schools applied, in similar measure and for essentially the same reasons, to the training of clergy and Nonconformist ministers. From the 1820s various schemes were introduced to increase the number of men in training as clergy in all branches of the Church and also to strengthen their knowledge of the Bible and Church doctrines. Theology, as a compendium of useful religious knowledge, embracing historical and apologetic subjects, gained acceptance. New colleges were founded, qualifications for ministerial acceptance were made more specific and, where necessary, financial assistance was made available with the aim of achieving these changes. The University of London introduced major changes in 1898 leading to the creation of a 'Faculty of Divinity' composed of teachers drawn from several theological colleges. The changes led to the introduction of a Bachelor of Divinity degree which offered a syllabus suitable both for ministerial training and for teachers of religion. It marked a significant turning point in establishing theology (never narrowly defined) as a viable subject among the Classical Humanities.[4] Because of its clerical associations it sought to combine pastoral proficiency with intellectual openness to historical and philosophical criticism of religion. At first the Divinity Department of King's College London resisted the introduction of the degree to its course list, but later, in 1908, it adopted the university scheme under Principal A.C. Headlam.[5] Other London colleges participated shortly afterwards and it became widely accepted by most church training colleges as a degree course suitable for ministerial qualification. Developments among churches to promote shared knowledge, widened understanding and open study of the Bible from many directions became a challenging ambition which the new national educational requirement could not ignore.

The Primitive Methodist Arthur Peake, who became a leading figure in the Society for Old Testament Study, played a major role in establishing a Faculty of Theology in the new University of Manchester and was at the centre of schemes to promote theological training for Methodist ministers and teachers of religion. Within a short period several developments at national level brought about schemes linking colleges with the universities of London, Oxford, Cambridge and elsewhere.[6] Similar developments in Durham and Manchester helped to promote theology as an academic subject within the Humanities accessible beyond the

4. Cf. my essay 'Reminiscences of a BD Finalist, London 1954', *Baptist Quarterly* 45 (2014), pp. 301-309.

5. The situation in London was particularly relevant because of the prestige of King's College as a major centre for ordination training outside Oxford and Cambridge. Cf. Sidney Evans, 'Theology', in F.M.L. Thompson (ed.), *The University of London and the World of Learning, 1836–1936* (London and Ronceverte: Hambledon Press, 1990), pp. 147-60.

6. Pusey House was opened in Oxford in 1884, originally as a library for the late professor's books, but developed as a college for students of theology. The Congregational Mansfield College followed in 1886 and the English Presbyterian College moved from Westminster, London to Cambridge in 1899, bringing with it a substantial number of leading Scottish academics. Cheshunt College (Congregational/Countess of Huntingdon's Connexion) followed in 1904 and various Methodist colleges followed in the early twentieth century.

requirements of seminary training for clergy or teachers in the national day schools. The ambition of improving the level of instruction in Sunday Schools which had begun in the mid-nineteenth century contributed further to the concern to promote knowledge of the Bible and to include modern critical interpretation as a feature of this. In the period prior to the First World War several leading churchmen, especially Nonconformists, were convinced that a critical understanding of the origin of the Bible, particularly the Old Testament, would help to counter the popular belief that science and religion were conflicting realms of knowledge.

2. *The Political Context*

In the more immediate political context it is evident that 1917 was a critical year of decision for the prosecution of the First World War which overwhelmed all other national interests. The fearful losses of the battle of the Somme in the previous summer made necessary the introduction of compulsory conscription to military service in 1916. The possibility that ministers and clerics, who had hitherto been exempt, might be included in this brought a fresh intensity to debate about the justice and divine sanction of human warfare. By this time most colleges training men for the priesthood of the Church of England or the Nonconformist ministry were either closed or taken over for military purposes. The Congregational Mansfield College in Oxford was an exception where a small group of active students remained.[7] A few prominent churchmen expressed opposition to compulsory military service, but the majority regarded it as an important national duty and published essays and books arguing the case for war. Notable among these were George Adam Smith, James Denney and P.T. Forsyth, but more widely influential was the support given by the national and church newspapers. Inevitably appeals to the Old Testament and its concern with warfare and national loyalty figured prominently.[8]

7. Elaine Kaye, *Mansfield College, Oxford: Its Origin, History, and Significance* (Oxford: Oxford University Press, 1996), pp. 162-65. For the impact of the war on Congregational churches, see Alan Argent, *The Transformation of Congregationalism, 1900–2000* (Nottingham: Congregational Foundation, 2013), pp. 79-109; for Baptist responses, cf. Ian Randall, *The English Baptists of the Twentieth Century* (Didcot: Baptist Historical Society, 2005), pp. 78-83.

8. Objection on grounds of conscience to compulsory military service became a major national issue which personally affected several biblical teachers and scholars. It remained a cause of dissension long after the war had ended. Cf. W. Ellsworth-Jones, *We Will Not Fight: The Untold Story of the First World War's Conscientious Objectors*

So far as the soldiers fighting the war were concerned, their experience was frequently an occasion of bewilderment and hostility towards the popular expositions of heroes and heroism they had been taught in Sunday School. These were usually simple adaptations of biblical tales of military prowess and courage intended to foster good citizenship and patriotic loyalty.[9] They retold the exploits of men like Moses, Joshua, David and others, presenting them as examples of personal courage and upholders of justice and right. Reconsidered in the light of the experience of the trenches of France and Flanders, the stories raised serious questions about the Bible's suitability as a handbook of moral teaching. Similar anger and confusion is evident in the parodies of popular hymns that became ribald soldiers' songs; the classical scholar Maurice Bowra declared these to be the most deeply felt front-line poetry of the trenches[10]—later portrayed forcefully by Joan Littlewood in *Oh What a Lovely War*.

With churches of all denominations strongly supporting the war and ordained ministers seeking commissions as military chaplains, the Bible's stories of military conflict and divine approval of warfare were hastily, and often simplistically, called upon to provide support for enlistment as a moral duty. Appeals to the Ten Commandments and other Old Testament texts by objectors summoned to appear before local tribunals set up for the purpose were invariably dismissed. From many sides the wartime situation made the narratives of the Old Testament an increased focus of attention after compulsory conscription was introduced as the war was entering its darkest phase. The realization that there would be no early victory and the necessity of extending the liability for conscription to almost the whole male population made Old Testament themes a focus of debate. Clergy and those in training for Christian ministry were exempted from this compulsion, but large numbers enlisted voluntarily. Many men in this situation accepted opportunities of offering themselves for duties regarded as comparable to national service in order to avoid public criticism. This was frequently with the YMCA or the Quaker Friends' Ambulance Unit.

(London: Aurum Press, 2008); F. Goodall, *A Question of Conscience: Conscientious Objectors in Two World Wars* (Stroud: Sutton Publishing, 1997); Karyn Burnham, *The Courage of Cowards: The Untold Story of First World War Conscientious Objectors* (Barnsley: Pen & Sword Books, 2014); John Broom, *Fight the Good Fight: Voices of Faith from the First World War* (Barnsley: Pen & Sword Books, 2015).

9. Valuable information regarding these issues is presented in Eryl W. Davies, *The Immoral Bible: Approaches to Biblical Ethics* (London: T&T Clark International, 2010).

10. Leslie Mitchell, *Maurice Bowra: A Life* (Oxford: Oxford University Press, 2009), especially pp. 40-45, 316-17.

In 1916 the celebrated Old Testament scholar George Adam Smith used his Moderator's Address to the Scottish United Free Church Assembly to press the case for military service as a necessary Christian duty. In similar vein the widely respected Primitive Methodist Arthur Peake pressed the case for military conscription in talks and lectures which were subsequently published as a booklet. He did, however, offer some biblical defence, for those who dissented from this view, from the example of the prophet Jeremiah.

In addition to the widespread public focus on familiar biblical stories of warfare, the frequent appeals to the biblical language of sacrifice as a religious offering to God made this feature of Old Testament religion a further topic of controversy. The popular evangelical doctrines of Atonement and Redemption gave great prominence to such language, as was the case also with several well-known hymns, which made them a ready target for parody. The idea of a loving and beneficent divine providence, which could only achieve its goal at great cost in human life, placed such thinking on a precarious level. Why did God demand the killing of so many people? In addition, reports of angelic visitations and miraculous acts of healing in biblical stories offered a source of false optimism which was readily linked to contemporary events in popular religious thought. Such flights of fantasy raised hopes of supernatural intervention which several chaplains found distressingly false.

Drawing on his experiences as a chaplain, Charles E. Raven became disillusioned with popular themes taken from the Old Testament and felt affronted by the enthusiastic militarism of one of the Cambridge professors of Divinity (this was, presumably, the Hulsean Professor W.E. Barnes of Peterhouse, who was to his life's end a strong advocate of military training).[11] Raven was later to express strong opposition to the Church's use of the Old Testament as incompatible with the fundamental Christian understanding of the love of God. The often very inadequate nature of the instruction and help given to Sunday School teachers, in spite of a considerable range of literature published for this purpose, left a wide gap which scholars from all church persuasions sought to bridge. Although Sunday Schools were not intended as a means of religious indoctrination, Old Testament stories had been freely used as a way of teaching adult values and good neighbourliness. Furthermore, the practice of linking Christian youth movements such as the Church Lads' Brigade

11. Raven's views became particularly important in view of his later theological eminence and strong support for a Pacifist religious viewpoint. He went so far as to suggest that the Old Testament should be discontinued from general church use except in a substantially shortened and modified form.

and the Boys' Brigade with special recruitment programmes added further to the suspicion hovering over the Old Testament that it was a sacred mandate for warfare and unsuitable as a literature of spiritual guidance and comfort.[12]

Overall the experience of war brought an end to the optimism and years of popular support enjoyed by churches of all persuasions. Only the more marginalized sections of the church which nursed a bleakly apocalyptic world-view were able to take some comfort from the devastating losses of the war by seeing it as a further sign of the imminence of the Second Advent. Such sectarian communities had been intermittently popular since the Napoleonic era, but the extension of the war into the Middle East, and in particular to Palestine, added a further impulse. The war itself was regarded as the most frightening 'sign of the times', confirming that the end of the present world order was imminent!

In this connection the year 1917 was regarded as especially significant, since General Allenby's Palestinian campaign culminated in a triumphal entry into Jerusalem in December of that year. Several evangelical Christians, including some respected politicians and public figures, linked this to biblical prophecies and their interpretation in accordance with a scheme which had never entirely been abandoned since the sixteenth century. In the light of the current turmoil and redrawing of national boundaries the war appeared as a divine judgment on humanity and a sign that the 'end' was near. The fact that during the nineteenth century more credible interpretations of the nature of the apocalyptic imagery of the Bible became available was ignored. The worldwide nature of the current conflict, and the desire to grasp at every hope that the war was part of a divine plan for salvation, gave new life to older discredited schemes of interpreting world history. Reports of Allenby's wresting of Palestine

12. The changing attitude of the various branches of the church to the war became increasingly evident as the war progressed. Even to the present day the issue of compulsion for military service has remained a subject of controversy as the devastating impact of the war on church membership has become increasingly evident. Leading theologians and biblical scholars of the period published books and adopted different positions; others reflected cautiously after the war was over when bitter social tensions remained. The majority of church youth organizations remained steadfast in their support for military duty in spite of the severe losses suffered. The Old Testament, on account of its extensive narratives of warfare as an expression of divine judgement or favour, figured prominently in such debates, as also did the language of sacrifice as a religious rite. Cf. Alan Wilkinson, *The Church of England and the First World War* (Cambridge: Lutterworth, 1978, rev. edn 1996; also *idem*, *Dissent or Conform? War, Peace and the English Churches, 1900–1945* (London: SCM Press, 1986).

from Ottoman control encouraged their revival, thereby presenting a fresh challenge to Old Testament scholars which they were not slow to face.

3. *The Old Testament and the Oriental World*

Adding still further to these issues calling for a better understanding of the Old Testament among Christians was the presence in Great Britain of an increasing number of Jews, including many recent immigrants from Germany and Central Europe, among which were scholars of distinction. With few exceptions the question of how the interpretation of the Jewish Hebrew Bible related to that of the Christian Old Testament had, until 1917, been largely left as the province of the Christian missionary societies devoted to work among Jews. Not surprisingly their message and interpretation was all too frequently limited and generally regarded by Jews as indicative of unwarranted Christian complacency. For the most part the Jewish background to the life and teaching of Jesus was left in the hands of Jewish converts to Christianity, several of whom became authors of publications dealing with such subjects as the Jerusalem temple and Jewish domestic life. Christian understanding of the world of Mishnah and Talmud remained sparse and almost non-existent.

By 1917 a number of Jewish scholars were established as recognized lecturers in British universities and several rose to positions of eminence. Israel Gollancz was appointed as a Professor in English Literature at King's College London in 1905. Since at the time many Christians simply equated the 'theology' of the Old Testament with the Judaism of the era of the New Testament period, there was an urgent need for a more critical understanding of the literature and content of Jewish teaching in the early Christian era. Many scholars openly interpreted the Gospel criticism of Jewish parties like the Pharisees as a rejection of the Old Testament. Quite evidently greater clarity and understanding were called for.

This was an area in which Claude Montefiore (1858–1938) and Israel Abrahams (1858–1925) made major contributions and both men became honoured members of the Society for Old Testament Study. The subject of Judaism and the Hebrew Bible became increasingly important in the wake of the rise of the 'History of Religions' School in Germany. Prior to World War I this gained a modest following in England through the work of J. Estlin Carpenter and Stanley A. Cook, both becoming influential members of the Society (Cook was president in 1925). In this new critical non-theological perspective Judaism was seen as the historical cradle of Jesus of Nazareth. The new viewpoint aimed to replace the traditional Christian emphasis on the Old Testament as a sequence of prophecies by relating it directly to the world of Jewish life and movements under Roman occupation. It gave rise to a new emphasis on the historical links and parallels between Christianity and Judaism to which W.O.E. Oesterley devoted an extensive range of publications. He was elected the Society's president for 1931 and sought to show the close relationship between Jewish and Christian forms of worship as well as exploring the prehistoric origins of Hebrew religion. Overall, as a liberally minded Anglican priest, he sought to promote an understanding of the fundamental nature of religion as an expression of human aspiration.

In line with this interest in Jewish interpretation of the Hebrew Bible, the task of furthering the study of the ancient Greek (Septuagint) translations of the Hebrew Bible entered a new phase of research at the beginning of the twentieth century, linking the biblical and classical civilisations closely together.[13] From being used primarily as a guide to the oldest Hebrew text, this monumental achievement of Hellenistic Judaism was recognized more broadly for its immense cultural importance. As a medium of popularizing Jewish religion in the Graeco-Roman world and linking it with Greek philosophy, it promoted ideas which were profoundly influential in the rise of Christianity. These issues were, however, only just beginning to be addressed by British New Testament scholars in the early twentieth century. Several of the men and women who were destined to become key figures in the Society for Old Testament Study made the subject of 'Early Judaism' (the quest for a suitable title to describe Jewish religious development in the Roman period remained open to many variations) a primary feature of their research. Most notable among these were Israel Abrahams (1854–1925), W.O.E. Oesterley (1866–1950), and G.H. Box (1869–1933).

These contemporary academic issues provided a fresh agenda for research and discussion by everybody engaged in biblical teaching and research in the years prior to World War I. The Edwardian years had been a time of stocktaking, when newspapers, religious journals and public lectures competed with each other to report on what were increasingly declared to be the 'assured results' of biblical criticism—even though this accolade for the new critical methods was unduly optimistic. The task of re-proclaiming the Bible and its message for humankind in the light of modern knowledge had taken on an element of glamour and adventure by the bringing back to Great Britain of a wealth of manuscripts and scrolls

13. Cf. William Horbury, 'The Septuagint in Cambridge', in N. de Lange, J.G. Krivoruchko and C. Boyd-Taylor (eds.), *Jewish Reception of the Greek Bible Versions* (Texts and Studies in Early Modern Judaism, 23; Stuttgart: Mohr Siebeck, 2009), pp. 9-38.

which had been preserved over many centuries in monastic libraries and storehouses in Egypt and elsewhere in the Middle East. Ancient languages such as Coptic, Syriac, Ethiopic and Armenian, which had previously appeared remote and esoteric, almost overnight became relevant tools for understanding how the English Bible had come down to the modern world. Exhibitions in the British Museum further stimulated public interest.

This was a branch of scholarship in which 'Orientalism' and 'Biblicism' overlapped, sometimes intermingled and frequently came into conflict with each other. A rivalry had arisen during the nineteenth century between these overlapping areas of learning and some of the causes of this lay with the retention of the *religious* 'tests' (actually a signed acceptance of the thirty-nine articles which formed the standard of faith for the national church) which until 1871 had governed entry in the two leading English universities. This contrasted with Germany where more numerous facilities and appointments for research in the field of Arabic, Syriac and other Oriental languages existed. As a result several leading experts in these languages in Britain were forced to seek employment in museums or left to retain an 'amateur' status with little financial support for research. In this context the founding in Finsbury Park, London of the School of Oriental Studies in 1917 marked a milestone for the promotion of the study of the languages and cultures of ancient Syria, Persia and Arabia. This was subsequently expanded to become the School of Oriental and African Studies in 1937. Although not directly concerned with the teaching of the Old Testament, or with theological issues, there was an inevitable overlap of interest in view of the range of ancient inscriptions and literature from Syria and Persia which had come to light.

These subjects had attracted a great deal of public interest in British society before the First World War since they not only concerned specific religious issues, but had a wider cultural and artistic appeal. There were many artefacts, writings and art works which exploration of the biblical lands had brought to light in the previous century. Egypt was especially a subject of intense interest. An Egyptian monolith, dubbed 'Cleopatra's Needle', was erected, after transportation difficulties, in the heart of London in 1876, and a related exhibit was placed in New York. Together with numerous expositions and museum displays, these attracted attention to the lost world of Egyptian civilization. Mesopotamia also was brought to light as a rediscovered world and drew W.E. Gladstone into publishing lectures reassuring the Bible-reading public that the new discoveries offered no occasion for alarm. For enquiring minds a range of relevant artefacts filled the galleries of the British Museum and similar institutions across the land. Babylon and the Bible became symbols of contrasting, yet inter-related, cultures.

The ancient world had been brought back, into the twentieth century. With it came questioning, and often a strong challenge to the greatly simplified and foreshortened understanding of human history portrayed in the Bible. No scholar more fully epitomised this new age of questioning than Sir James Frazer of Trinity College, Cambridge, whose work *The Golden Bough* (published in 1890) ran into many editions and described the beliefs and customs of the pre-Christian world in ways that appeared startling and offensive to many. The rediscovery and decipherment of ancient texts showed that several of them had links with the Bible; their contents laid bare a world that had disappeared below the horizon of history until nineteenth-century scholars brought it back to life. Such achievements of scholarly ingenuity and patience were themselves major intellectual milestones, shedding new and unexpected light on the world from which the Christian Bible had originated. They further raised the question, 'In what way is the Bible unique?'

The idea of bringing together persons who shared a common interest in the Old Testament was certainly not new in 1917, since, as noted above, for almost a century various projects were initiated to encourage ministers, teachers and all interested persons engaged in teaching the Bible, to meet to share information and to participate in discussion. Prominent among these were the two Mansfield Summer Schools held in that College in 1892 and 1894, followed by the first Oxford and Cambridge Summer School in Biblical Studies that took place in 1904.

While these activities were an encouragement to persons, especially teachers, interested in the latest developments in biblical scholarship, these were not the persons best placed to allay the fears of men and women who had mistakenly thought that the authority of the Bible was undermined by biblical criticism and that as a consequence the ideal of a Christian foundation for citizenship would be lost.

Throughout the Edwardian years of the twentieth century several leading scholars, both Anglican and Nonconformist, participated in an extensive effort to popularise the findings of biblical criticism through preaching, special addresses and publishing books intended to show that the Church had nothing to fear from new knowledge. It was hoped that a critical understanding of the Old Testament would remove the fear that modern science contradicted the Bible. The shadow of Charles Darwin was a long one. The first efforts at resolving such fundamental tensions, however, met with only limited success and had, on some notable occasions, encountered violent public opposition. Several widely read religious newspapers and journals joined in the attempt to promote the value of critical scholarship, but, on this front also, those who received the message were usually those who, by training, were already well schooled in understanding the character and nature of ancient texts. The education focused on Greek and Latin classics imparted in the British Public (Independent) Schools offered a basic understanding of how an ancient society differed from a modern one. However, such educational expertise was expensive and had, before the First World War, hardly begun to embrace Nonconformity; still less could it be carried over to the wider audience of national schools.

There was therefore in 1917 a readily identifiable and strongly felt need to improve opportunities for assisting those responsible for teaching and interpreting the Old Testament to understand the work of modern scholars. In the emotional turmoil of war, conflicting voices were to be heard from many quarters appealing to the Old Testament as unassailable proof of the divine justice of the British conflict with Germany. In contrast some leading public figures were stricken in conscience that two such cultured and self-proclaimed Christian Nations should find themselves locked in such a deadly struggle. Nevertheless few doubted that, in a host of ways, fundamental religious and moral values were at stake. The advent of compulsory conscription in 1916 put increased pressure on individuals to think deeply about the nature of patriotic responsibility and the divisions of loyalty between Church and State.

4. *Some Leading Personalities*

The national context of debate and controversy in 1917 that made the idea of a Society devoted to the study of the Old Testament significant is well shown by looking at the background and work of four key personalities who took the lead in planning, organizing and promoting its inauguration. Their interests and the reasons for their particular engagement with the Old Testament illustrate the character of the Society and point to the reasons for its wide and open non-confessional constitution.

Mention should first be made of William H. Bennett (1855–1920), a Congregational minister and scholar who had the distinction of becoming the first Christian Nonconformist ministerial candidate to be elected a Fellow of a Cambridge College, when he was elected a Fellow of St John's College in 1896. His experience and popularity as a teacher highlights the social and educational issues which had built up over more than a century. He had, after attending the City of London School, proceeded to the University of Manchester (where he took an MA in Mathematics) and the (Congregational) Lancashire Independent College, and subsequently to Cambridge (where he took an MA in Theology). On the basis of his publications he was awarded the Cambridge degree of DLitt in 1902.[14]

The most notable of Bennett's publications were annotated volumes on *Genesis* and *St Matthew's Gospel* in the Century Bible series of 1900–1912, which were under the general editorship of Bennett's Manchester colleague W.F. Adeney (1849–1920). Bennett returned to teach there in 1913, working alongside Adeney, and he was, along with Alfred Garvie and A.S. Peake, an eager populariser of the results of biblical criticism.[15] Together they established a strong Nonconformist reputation for this and through their publications they took a lead in efforts to improve Sunday School teaching and the training of ministers. On the strength of this educational background Bennett was elected the first president of the newly constituted Society, serving it until 1919. He died at the age of sixty-five in 1920. In view of the wartime conditions no meeting of the Society was held in 1918, but meetings resumed in 1919 under Bennett's presidency, and in 1920 A.R.S. Kennedy was elected as the new president.

The second key figure among the 'founding fathers' of the Society for Old Testament Study was Robert H. Kennett (1864–1932), in several respects a unique and unusual scholar who represented a different ecclesiastical tradition from that of Bennett. He arrived as a student at Queens' College, Cambridge in 1886 to read theology with the intention of becoming ordained in the Church of England. Although firmly evangelical in his church loyalty, he embraced warmly the critical viewpoints that had recently been introduced into the university by Fenton Hort and William Robertson Smith. As a competent Hebrew scholar, having been a pupil at the exceptional Merchant Taylors' School in London, he was persuaded by Stanley A. Cook to attend lectures by William Wright, the university's Professor of Arabic, and to study Semitic languages. After obtaining first-class honours in that subject in 1886, he was appointed Regius Professor of Hebrew in 1903 after the resignation of Alexander Kirkpatrick. Cook had held similar ambitions for a career but, after being deeply influenced by William Robertson Smith, his attention focused on the place of the Old Testament among the peoples and religions of the ancient Near East. Kennett and Cook were to become long-term friends and colleagues in Cambridge, where both spent their academic careers.

14. This information is taken from A.P.F. Sell, *Hinterland Theology: A Stimulus to Theological Construction* (Milton Keynes: Paternoster, 2008), p. 359 note.

15. See Sell, *Hinterland Theology*, pp. 355-416.

Between them they promoted the importance of comparative Semitic methodology in the lexicography and grammar of Hebrew, which, at the time, was still a subject of controversy.

In retrospect Kennett's work reveals several of the unresolved tensions affecting the study of the Old Testament in the early years of the twentieth century. His strong evangelical churchmanship was linked with advanced critical views about the authorship of several Old Testament books and about the role of the Old Testament in the Christian biblical canon. These views contrasted sharply with those of his contemporary Alexander Nairne (1863–1936), especially when the latter was elected to the Regius Professorship of Divinity in Cambridge (1923–1932).

Kennett's inaugural lecture to the first meeting of the Society for Old Testament Study in January 1917 was on 'The Origin of Deuteronomy' and marked out a subject that was to become closely linked with his name. It was also one in which other members of the new Society took a close interest since it was seen as a pivotal issue for the Graf–Wellhausen theory of the origin of the Pentateuch. The initial British reluctance to engage in detail with particular aspects of this hypothesis was further abandoned when Kennett's radical views were challenged by other, more conservative, alternatives. Overall, however, the issue indicated a new confidence and vigour in British biblical scholarship and a willingness to depart from a near total dependence on S.R. Driver's views, which were beginning to dominate British scholarship. For the rest, like several British scholars of the period, Kennett's interests were focused on problems of translation—a legacy of the negative popular reaction to the Revised Version of 1885.

Kennett's commitment to the newly formed Society indicated a renewed eagerness on the part of British scholars to engage in critical work on a wide range of issues, rather than simply record and explain what German scholars were advocating, which is the major part of what Arthur Peake achieved. The founding of the Society marked a new level of critical confidence and, after a delay following the ending of the war, the beginning of a new era of international dialogue on biblical subjects. The Society was well placed to play a large part in accelerating this development, gaining an enviable reputation for doing so.

Overall the war increased popular British distrust and disaffection with all things German, from pianos to philology and biblical interpretation, and this situation provided a challenge when the war ended. With the collapse of the post-war German economy in 1922–23 the Society, through its energetic secretary Theodore H. Robinson, found an opportunity for re-establishing contacts with contemporary German scholars and scholarship, initially by supporting the continued publication of the internationally respected journal *Zeitschrift für die alttestamentliche Wissenschaft*, threatened by the financial chaos in Germany.

Following the name of Robert Kennett among the leading figures who promoted the new Society must be mentioned that of Arthur S. Peake. He was a Primitive Methodist layman who had come to Manchester from Mansfield College, Oxford in 1901 to establish a college for the training of men for the ministry. To this end he received funding from the Liverpool jam manufacturer W.P. Hartley. The son of a Primitive Methodist minister, Peake entered St John's College, Oxford in 1890–93, subsequently gaining election as a tutor in Merton College and turning to the study of theology. He at one time contemplated being ordained in the Church of England, but accepted a teaching Fellowship in the Nonconformist Mansfield College before taking up the challenge presented by W.P. Hartley to move to Manchester and train Methodist ministers.

In Oxford he was profoundly influenced by Samuel Driver, from whom he learnt the Hebrew language and acquired a profound love of the Old Testament. In Manchester he was closely involved in the foundation of the new University and published in 1913 a comprehensive volume on the modern study and criticism of the Bible. This commended the importance of the new critical interpretation, centred on the re-conceived historical order of the composition of the Old Testament literature. He emphatically regarded the new understanding as support for the Christian claim concerning the revelatory nature of its message. Most importantly, he believed that the critical approach removed the necessity for regarding scientific and religious views of creation as in conflict with each other. As he saw the situation, the modern criticism of the Bible, which had developed amid controversy in the nineteenth century, offered the prospect of a new reformation of the Christian Church. Another major publication was a two-volume commentary on the book of Jeremiah in the Century Bible series (1910, 1912). This was to gain fresh attention in 1916 when Peake became involved in public debate about compulsory military service.

To follow these early writings, Peake planned to edit a substantial commentary on the entire Christian Bible in a single volume, with contributions from a wide range of leading scholars. The commentary proper was to be supplemented with introductory articles on biblical subjects. It was intended to serve as a comprehensive guide to the 'modern' view of the Bible with contributors drawn from all branches of the Christian faith. Difficulties in editorial preparation, followed by the outbreak of war and a breakdown in Peake's health, delayed publication until 1919.

Nevertheless, this one-volume presentation of the 'new look' of the Bible through the eyes of a new generation of scholars became a widely read handbook for teachers, ministers and lay persons. Further problems of health and involvement in proposals for union within the various Methodist churches prevented Peake's attendance at the first meeting of the Society for Old Testament Study. Nevertheless, he quickly became one of the strongest supporters of its aims and work.

The fourth of the key personalities involved in the planning and promotion of the new Society was at the time the person least known nationally, but nevertheless one who was destined, over the next twenty years, to take a lead in shaping the Society's character. This was Theodore H. Robinson—a young Baptist minister, the son of a Baptist minister and the great-grandson of a Baptist missionary to India. This denominational connection was to prove significant at a time when the denomination was undergoing major reorganization and change, especially as these changes were closely involved with Robinson's teacher in Greek and Latin languages in Cambridge, T.R. Glover. He too was the son of an eminent Baptist minister, Richard Glover of Bristol, and as a Cambridge University Lecturer in Latin he was a prominent figure in the university and in Baptist church developments. In particular he took a role in promoting the ideal of a united denomination with broad ecumenical links.

Born at Edenbridge in Kent in 1881, Theodore Robinson was educated at the celebrated Mill Hill School, London and St John's College, Cambridge (1901–1903), where he came under Glover's influence. From Cambridge he returned to London to study theology and Semitic languages at Regent's Park College (1904–1905), being ordained as a Baptist minister. After two years teaching in the Quaker Woodbrooke Settlement in Birmingham, he went to Serampore, India to teach biblical studies and Semitic languages; while there he published a tutorial primer for the study of Syriac—a book still in print with later supplements more than a century later. He returned to University College Cardiff in 1915 to teach theology and Semitic languages, and this was to remain his academic workplace until retirement in 1944. In this capacity he was one of the examiners for the University of Wales who first proposed the formation of a Society specifically devoted to the study of the Old Testament, and he became its first Honorary Secretary.

Congregational churches, along with Baptists and Methodists, were heavily engaged in major educational and administrative changes at the turn of the century with the aim of closer union and co-ordination of practice. This was linked to plans for a more educated ministry, coupled to ambitions for the extension of nation-wide education and greater co-operation between churches. Not surprisingly, these developments encountered resistance and there was concern to dispel the misconception that modern critical interpretation of the Old Testament was an especially Nonconformist development, intended to undermine the claim of the established Church of England to be truly national in character.

Other suspicions also surfaced, linked particularly with the aggressive 'holiness' movements of the period. In the wider intellectual setting, debate became increasingly focused on critical issues regarding the historicity of the Bible similar to those which had arisen over the historical roots of ancient Greek (Homeric) traditions. Robinson was familiar with these debates and convinced that, when properly understood, a critical understanding of the biblical literature could serve as its own commendation. Instead of undermining the claims of theology and its biblical inheritance, it freed them from false objections. Modern criticism served to uphold a historically based reassurance of the truth of the biblical story which would reinforce Christian claims concerning its unique revelatory character. Not surprisingly, the reconstruction of a history of ancient Israel became a major goal of his academic career, for he saw such a history as a platform on which wider theological issues could be built.

The fuller unfolding of this perspective, and its limitations, belongs to the later years of twentieth-century scholarship, but its recognition as a major issue in 1917 is well attested. Robinson's commitment to scholarship, and his concern that it should be pursued on the widest possible basis between all interested persons and that it should be conducted without prejudice and emotional rancour, were important. He was to steer the newly formed Society for Old Testament Study through some difficult years, to initiate important projects, and especially to give it an international outlook which set it in the vanguard of progressive research.

5. *The Central Issues—National and Religious*

Why was the Society for Old Testament Study formed in 1917? It was a year of turmoil, grief for many and national anxiety for all; it was certainly not a period when, in quiet contemplation, new ventures could be comfortably planned and launched. Nevertheless, knowledge of the background of events sheds a great deal of light on why a new pioneering Society, devoted specifically to the teaching and interpretation of the first half of the Christian biblical canon, should have been started in that year, implementing a proposal made a few months earlier. The Old Testament was in the centre of passionate arguments about the right and duty of patriotic military service. It was not the organization and administration of the national Church that was at issue, of the kind that had persisted throughout the preceding century and which promoted a new era of ecumenical discussion, but rather the rights and duties of citizenship that were uppermost in this public debate. How is a Christian man or woman related to other citizens and how, in a world perspective, are nations related to each other? Does the idea of divine providence still carry meaning? The issues were many, making simple answers unsatisfying and sometimes self-contradictory. Popular opinion attached greater authority to the Bible than to ecclesiastical pronouncements and creeds. This presumed authority had been placed under threat by over-simplistic use of biblical narratives in Sunday School lesson-making and by a vague perception that modern science debunked the Bible's teaching about God and creation. Reflection on the circumstances surrounding the original proposal to form a new Society points to three major issues which exercised a strong influence.

The first derives from the way in which the Old Testament had been interpreted and used during the Victorian era. Prominent in this regard was the work, and remarkable success, of the Sunday School movement in which the Bible had been used as the primary handbook of responsible adult citizenship, fostering a sense of self-worth, integrity and national pride. Doctrinal issues were deliberately kept in the background. The Old Testament was interpreted as a panorama of responsible and adventurous adulthood, often aggressively muscular and fearless in its outlook, since life itself was recognized to be fraught with threats and hazards. In this context, the geographical and political horizon of such teaching was linked to the missionary outreach of the Christian churches and, in a still wider setting, to expectations of British imperial expansion. The world itself was expected to become progressively more Christian as the ethical impact of these developments was felt. Such hopes were dealt a sharp blow by the outbreak of war with Germany in 1914 and their weaknesses exposed.

Various schemes to moderate, redefine and qualify the Christian world-view of popular teaching in the Sunday School movement were in process of consideration and implementation by the time this occurred. Churches of all persuasions became anxious to impose a closer doctrinal supervision of what was taught in the schools that were usually, but not always, conducted in church premises. The popularising of fundamental scientific breakthroughs during the nineteenth century (Charles Lyall, Charles Darwin and others) made it essential that over-simplified beliefs in divine creation and providence were either avoided or at least qualified by further comment. Church doctrine and scientific teaching had fallen seriously out of step with each other. The passing of the Education Bill of 1902, with its provision for nationwide teaching of religion in all schools, had unfortunately rekindled old rivalries and distrust between churches. Biblical criticism, broadly understood as a way of interpreting the Old Testament on its own terms and in full recognition of the limitations attendant on the circumstances and historical context of its origins, was regarded as a vital tool for achieving this end. Accordingly assistance for the promotion of this fuller, revised interpretation of the Old Testament was seen to be a highly desirable goal. A Society in which scholars, teachers and lay persons could meet together to hear what scholars were saying and where scholars could themselves debate and discuss the seemingly endless flow of hypotheses and conjectures about the literature would be a welcome introduction. Such at least was a primary concern in the minds of the men who made the first proposal that such a Society was needed and would be well received.

A further consideration is also highly relevant. This concerns the legacy of the Revised Version of the Authorised (King James) Version of the Bible in 1881/5. The work of the revisers was not well received. Lovers of English literature and church liturgy regarded it as the betrayal of an incomparable heritage. In contrast, scholars and doctrinal experts regarded the failure to introduce clearer and more precise textual and linguistic accuracy, if necessary supported by notes, as a negation of the labours of accredited experts. A prolonged period followed the first publication with the issuing of copious notes, explanations and addenda for and against the work of the Revision Committee. It was a clear instance where the needs of the many different groups who shared a common interest in the Bible were at variance with each other. Yet the proposal to prepare the Revised Version had been the boldest and most eagerly supported religious undertaking of the Victorian age in which all the major church communities and denominations were involved. It enjoyed substantial financial backing from the publishing privileges accorded to the two major university presses. It had been expected that this broad basis of national and ecclesiastical support would enable it to avoid major protests and opposition. But this was not to be the case.

Alongside this specifically religious project, the period of Near-Eastern exploration and the birth of tourism to the Bible lands had added a broad secular, cultural colouring to knowledge of the world from which the Bible had come. It was a source of art, invention and strange customs, made all the more alluring on account of the popular attraction of 'Oriental' culture to Victorian minds. The Bible was no longer bound in a cloth decorated with modern, or medieval, symbols, but had been opened and could be understood on its own terms in its own setting.

Thirdly, and perhaps rather ominously in view of developments that occurred later, the first stirrings of a fundamentalist interpretation of the Bible were being felt.[16] Biblical criticism was viewed in the minds of such scholars as William Bennett and Arthur Peake as its own best commendation. 'Teach it, and readers will see that it is right' could have been the motto which such men adopted. When rightly understood the Bible could be read 'like any other book', to use the phrase linked inseparably with the name of Benjamin Jowett. So, in the minds of those who had learnt to read the Bible with the guidance and enlightenment that scholarship had made possible, the new knowledge would make its unique character more fully evident.

Throughout the discussions, plans and early meetings of the Society for Old Testament Study, its broad basis, freedom from confessional restrictions and aloofness from religious prejudice were strongly upheld. It was to be exploratory, outward-looking and inclusive. All that was deemed to be essential was that the Old Testament should be read on its own terms, in its own language (Hebrew) and with its own openness of spirit.

16. Cf. Harriet A. Harris, *Fundamentalism and Evangelicals* (Oxford: Oxford University Press, 1998).

Summer Meeting 1927, at Keble College, Oxford.
The front row comprises (left to right) Otto Eissfeldt, Antonin Causse, Herman Obbink, Frank Rockstro (Treasurer), Paul Volz, David Simpson (President), Adolphe Lods, Theodore Robinson (Secretary), Bernardus Eerdmans, Powis Smith, and Willi Stark.

The Society for Old Testament Study: 1917–2017*

Eryl W. Davies

1. *Beginnings*

The documents relating to the history of the Society over the past century, housed in the archive of the library at Bangor University, indicate that the first suggestion which led to the formation of the Society was made at a meeting of examiners in Hebrew to the University of Wales in the early summer of 1916. The three people present—namely, T. Witton Davies, William H. Bennett and Theodore H. Robinson—decided to invite others to a meeting of Old Testament scholars to be held in Cambridge during the following summer in order to discuss the matter further. This time there were nine present (including such eminent scholars as A.S. Peake, S.A. Cook, G.B. Gray, and J. Skinner) and they agreed that a Society of those engaged in the study of the Old Testament should be formed and that a circular be sent inviting all well-known British Old Testament

* In writing this chapter I have made extensive use of the material available in the Society's archive housed in the library of Bangor University, and I wish to express my thanks to the archivist, Mrs Elen Wyn Simpson, for her patience and assistance in locating the relevant material. All quotations in this chapter, unless otherwise stated, are from the Minutes of the Society's General Committee meetings or from the Minutes of its Business Meetings or from the annual Bulletin sent out to members. I have profited greatly by the 'Short Histories' of the Society, written by G. Henton Davies (1950), D.R. Ap-Thomas (1967) and John Rogerson (1992), and the brief account of the Society's history written by George W. Anderson and published in *Vetus Testamentum* (vol. 17 [1967], pp. 123-26) to mark the Jubilee of the Society's foundation. I wish to thank a number of scholars who have allowed me to consult them on a variety of issues, including John Day, Lester Grabbe, Walter Houston, Alastair Hunter, Paul Joyce, and Jonathan Stökl. I am also grateful to the editor of the volume, John Jarick, for helpful comments on earlier drafts of the chapter.

scholars to participate. The circular noted that 'there has been for many years a feeling amongst British Old Testament Students that there has been too much isolation in the work of individuals', and that there had been little opportunity hitherto to meet and exchange views. The circular continued: 'It is, then, with a sense of the need for closer co-ordination of Old Testament research in this country that we venture to suggest the formation of a British Society for Old Testament Studies'. The circular conceded that the timing of the new venture—three years into the War—might be regarded by some as not particularly propitious, but it was felt that it would be beneficial for the Society to be already in existence at the close of the War and thus 'in a position to make use of the opportunities which will be presented on the re-establishment of European peace'.

The replies received to the circular were positive, and the first Meeting of the Society was arranged for 3rd January 1917 in London, the authorities of King's College having kindly agreed to place a room for the day at the disposal of those who were able to attend. Fourteen scholars were present, and their names and denominational affiliations were carefully documented (G.B. Gray, Congregationalist; L.E. Elliott-Binns, Anglican; J. Skinner, Presbyterian; A.S. Geden, Wesleyan; T.H. Robinson, Baptist; etc.). In some respects, this Meeting did not get off to the most auspicious start: only two scholars had been invited to read a paper, and one of those (A.R.S. Kennedy) had been unable to attend. Although Kennedy had sent a copy in advance of the paper he had intended to read, in view of his absence and the fact that his paper was expected to appear in print, 'it was decided not to hear it'. Despite this apparent setback, some important decisions were taken at this Meeting, not the least of which was that 'a Society be formed for the promotion of the study of the Old Testament' and that it be officially known as 'The Society for Old Testament Study'. It was decided to elect W.H. Bennett as its first President and T.H. Robinson as its first Secretary. Meetings would be convened twice a year and membership subscription would be five shillings per annum. The original members of the Society were deemed to be those present at the January meeting, but it was resolved that others who had been unable to be present but had signified their approval of the proposed Society be invited to join it. By September 1917 those deemed to have enrolled as members numbered thirty.

2. *The War Years*

Although the resolution to form a Society was passed, unanimously, in January 1917, members were informed in a Notice sent out on 20th March 1918 that, owing to the War, no further Meeting of the Society would take place ‘until greater facilities for travelling are resumed’. The next Notice appeared on 22nd August 1918, informing members that, due to the prolongation of the War and the increasing difficulties of travelling, it would not be possible for the Society to meet in the foreseeable future but that a Meeting would be arranged ‘as soon as it is practicable to hold one’. An almost audible sigh of relief can be heard in the Notice sent out on 12th March 1919: ‘The conclusion of active hostilities in the main theatres of war, and the near prospect of a general peace, give us reason to believe that we may be able to resume our activities’. The Committee thus arranged for a General Meeting to be held at the Dalton Hall, Victoria Park, Manchester, during the third week in the following July, at which the President would deliver an address on the general policy of the Society. Unfortunately, only five members were able to be present, a further thirteen members having sent their apologies for ‘unavoidable absence’; those present, however, expressed their gratitude to the Secretary, T.H. Robinson, for his sterling efforts to maintain the work of the Society ‘under war conditions’.

Following the Meeting in July 1919, the Society met regularly, twice a year, until the outbreak of the Second World War. The 21st Summer Meeting of the Society was held during 18th–20th July 1939, at Queens’ College, Cambridge, with 55 members present, and the report of the Meeting contained a Notice to the effect that ‘in view of the War situation the Committee is of the opinion that the Winter Meeting should be cancelled’. In the meantime, the interests of the Society would be cared for by the Officers and Committee as elected for 1939. The possibility of holding a Meeting during the following summer would be ‘considered in the light of whatever turn events may take in the next few months’. In order to keep members informed of developments in Old Testament scholarship it was decided that records would be kept of scholarly publications, and that a comprehensive list would be issued ‘when conditions make it possible’. The Committee tentatively suggested that a Meeting be held in the summer of 1940, but before reaching a final decision on the matter ‘the Secretary would be glad to hear from members who anticipate that they would be able to attend a meeting if one were arranged’. The response of members appears to have been positive for, initially, plans were in place to hold a Meeting in July 1940, but in view of ‘developments in the past weeks’ the Committee had felt obliged to cancel it at short notice; members were, however, reassured that ‘we are ready to resume active operations as soon as conditions permit’. Consideration was given to holding a Meeting of the Society in the summer of 1942, but ‘in view of all the difficulties and uncertainties' decided against. Members were informed through the Bulletin issued in March 1943 that there would be no Summer Meeting in that year either, since 'our membership is very scattered' and it was thought that few would be able to attend. As it turned out, the next Meeting of the Society did not take place until January 1946, its 22nd Winter Meeting, at which T.H. Robinson presided, with 54 members present. H.H. Rowley, the Society's newly appointed Foreign Secretary, reported that he had managed, during the War years, to keep in touch with Old Testament scholars from nine European countries, 'though not with Germany'; his report was deemed to be of great interest and was circulated privately among members of the Society. It is interesting to note, in passing, that members attending Meetings of the Society during the years immediately following the War were duly warned 'to provide their own towels, serviettes, soap and shoe cleaning materials', and some were even required to bring 'their own sheets and pillow cases', though no doubt all would have been relieved to know that 'ration books are no longer required'.

3. *Officers of the Society*

The first President of the Society was W.H. Bennett and the first Secretary was T.H. Robinson, both of whom were appointed to office during the inception of the Society in 1917. Sadly, W.H. Bennett died three years later, on 27th August 1920, but T.H. Robinson was to serve as Secretary for almost thirty years, as sole Secretary until 1927 and thereafter as Joint Secretary with C.R. North. Throughout this period Robinson was responsible for the international contacts of the Society and it was he who edited the *Book List* from its first issue in 1933 until 1940, when it ceased to appear for the duration of the War. In 1928 the Society elected him as its President, and upon his retirement from the office of Secretary in 1946 he was elected President for a second time in recognition of his immense contribution to the Society over the years. At the 22nd Winter Meeting held at Regent's Park College, Oxford, in 1946 it was decided that a volume of essays should be presented to Robinson in recognition of his long and distinguished service to the Society. In the following summer the Society's Meeting was held in Cardiff, with T.H. Robinson as President, and on the Monday evening members and visitors were entertained to dinner at the Park Hall Hotel at which the President was formally presented with a volume (in manuscript) of 13 essays 'in token of his great services to the Society over twenty-nine years'. At the same event,

S.A. Cook, on behalf of the British Academy, presented Robinson with the Burkitt Medal for Biblical Studies. The volume, entitled *Studies in Old Testament Prophecy*, and edited by H.H. Rowley, was not published until four years later, the long delay evidently due to difficulties precipitated by post-war conditions.

Another scholar who served the Society with distinction for many years was C.R. North. He was elected as a member in 1924 and served as Joint Secretary (with Robinson) from 1927 until 1948—a period of rapid growth in the Society's membership—during which time he guided the Society with considerable skill and foresight. He was elected President in 1949, and again (as 'acting President') in 1958 during the incapacity of L.E. Elliott-Binns. He was appointed Treasurer in 1952, serving in this capacity for six years, and the Society's Minutes note that during his period as Treasurer its financial position had steadily improved, for he had 'continuously endeavoured (often, it has seemed, with considerable success) to make two blades grow instead of one'. When C.R. North indicated his desire to resign as Secretary, having served in this capacity for 21 years, the Society thanked him for his service over such a long period, and not least 'for his exceptional labours in reviving the activities of the Society after the Second World War'. At the 1952 Summer Meeting of the Society it was agreed to recognize North's 65th birthday by presenting him with a piece of antique silver, suitably inscribed, and an appeal was circulated for five shillings per member ('more or less being equally welcome') in order to purchase the gift. D. Winton Thomas was appointed to act as treasurer of the fund. At the 29th Summer Meeting of the Society in 1953, held in Cambridge, Winton Thomas and his wife entertained members to a garden party at which T.H. Robinson paid warm tribute to C.R. North for his distinguished service to the Society as Secretary, Treasurer and President. North was then presented with a silver salver inscribed with the words: 'Presented to Christopher Richard North by members of the Society for Old Testament Study as a token of their affection and their appreciation of long and memorable service'.

During the Second World War and its aftermath few scholars did more than H.H. Rowley to foster contacts with continental colleagues. He was appointed as the Society's first Foreign Secretary in 1946 and held the post until 1960, during which time he worked assiduously to strengthen ties with scholars and kindred societies abroad. Rowley also served as editor of the *Book List* from 1946 until 1956, and it was under his editorship that the List was considerably enlarged in size and scope. The Society accepted his resignation as editor 'with the greatest regret', recognizing that he had given unstintingly to the task of making the *Book List* a comprehensive and discriminating guide to current publications in the field of Old Testament study. He was elected President of the Society for 1950, and at the Society's Summer Meeting in Birmingham in 1955 a *Festschrift* (edited by D. Winton Thomas and Martin Noth), to which no fewer than 23 scholars from 13 countries had contributed, was presented to him on behalf of the Society and the Editorial Board of *Vetus Testamentum*. In an obituary published in *The Times* Edward Ullendorff noted that 'his work for the Society for Old Testament Study gave that learned body a standing in biblical scholarship which his successors will have to strive hard to maintain'.

Mention should also be made of G. Henton Davies, who succeeded C.R. North with responsibility for the domestic affairs of the Society, and he served as its Home Secretary for 15 years. From 1961 to 1963 he also served as the Society's Foreign Secretary, and he was elected President for 1966. As George W. Anderson notes in a Jubilee Year tribute to the Society in *Vetus Testamentum*, 'it is no disparagement to the work done by others to state that these four scholars, Robinson, North, Rowley, and Henton Davies, exercised the most important influences on the development of the Society during the first half-century of its life'.

Another member who served the Society with considerable energy and enthusiasm was George W. Anderson. He was the editor of the *Book List* from 1957 until 1966 and served as Foreign Secretary from 1964 until 1974, during which time he built upon the foundations laid by H.H. Rowley and did much to enhance the Society's reputation at home and abroad. It was his idea to include succinct reports on each Meeting in the annual Bulletin, an innovation welcomed by all, and especially by those unable to attend the Society's Meetings in person. He provided the Society with particularly close links with Scandinavian scholarship, and it was entirely fitting that his last year as Foreign Secretary coincided with his Presidency of the International Organization for the Study of the Old Testament.

As the Society grew in number it became necessary to appoint other officers to shoulder some of the responsibilities of the Secretary and Treasurer. In 1946 it was resolved to appoint a Foreign Secretary responsible for maintaining links with scholars and kindred Societies based overseas, thus enabling the Secretary—now designated as the Home Secretary—to focus on the Society's domestic affairs. These titles of 'Home Secretary' and 'Foreign Secretary' were to be used for more than half a century, until in 2008 the title of 'Secretary' was reinstated for the former and the title of 'Secretary for Honorary Members' was introduced for the latter, in part to overcome a widespread misunderstanding that the so-called 'Foreign Secretary' dealt with matters concerning foreign members while the so-called 'Home Secretary' only dealt with matters concerning British-based members. At the 29th Winter Meeting of the Society in 1954 the office of Publications Sales Secretary was formed, with the main tasks of monitoring the sale of the *Book List* and other publications of the Society and of reporting regularly to the Treasurer 'for monies thus gained'. D.R. Ap-Thomas was the first to hold this post, a position which he held from 1953 until 1960, and which he relinquished only to then serve as the Society's Home Secretary from 1961 until 1972.

It was in 1954 that the Society appointed its first Hospitality Secretary who was responsible for the domestic arrangements of its Meetings. The first holder of this office was A.S. Herbert, and over the years the Society has been indebted to a long line of Hospitality Secretaries who have ensured that the Meetings run smoothly and that any problems are resolved with the minimum of fuss.

The possibility that the Society should consider establishing its own archive was raised in 1987, but it was not until the 1999 Winter Meeting that the Society decided to create the post of Archivist. John Rogerson was appointed as the first holder of the office, and his access to the archive enabled him to write a valuable *Short History* of the Society, covering the period 1917–92.

During the 1991 Winter Meeting the Society resolved to create the position of 'Honorary Research Officer', though it was later decided that 'Information Officer' would be a more apt title for the post. Philip Jenson was its first holder, and it was largely due to his pioneering work that the Society, by the summer of 2000, was able to boast its own website. By today the website has become a valuable repository for material relating to the Society, containing information for those wishing to join, details about forthcoming meetings, links to other relevant sites, and details of publications sponsored by the Society.

It was at the 1996 Winter Meeting that the suggestion was made to create the post of Membership Secretary to relieve some of the Treasurer's duties. Heather McKay was elected as the first Membership Secretary. She created a database containing the names and addresses of all members and carefully monitored the payment of their subscriptions. Now, at the click of a button, it is possible to discover how many members there are in the Society, whether they belong to the category of Ordinary or Honorary members, which countries they come from, and the ratio of male to female members.

Over the century very many members have given unstintingly of their time to serve on the General Committee, or to undertake the sometimes onerous duties of office, and the Society owes a debt of gratitude to all who have contributed to its success during the last hundred years of its existence.

4. *Meetings*

a. *General Arrangements*

Apart from the War years the Society has met regularly twice a year, usually in January and July. Meetings have tended to follow a similar format throughout the century: papers are read and discussed, and matters of direct interest to the membership are debated. At the Winter Meeting in 1993, however, it was decided to experiment with the usual format, and the morning session was devoted to two parallel programmes of short papers, with the opportunity for members to switch between groups depending on their particular interests. The experiment proved successful and was repeated at the Summer Meeting the following year in Edinburgh. The format was changed again when the Society held its Meeting in Sheffield in 1996, for here it was decided to have a themed programme under the title 'The Quality of Life in Ancient Israel', and this Meeting consisted of *three* concurrent sessions (on 'family', 'learning' and 'power') in the morning which were repeated in the afternoon and again during the following morning to enable members to attend and participate in all three discussions. Delivering a paper to the Society, however, was not always without its potential hazards, as James Kennedy was to discover when he read a paper on 'Selah' to the Summer Meeting of the Society, held in Birmingham, back in 1923. It seems that Dr Kennedy 'had the misfortune to slip and fall as he was delivering his paper, sustaining a fractured thigh', which resulted in his having to stay at a nursing home in the city for six weeks. Fortunately, such incidents were a rarity, and most members over the century have managed to read their paper without coming to any undue harm!

b. *Notable Meetings*

In order to celebrate the 21st anniversary of the Society's foundation it was resolved at the Winter Meeting 1936 to publish a volume of essays under the title *Record and Revelation*, and edited by H. Wheeler Robinson. As a further mark of the Society's celebration, it was decided that, instead of the usual three-day meeting in July, a four-day meeting would be held at Keble College, Oxford, on 20th–23rd September 1938. Members were duly warned, however, that ‘there will not be sleeping accommodation for ladies at Keble, but arrangements are being made whereby they may have their meals there’. Papers for the occasion were invited from scholars overseas, including W.F. Albright, J. Hempel, A. Lods and J. Pedersen (though, in the event, Hempel was unable to attend, due to the ‘international situation’). T.H. Robinson read a short paper at the Meeting reviewing the history and work of the Society. Messages of congratulation and good wishes were received from the Royal Asiatic Society, the British and Foreign Bible Society, the American Oriental Society, the Society of Biblical Literature, the Canadian Society of Biblical Studies, the Palestine Exploration Fund, the Deutsche Morgenländische Gesellschaft and the Studiorum Novi Testamenti Societas. At the Meeting, manuscript copies of *Record and Revelation* were open for inspection by members, and it was reported that the book would be published in October 1938.

In July 1949, the Society celebrated its ‘Silver Jubilee of Summer Meetings’ in Bangor, with C.R. North as President, and papers were read by such eminent scholars as W.F. Albright, G.E. Wright and Gerhard von Rad, among others. Von Rad was later to publish his paper (on ‘The Holy War in Israel’) in expanded form as a monograph, which he dedicated to the Society. During this Meeting it was noted that the BBC had invited members to give a series of talks on the ‘Third Programme’ on the present state of Old Testament studies as part of the Society’s celebrations; among the talks (each lasting 20 minutes), which were aired the following October, were disquisitions on archaeology and the Old Testament (J.N. Schofield), the literary study of the Old Testament (H.H. Rowley), the thought of the Old Testament (T.H. Robinson), the theology of the Old Testament (N.W. Porteous) and the revived interest in the Old Testament (C.R. North). The Jubilee celebrations continued during the following Winter Meeting held in King’s College Hostel, Vincent Square, London, with H.H. Rowley as President. A special dinner was held to celebrate the event, the occasion being graced by the Archbishop of Canterbury, the Moderator of the Free Church Federal Council, the Chief Rabbi, the Dean of Westminster, and Sir Frederic Kenyon, and messages of good will were received from Societies all over the world.

The 32nd Winter Meeting of the Society, held at King’s College Hostel in 1957, was particularly notable since ‘for the first time more than one hundred members were present’ (the actual number was 103). It may be that more members than usual had endeavoured to attend this Meeting since on the Tuesday evening the Society entertained the four surviving Founder Members of the Society: T.H. Robinson, L.E. Elliott-Binns, W.A. Davies and B.M. Pickering. Aubrey R. Johnson welcomed the Founder

Members, and Elliott-Binns, who had seconded the original resolution to form the Society, responded. The Bulletin for 1957 commemorates the occasion as follows: 'Thus quietly the first forty years of the Society were celebrated. The Society again records its gratitude for the imagination and leadership of the Founder Members and its delight that all those surviving from 1917 were able to be with us on the 1st of January, 1957.'

At the Winter Meeting 1951 the suggestion was considered that the Society might convene a Meeting in Rome, and it was felt that the Easter vacation, 1952, would present a convenient opportunity. After much discussion at the Business Meeting, a large majority was in favour, provided that no fewer than 30 members were prepared to make the journey. The Rome Meeting would last a week, allowing ample time to hear a variety of papers and to make excursions to numerous places of interest. Thus it was that the 55th Meeting of the Society was held at the Pontifical Biblical Institute in Rome, with 31 members of the Society and 18 guests present. The Revd Father R.A. Dyson, S.J., met the party when they arrived at the train station in Rome ('some five hours late') and it was he who acted as their constant guide and companion throughout the week. Tours had been arranged for the visitors to the Trevi Fountain, the Pantheon, the Protestant Cemetery containing the graves of Keats and Shelley, various churches, temples and museums, the Sistine Chapel, and the Vatican Library, where 'we were allowed both to see and to handle several treasures including some leaves of Codex Vaticanus'. On the Thursday morning members of the Society were accorded a private audience with Pope Pius XII, during which he read an address to the visitors in English and greeted each of them personally. The fact that the audience took place in the part of *L'Osservatore Romano* which was usually reserved for papal pronouncements clearly added to the significance of the occasion. At the closing meeting during the last evening of the visit, D. Winton Thomas, the Society's President-elect, expressed gratitude for the hospitality which had been extended, noting especially that 'in the days to come our thoughts will turn many times to that morning in the Vatican, and we shall live again in our memories an experience which none of us is ever likely to forget'. In the annals of the Society, he continued, 'this meeting will ever remain a historic and unique occasion'. In 1957 it was reported that Pope Pius XII's address to the Society's Rome Meeting had been given permanent record in *The Canon Law Digest*, the editor of which had added a note to this effect: 'We report this address as an example of the sort of gracious and cordial courtesy which the Holy Father is happy to show toward a scholarly association which is *not distinctively Catholic*' (his italics).

This was not the only occasion for the Society to hold its Meeting outside the British Isles. At the Summer Meeting in 1925 it was suggested that arrangements might be made for a party of members to visit Palestine, though, at that time, nothing seems to have come of the suggestion. The idea was resuscitated during the Winter Meeting of 1932, and C.R. North was given the task of investigating whether such a visit would be viable, but owing to economic conditions it was decided to postpone any consideration of such a trip. It was not until the mid-1960s that the projected visit was finally realized, and that was in no small measure due to the persistence of Henton Davies. Ever since he became Home Secretary of the Society in 1946 he had patiently advocated that the Society should visit Palestine and hold a Meeting there. His advocacy was without success until it was realised that it would be a shame if the Society reached its Golden Jubilee in 1967 without ever having visited the Holy Land. Appropriately enough, in the year that Henton Davies (the Principal of Regent's Park College, Oxford) was President, the Society held its long heralded Meeting in Israel. The Meeting took the form of a topographical and archaeological tour of the Holy Land from 29th August until 12th September 1966. A full itinerary was arranged, including an illustrated lecture by A.D. Tushingham of the British School of Archaeology in Jerusalem, and visits were made to a variety of locations, including Qumran, Jericho, Gibeon, Hebron, Bethlehem, Bethel, Ai, Shechem, Samaria, Ashdod, Lachish, Megiddo and Hazor, all under the expert guidance of Roland de Vaux, Martin Noth (two of the Society's Honorary members) and R.B.Y. Scott. As D.R. Ap-Thomas, who had arranged the tour, notes in his *Short History* of the Society 1917–67, 'few parties can ever have visited Palestine under such authoritative and generously dispensed guidance'. The usual Business Meeting of the Society was held in the Presbyterian Hospice at Tiberias, on the shore of the Sea of Galilee. During that Meeting a tribute was paid to Henton Davies by a senior ex-President of the Society, Norman Porteous who, having expressed the Society's indebtedness to Henton Davies for his valuable contribution to the Society over the years, concluded with these words: 'We all have our dreams and many of them we do not fulfil. But there is one man here—our President—who has cherished a great dream for many years and now has fulfilled it, and we have all shared the benefit.'

The study tour of Israel provided an ideal curtain-raiser to the Society's Jubilee Year in 1967. There had been much discussion since 1963 as to how to celebrate the Society's 50th year. One suggestion was that it should seek royal patronage, and Henton Davies was asked to look into the implications and possibilities. He discovered that the use of 'Royal' might be obtained in two ways: on application for such permission by an 'influential person' or 'by incorporation' (a more complicated and expensive procedure); after some discussion, however, it was eventually decided not to pursue the matter any further. One idea which *did* meet with approval, however, was to inquire whether F.D. Coggan, Archbishop of York (and a member of the Society), would accept nomination to be President for the Jubilee year. The Society would do whatever was necessary to adapt itself to the demands of Dr Coggan's time, but it was felt desirable that the President be able to attend the Jubilee Dinner to be held in London during the Winter Meeting of 1967, to which a number of distinguished guests would be invited. The Dinner was to be held on the Wednesday evening, at which His Grace the Archbishop of York would preside in the splendour of the Ballroom of St Ermin's Hotel, Westminster, and his speech at the Dinner would be regarded as his Presidential address. Among the dignitaries to be invited would be the Archbishop of Canterbury, the Moderator of the Church of Scotland, the President of the British Academy, the Chair of the Palestine Exploration Fund, the Chair of the British Association of Jewish Studies, the President of the Society for New Testament Studies, the President of the Dutch Oudtestamentisch Werkgezelschap, and a representative of the Society of Biblical Literature. The event, by all accounts, was a most memorable occasion, the only regret being that not one of the Society's Founder Members had lived to witness the occasion, W.A. Davies and B.M. Pickering having died the previous year, and T.H. Robinson—fondly known as the 'Father of the Society'—having passed away in 1964.

c. *The Business Meeting*

Most of the issues and concerns relating to the day-to-day running of the Society are discussed in the first instance by the General Committee which makes recommendations to the Business Meeting. Exigencies of space preclude a detailed account of the myriad issues raised over the years, but three items have appeared regularly on its agenda: the venue, the number of Meetings to be held each year, and whether or not the Society would benefit from having Meetings centred on a particular theme.

(i) *Venue.* The first meeting of the Society in January 1917 was held at King's College, London, and for most of the twentieth century the Winter Meetings have been held in one of the Halls of Residence of King's College. Indeed, at the 50th Winter Meeting of the Society a special dinner was held to mark the long association between King's College and the Society, at which the Assistant Principal of King's College was the guest-of-honour, and the President (Baroness E.F. de Ward) spoke appreciatively of the Society's long association with the College. Until 1969 the Winter Meetings were held in Vincent Square, but owing to the increase in the number of members attending it became necessary in 1972 to move to another of King's College Halls of Residence, Halliday Hall, on Clapham Common, where the Society's Winter Meeting was accommodated for 19 years. In 1984 a small group was set up to look at possible alternative venues for the Winter Meeting, not necessarily in London. Other venues such as Birmingham, Manchester and Sheffield were considered, but it was decided that for many members the advantages of meeting in London outweighed the disadvantages and that there were strong reasons to continue to meet in the capital.

In 1990, however, the Society was informed that Halliday Hall would not be available in future, King's College having decided to sell the property, and this gave rise once again to a discussion as to whether a venue outside the capital might be considered for the Winter Meeting; but, once again, most favoured a London venue, though others stressed the advantages of a location more central to Britain as a whole. For various reasons it became impractical to continue with the Society's Winter Meetings in London, and since 1992 the Winter Meetings have been held in various locations outside the capital. The tradition that the Summer Meeting be held at a venue of the President's choice has continued unabated over the years.

(ii) *One Meeting or Two?* Apart from the War years the Society has met regularly twice a year, although at various times it was suggested that one Meeting a year would be sufficient. In 1948 there was no Winter Meeting due to a fuel crisis, and two years later the Committee recommended that in future only one Meeting per year should be held, partly because of the increasing difficulty in finding accommodation in London for the December or January Meeting and partly because of the expense incurred by members attending two Meetings a year. It was also agreed that the Meeting should be held in the north and south alternatively and that it should take place in the second half of July. Despite the Committee's recommendation, however, the pattern of two Meetings a year was maintained. In 1978 the issue was raised whether the Society should dispense with its Summer Meetings in those years when a meeting of the International Organization for the Study of the Old Testament occurred or when a Joint Meeting with the Dutch Society was held outside Britain, but it was felt that this would deprive many members of a summer meeting altogether since a relatively small number were able or willing to attend meetings outside the United Kingdom.

The most serious threat to the continuation of the Winter Meeting came in 1993, when it was observed that by the Winter of the following year most Universities would have moved to the semester system, leaving a very short Christmas break, and precluding a Meeting in either of the weeks during which the Winter Meeting had traditionally been held (the third week in December or the first week in January). For many these dates would fall during term time, and thus the very future of the Winter Meeting was brought into question once again. Indeed, notice was given that 'the January 1994 Business Meeting may have to discuss the motion that there in future be no Winter Meeting of the Society'. In the meantime the Home Secretary would write to all Universities and Colleges from which British and Irish members came, inquiring about moves towards a semester pattern. When the data was duly presented to the Committee, it was concluded that the impact of such changes was not so significant as to call for an abandonment of the Winter Meeting. Thus with very few exceptions, both Winter and Summer Meetings of the Society have been held annually.

(iii) *Themed Meetings.* At the Summer Meeting in 1950 it was announced that a letter had been received from the Faith and Order Department of the British Council of Churches inviting the Society to consider devoting a special meeting to the subject of eschatology. It was agreed that at the Society's Meeting in Norwich in the following year the main theme would be the eschatology of the Old Testament, and papers would be invited bearing on this subject. Over the years, however, although a few themed Meetings have been held, these appear to have been the exception rather than the rule. The Summer Meeting of the Society held at the University of Nottingham in July 1998 was based around the theme of 'Apocalyptic'; the Winter Meeting of the Society two years later in St Catherine's College, Cambridge, centred on the book of Isaiah; and the Winter Meeting in Birmingham in 2003 was based on the theme 'The Hebrew Bible against its Ancient Near Eastern Background'. The Meetings of the Society held jointly with the Dutch-Flemish Oudtestamentisch Werkgezelschap, however, have regularly adopted a themed programme, since the papers given are intended for publication in a themed volume of *Oudtestamentische Studiën*. The joint Meeting held in Durham in 1991, for example, was based on the theme 'Texts and Versions', while the joint Meeting held in the summer of 1994 took as its theme 'Synchronic or Diachronic? A Debate on Method in Old Testament Exegesis'. At the Durham Meeting there was a lengthy discussion of the advantages and disadvantages of having a themed programme in the regular Meetings of the Society, but it was felt that, while there was undoubtedly a place for thematic elements to be included in the programmes occasionally, the themes chosen should not be too narrow and the programme should aim to include 'something for everyone'.

5. *Membership*

a. *Ordinary Members*

At the Winter Meeting of the Society in January 1921, T.H. Robinson, the Secretary, noted the rapid progress which the Society had made during the four years since its inception. Twelve months previously, the membership stood at 40; by now it numbered 59, an increase of almost 50% in one year. However, the age (though evidently not the gender!) of its members seemed to cause him some concern, for he emphasized the need to 'keep before us the possibility of introducing the younger men'. Some members felt that it was appropriate, in view of the probable further increase in numbers during future years, to consider the question of the conditions of membership, and the Committee was instructed to make recommendations on the matter. At the Meeting of the Society held in the summer of 1920 the Committee resolved that the only condition should be that every application for membership must be supported by two members of the Society. Four years later, however, it was felt that the qualification for membership should be further refined, and it was now resolved that future members should possess at least one of the following qualifications: they must have either (a) published contributions on the study of the Old Testament; or (b) occupied a recognized teaching post which involved giving instruction in Old Testament subjects; or (c) obtained a University degree or similar diploma involving 'the study of the Old Testament in Hebrew'. The rules regarding membership were refined further still during the Winter Meeting of 1935. It was now resolved that the nominations supported by two members of the Society must be carefully considered by the Committee; those approved would be submitted to the next business session of the Society, which would, in turn, either accept or reject the Committee's recommendations. Those elected would be required to pay an annual subscription, which would be due on 1st January each year, or, in the case of new members, on their election, and any member whose subscription was more than three years in arrears would be deemed to have resigned.

Of course, not all persons who applied for membership of the Society were automatically accepted, and over the years the Committee diligently scrutinized each application in turn. Often nominations were deferred ‘pending further enquiries regarding knowledge of Hebrew’, or were rejected outright on the ground that sufficient knowledge of Hebrew had not been demonstrated. At the Winter Meeting 1962, for example, 17 nominations had been received, but only 9 were accepted. Interestingly, details are given in the Society’s Minutes as to why some of the 8 unsuccessful applications had been rejected or deferred. Two nominations had evidently lacked a seconder; one applicant was deemed to be still *in statu pupillari*; in the case of three other nominations it was unclear how much knowledge of Hebrew the candidates possessed; and in the case of one applicant it was decided, rather bizarrely, that the Society ‘should invite him to some meetings so that members may get to know him’. In 1951, one (male) applicant was rejected because he ‘showed little evidence of direct interest in the Old Testament’, while in the following year a (female) applicant was rejected on the rather vague grounds that ‘she was not really suitable for membership’, though she might be permitted to attend Meetings of the Society at the discretion of the Secretary.

b. *Honorary Members*

It was at a Meeting of the Society in December 1926 that the issue of Honorary Membership was first broached, and it was resolved that such membership should be confined to outstanding foreign scholars; persons normally resident within the British Isles would, therefore, not be eligible. It was also decided that the number of Honorary Members should not exceed 12 at any time and that, except at the first election, not more than one per annum should normally be elected, though in exceptional circumstances the Society may elect two. Thus, as from 1927, there were two categories of membership within the Society: Ordinary and Honorary. Honorary Members would not be required to pay a subscription and would receive free of charge the same publications as Ordinary Members. In 1949 it was agreed that the number of Honorary Members should be increased to 15, and in 1953 it was increased further to its present 20. Clearly, those who have been elected as Honorary Members over the years have greatly appreciated the accolade, and some (such as W. Eichrodt, G. von Rad, H.W. Wolff and O. Kaiser) have dedicated volumes to the Society in recognition of the honour bestowed upon them.

c. *Associate Members*

At the Winter Meeting 1937 the issue was discussed of election to membership of the Society of scholars who were resident overseas. This had been precipitated by a letter from a Canadian scholar inquiring whether membership was open to those who resided outside the British Isles. It was decided that scholars resident abroad should be allowed to become members and that their method of election should be the same as that for scholars resident in the British Isles. The rules regarding membership of foreign scholars were not formalized, however, until the Winter Meeting of 1949, when the Society introduced, for the first time, the category of Associate Members, making it possible for non-British scholars (in addition to Honorary Members) to share in the Society's activities. Each application for Associate Membership was to be considered by the Committee, and the names of those who had been approved would be submitted to the next business session of the Society, which would approve or reject the Committee's recommendation. Associate Members would be subject to the same rules as Ordinary Members in regard to the payment of subscriptions and would receive the same publications; they would have the right to attend any Meeting of the Society but, unlike Ordinary Members, would not to be permitted to vote at the business sessions. For the most part, however, the rules pertaining to Ordinary and Associate Members were very similar—so much so, indeed, that in 1974 the question was raised as to whether the distinction between them needed to be maintained. In 1994 a Working Party was established to consider the future direction of the Society, and one of its recommendations was that the category of Associate Membership should be abolished. The recommendation was accepted by the Business Meeting, and the Bulletin for 1997 is the first to appear in which no distinction is drawn between Ordinary and Associate Membership in the list of those who had been elected as members of the Society.

d. *Election of President*

In 1947 it was decided to clarify the means by which the Society's President was to be elected: nominations for Presidency of the Society should be sent to the President in office prior to the meeting of the General Committee at which the election was made; in the event of there being more than one nomination, a secret ballot would be held among the Committee members. In 1966, however, Peter R. Ackroyd suggested a new procedure for electing the President, which was subsequently adopted by the Society. As from January 1967 names should be submitted to the Committee and considered for the Presidency *two years hence*. The Committee would then discuss the names suggested and arrange them in order of choice. Then the President would invite them in that order to accept nomination, and the first person approached who accepted would be recommended by the Committee to the Business Meeting to become President-elect in the following year and President in two years' time. In 1988 it was agreed that a notice should be included in future programmes for the Winter Meeting reminding members that any member could submit a suggestion for a future President of the Society to the Committee via the Home Secretary.

e. *The Presidential Bible*

It was at the Summer Meeting of the Society held at Handsworth College, Birmingham, in 1932 that the idea first emerged of obtaining a Hebrew Bible which would be the property of the Society. The signatures of past Presidents who were deceased would be copied into it, and future Presidents would sign their names in the Bible as their first act upon entering their Presidential year. For this purpose, A.R.S. Kennedy offered to present a copy of a rare Bomberg edition to the Society, an offer which was gratefully accepted. The Bible was duly presented to the Society at the 15th Winter Meeting in 1933, and it was used for the first time at the installation of the then President, W.L. Wardle.

At the last Meeting of the Society before the outbreak of the Second World War, the President, Herbert Loewe, reported that he had been concerned for the proper care of the Society's Bible and he had ventured to take measures to ensure its safe preservation. To this end, he had arranged for a casket to be made of acacia (*shittim*) wood to house the Bible, and he had even taken the precaution of insuring the Bible for £25, paying the initial premium of 15 shillings himself. He had also ensured that 'the binding had been refurbished and the worm destroyed', and that the title and signatures of past Presidents had been photographed.

At the Winter Meeting of the Society in 1956 the Secretary 'hinted' that it was desirable that the Society's Bible and its casket should be transported to and from Meetings in an appropriate carrier, and S.H. Hooke, taking the hint, informed the Society that he and his wife wished to make a gift of a suitable case to the Society in token of the fellowship which he had enjoyed during the 25 years of his membership. Thus at the following Summer Meeting in Cardiff, S.H. Hooke presented the Society with a handsome red leather case suitably made to hold and carry the Bible in its casket.

In 1978 the Secretary was asked to arrange to have the Bomberg Bible with its box insured for £250, the sum to be adjusted at a later date in the light of a professional valuation. However, it was not until 1993 that it was decided to have the Bible valued. A letter from Sotheby's, dated 24th August 1993, and addressed to R.J. Coggins, the Society's President for that year, reads as follows: 'Our consultant has now had the opportunity to look at your Hebrew Bible, which was printed in Venice between 1525–1529, the third to be printed by Daniel Bomberg. We would value it for sale at auction at £1500-£2000.' The letter goes on to note that the casket had been inspected by the Furniture Department, which reported that, 'although a fine piece of workmanship', it did not add significantly to the value of the book.

6. *Correspondence*

While most of the information concerning the Society's activities and deliberations over the past century can be gleaned from the Minutes of its various Meetings, an interesting sidelight is thrown on various aspects of its activity by items of correspondence that have been preserved in the Bangor archive.

One letter was sent in August 1939 in the name of the Society's Officers and Committee to individual members concerning the plight of Paul Kahle, who would have been well-known to members not only as the editor of the third edition of Kittel's *Biblia Hebraica* (1937) but also as an Honorary Member of the Society. The letter reminded its readers that Kahle, on account of the sympathy displayed by his family to members of the Jewish faith, had been deprived of his Chair at the University of Bonn, and that 'his future, and that of his wife and five sons, is a matter of great anxiety both to himself and his many friends in this country, where he has decided to make his home'. The gist of the letter was to suggest that members of the Society might wish to afford some practical help to Dr Kahle by contributing to a fund designed to pay the fees to enable one of his sons (who wished to specialize in the Semitic field) to be educated at London University. It was estimated that the fees would amount to about £50 per year for three years, but if the bulk of the Society's members ('who number well-nigh two hundred') were to contribute ten shillings a year for three years, enough money would be raised. In the Bulletin for January 1940 it was reported that the contributions to the Kahle Fund during 1939 had amounted to £48. The Bulletin for March 1942, however, noted that little had been contributed since the previous Bulletin 'and we think it best that the fund should now be closed'.

It is often through the letters written by officers of the Society to each other that one is able to appreciate how various crises which beset the Society from time to time were dealt with. One such crisis faced the Society during 1957–58. In mid-December 1957, the then Secretary of the Society, G. Henton Davies, wrote to members of the General Committee indicating that Elliott-Binns' wife had died at the end of November, and a letter had been received from his son indicating that his father was in 'failing health, both physically and mentally', and would almost certainly not be able to take part in any of the proceedings of the Society during the following January. This was a matter of considerable concern, since Elliott-Binns was due to be installed as President during that January Meeting. Thus the Committee was faced with the task of finding an alternative President at very short notice. H.H. Rowley wrote to the Secretary suggesting a 'Joint-Presidency' for the year by inviting C.A. Simpson to act in this capacity ('if he would accept appointment at this late hour'); Rowley pointed out that, in practice, Simpson would then be the sole President for the Winter Meeting and, in all probability, for the Summer Meeting also. However, C.R. North, in a letter dated 11th December 1957, pointed out an obvious difficulty with this suggestion: whether someone had been or was President of the Society depended, in the last resort, on their having signed the Presidential Bible, and if Elliott-Binns could not be present he could not sign the Bible; besides, the person acting as 'Joint President' might feel that 'he was just being made a convenience'. North thus favoured asking C.A. Simpson to become sole President for the year, and such action would be a recognition of the value to the Society of Associate Members, of whom many by now were American. Aubrey R. Johnson, on the other hand, was deeply wary of both suggestions, pointing out that Simpson's name had not yet even been considered by the General Committee as a potential President; it would be far better to fall back on someone who already enjoyed the confidence of the Society in this respect, and his favoured solution was to ask C.R. North to serve as a President for a second term during 1958 ('after all he has done for the Society over the years this seems to me no more than he deserves'). After much discussion, and 'in view of the fact that Canon Elliott-Binns is still alive and had not withdrawn', it was decided to install C.R. North as 'acting President' for 1958.

Some of the letters in the archive are tinged with an element of sadness. In a letter dated 13th April 1970 C.R. North thanked Henton Davies for his wishes of 'many happy returns' on his 82nd birthday, but said that he now felt old and permanently tired; he had given up writing ('except letters, of which I write a good many'), but he did manage to preach occasionally, and 'when it comes to the end I feel more the Methodist Minister than I do the University Professor'. In *his* letter Davies had evidently asked what North thought of the NEB translation, especially the rendering of Isaiah 53 (North having written a volume on the so-called Suffering Servant Songs); in his reply, North seemed rather dismissive of the translation, noting that the panel had managed to translate the whole of Isaiah 52 and 53 'in one short evening session'. North himself had been unable to be present and had left his detailed notes on these chapters on the table for the translators to consult, 'but they didn't make any use of my suggestions, such as they were'. One member, he claimed, had been 'pretty overbearing' during the discussions, and North had threatened to give up his membership of the panel. He was only dissuaded from such precipitate action by W.D. McHardy, who told him: 'Don't do that, Chris; you're the only man who can stand up to him!'

Of course, in more recent years, communication between officers of the Society has tended to be by emails, an innovation which, while having the obvious advantage of eliciting an almost spontaneous response to pressing issues and facilitating rapid exchange of ideas and views, has the disadvantage of being a form of communication that can all too quickly be eliminated at the click of a button, and those who will be writing the history of the Society over the next century will sadly be deprived of a rich and valuable source of information.

7. *International Outlook*

In the Society's Rules it is stated that one of its aims was 'the promotion and co-ordination of Old Testament studies in Great Britain and Ireland and the maintenance of relations with Old Testament scholars abroad'. Over the years the Society has done much to foster international co-operation by inviting a number of foreign scholars to read papers at its meetings and by electing some of them as Honorary Members. It has also striven to maintain cordial relations with similar learned societies in other countries. Indeed, almost from the inception of the Society, overtures were made to foreign institutions concerned with Old Testament research. During the Winter Meeting 1923, for example, attention was drawn to the fact that the *Journal of the American Oriental Society* printed regular reports of Meetings of Societies concerned with oriental subjects, and the Secretary was instructed to communicate with its editor with a view to securing Notices of the SOTS Meetings in the Journal. During the same Meeting in 1923 it was reported that the *Zeitschrift für die alttestamentliche Wissenschaft* was in grave financial difficulties and was in serious danger of having to suspend publication. Such was the dire financial situation of the Journal that all four numbers for 1923 had to be published as a single issue. A donation of £10 was sent by the Society from its meagre resources, and as a result of further correspondence with the editor of the *Zeitschrift* it was agreed that the Journal would henceforth accept and publish a limited number of articles in English, while members of the Society would reciprocate by helping to increase its circulation through personal subscription, which would preferably be paid through the Society. By December 1924, 29 members of the Society had subscribed to the Journal. The 1924 issue of the *Zeitschrift* was notable for the fact that it contained, for the first time, four contributions in English, three of which were written by members of the Society. The experiment was clearly due to continue for the foreseeable future, since it clearly worked to the advantage of both the periodical and the Society: members of the Society had a new outlet for their publications while the *Zeitschrift* could boast of being 'a genuinely international Journal'. Indeed, according to the Secretary's report to the Summer Meeting 1924 it was the 'sincere desire' of its editor 'to secure hearty co-operation amongst the Old Testament scholars of his country and ours'. When the Treasurer of the Society, F.B. Rockstro, indicated his wish to retire from the role after a period of some ten years, mention was made of the fact that he had 'carried out with unfailing regularity the intricate arrangements between the Society and *ZAW*, so making possible that close relationship with world-wide Old Testament scholarship which it has been one of the first objectives of the Society to achieve and to maintain'.

It was at the Winter Meeting of the Society in 1925 that the idea was mooted, for the first time, to invite distinguished continental scholars to attend and read a paper at the Society's Meetings, the Society expressing a willingness to defray the travel expenses involved and offering a fee to the speaker. Having made tentative inquiries, it was clear that 'no foreign scholar would expect a fee if asked to read a paper before the Society'; nevertheless, it was deemed entirely reasonable to offer a sum for travelling expenses, and while this would obviously vary according to the distance travelled, '£15 might be regarded as a fair average'. The first distinguished scholar to be invited was Hugo Gressmann of Berlin, who read a paper to the Society in January 1926 under the title 'Foreign Influences in Israelite Prophecy'.

In order to mark the tenth anniversary of the Society in 1927 arrangements were made for an international gathering of scholars at Keble College, Oxford, at which Hermann Gunkel and A. Lods (both Honorary Members of the Society) would read papers. Scholars could read their papers in English, French or German, as they desired, and abstracts in the three languages would be available at the Meeting. Over 80 members and guests were present; the President was T.H. Robinson (C.R. North having agreed to act as Secretary during his Presidency). The 16 papers read at the Meeting in Keble were subsequently published in a volume entitled *Old Testament Essays*, edited by T.H. Robinson.

No International Society was established following the 1927 Meeting, as some had hoped, but in the Winter Meeting 1935 the Society received an invitation to attend an international gathering of Old Testament scholars to be held in Göttingen, and the Society welcomed the invitation, the dates provisionally fixed for 4th–10th September 'which will enable foreign visitors to take advantage of the special railway concessions offered by the German Government'. The Meeting was to be organized on the plan followed at Oxford in 1927, with several short papers (in English, French and German) delivered during the morning sessions, and one longer paper during each of the evening sessions. The gathering was evidently a great success, with about 80 delegates present, representing 14 different nationalities. The British delegation numbered 14, of whom 12 were members of the Society, and four members had been invited to deliver papers. The delegates received a warm welcome and were provided with excellent accommodation by their German counterparts, and there was 'every ground for believing that the Meeting will have helped to draw the Old Testament scholars of the two countries closer together'.

Another international gathering of scholars was organized for the Society's Meeting in Cardiff in September 1946 when, in addition to the 44 members present, there were a number of visitors from overseas, including A. Bentzen (Copenhagen), I. Engnell (Uppsala), W. Baumgartner (Basel), J. Coppens (Louvain), P.A.H. de Boer (Leiden), A. Parrot (Paris) and T.C. Vriezen (Groningen). Four years later, at the Winter Meeting 1950, it was announced that the Dutch Society for Old Testament Study intended to hold an International Meeting of scholars at Leiden during the following August and members of the Society were duly encouraged to attend, especially given that many of their Dutch counterparts had made every effort to attend the International Meeting at Cardiff. Members who were considering attending were to inform the Secretary well in advance, since 'a party of 15, travelling together, will receive a 10% reduction'. It was at the Leiden Meeting that the International Organization for the Study of the Old Testament was formed, and its quarterly Journal, *Vetus Testamentum*, was launched. The newly formed Organization would have its first meeting in Copenhagen in 1953, with A. Bentzen as its President.

The Society agreed to invite him to become one of its Honorary Members, an invitation which he gladly accepted, although, sadly, Bentzen died within six months of his election as Honorary Member.

Over the years the Society has enjoyed a particularly close relationship with its Dutch counterpart. The Old Testament Society in Holland—Het Oudtestamentisch Werkgezelschap (OTW)—was founded in July 1939, and continued to meet throughout the years of the War, albeit in secret, and it even managed to publish three volumes of *Oudtestamentische Studiën* between 1941 and 1943. A Joint Meeting between OTW and SOTS was held in the Netherlands during September 1970, and this was to be the first of regular triennial Meetings between the Dutch Society (now the Dutch-Flemish Society) and SOTS over the years to come. In these days of easy travel it is sometimes difficult to appreciate the effort that would have been involved in attending such Meetings abroad. D.R. Ap-Thomas, then the Home Secretary of the Society, was given charge of the travel arrangements for delegates who wished to attend this first Netherlands Joint Meeting. Members were instructed to congregate at Victoria Coach Station in London by 4.00 p.m.; they would arrive at Ostend by 10.00 p.m., having travelled by hovercraft from Ramsgate for the 40-minute crossing; after an overnight stop at Ostend they would depart at 9.00 the following morning and would arrive at the conference by 5.00 p.m. 'in good time for an evening meal'.

8. *The Society's Publications*

a. *The Society's 'Journal'*

Throughout its history the Society has produced or sponsored a wide variety of publications, which have served a public much wider than its membership. In the circular which was sent out to prospective members in 1916, the hope was expressed that the Society would eventually issue a periodical of its own, although it was deemed wise to postpone such an ambitious undertaking 'till a more settled time'. It was therefore suggested that, in the meantime, the Society should confine itself to correspondence, and that papers contributed by its members should be circulated in typescript; such a collection of papers would then form the nucleus for the first issues of the proposed periodical 'when the time is ripe for its appearance'. During the very first meeting of the Society following the War, consideration was given to the feasibility of publishing a *Journal of Old Testament and Semitic Studies*.

Although it was realized that the Society would be unable to produce such a Journal without financial assistance, it was resolved that representations be made to Cambridge University Press to discuss the possibility of establishing a periodical reflecting current research in Old Testament studies; at the same time, members of the Society would be consulted as to their willingness to subscribe to such a publication and contribute articles to it, should it ever see the light of day. A meeting was therefore arranged between representatives of the Society (S.A. Cook, R.H. Kennett and T.H. Robinson) and representatives of the Syndics of the Cambridge University Press on 13th October 1919. It was pointed out that the amount of research work carried out in the area of Old Testament studies by scholars from the British Isles would provide ample assurance that sufficient material for inclusion in the Journal would be forthcoming. The Press intimated that the subscription for the Journal would probably be about ten shillings per issue, though it was suggested that members of the Society might receive it at a reduced rate. Contributors would receive no financial remuneration, though they might be given a limited number of offprints of their article, while reviewers would just receive a copy of the volume to be reviewed. The Press was generally very sympathetic to the proposal to establish the Journal, but emphasized that it was normal for a learned periodical to start with an endowment or a guarantee fund (of about £300 for two years if the periodical was to appear quarterly). Given that the cash balance of the Society at this time was just over £6, and that the War Loan Certificates were valued at just over £9, the cost of publishing a Journal was clearly deemed to be prohibitive, and it was suggested that attempts be made to consult other publishers who might be able to provide more favourable terms.

Thus, on 1st January 1920, three representatives of the Society (G.H. Box, R.H. Kennett and T.H. Robinson) met with a representative from SPCK. They pointed out that British scholars engaged in Old Testament research had no adequate outlet for the publication of their work, and that, as a result, the research of British scholars suffered by comparison with that produced in Germany and America. The representative of SPCK appeared sympathetic to the idea of publishing a half-yearly Journal, though demanded some guarantee that the material contained therein 'should not be anti-Christian'. The Society's representatives did not see this as a problem; they quickly realized, however, that what might prove far more problematic was the *financial* guarantee that would be expected were the Press to proceed with the project. In a letter subsequently sent to the Society, SPCK calculated that the cost of producing such a Journal, allowing for a circulation of about 350, would be about £94 per issue. Once again, the cost was deemed to be prohibitive, and it was decided that no further progress should be made concerning the idea of establishing the *Journal of Old Testament and Semitic Studies*.

b. *Bible Translations*

In one of the first Notices sent to members of the Society on 20th March 1918, it was suggested that a record be kept of their published contributions, and the Secretary thus invited members to send him information regarding any books or articles which they had had published during the previous year. The first list of published contributions (six by three different authors) appeared in the Notice sent out to members on 22nd August 1918. Among the publications listed in the Notice sent out the following year was an article which had appeared in the May 1918 edition of the *Expositor* by W.H. Bennett under the title ‘On the Impossibility of Translating the Old Testament’. It may well have been in reaction to that publication that G.B. Gray was invited to read a paper at the first Meeting of the Society following the War on ‘The Possibility of Issuing a New Translation of the Old Testament’. Although Gray was unable to attend in person to deliver his paper, the members present thought it worthwhile to discuss the desirability and practicality of issuing a new translation of the Old Testament. It was emphasized that the need for such a translation was widely felt, especially ‘amongst organizations undertaking aggressive Christian work with working men and students’, and it was resolved that the Secretary should arrange a meeting with a representative of the Student Christian Movement in order to pursue the matter further. At this meeting it was agreed by both parties that ‘there was grave need of some means whereby the message of the Old Testament could be brought home to the student world’. While members of the Society clearly had in mind the possibility of a new translation of the Old Testament, the representative of the Student Christian Movement was of the view that the most urgent need was a rearrangement of the Old Testament material in some sort of chronological order so that its readers could better appreciate ‘the evolutionary element in the religion of Israel’. Representatives of the Society were quick to point out the difficulty involved in undertaking such a task, not the least of which was that only small portions of the literature could be dated accurately. In the event, it was resolved to publish the Pentateuch in separate documents, J, E, and P, so that each could be read continuously, thus enabling an outline sketch of the main lines of the development of Israel’s religion from earliest times to emerge.

Despite the success of this initial undertaking, there seemed little appetite among members of the Society to produce the kind of material requested by the Student Christian Movement, though they readily recognised that 'much could be done to encourage the popular study of the Old Testament if organizations like the Student Movement could be brought into closer touch with the leading scholars of the country'. Members of the Society seemed far more amenable to a suggestion by the Adult School Movement that some of the books of the Old Testament be translated into 'modern colloquial English'. A draft translation of the book of Amos was prepared to the evident satisfaction of the Adult School Movement, and it was decided that the Society might produce further translations along the same lines, with T.H. Robinson acting as co-editor with G. Currie Martin. *The Book of Amos in Colloquial English* duly appeared in 1921, published by the National Adult School Union, and in the Winter Meeting 1922 it was reported that it had sold no fewer than 3,000 copies. It was quickly decided that translations should now begin on other books of the Old Testament, and competent scholars were commissioned to translate Genesis and Jeremiah, among other books. The popularity of these translations can be gauged by the fact that by July 1928 sales of the translation of Amos had increased to 10,200; the translation of Genesis had sold 7,000 copies, and that of Jeremiah 4,900. By 1939, the last year for which reliable figures are available, the total sales of the translations of the various books of the Old Testament had reached 42,000.

Popular as these colloquial translations proved to be, at the Winter Meeting of the Society in 1921 a special committee met to discuss a memorandum prepared by W.B. Stevenson, of Glasgow University, concerning the possibility of preparing a new translation of the entire Old Testament into 'dignified modern English'. The committee was of the view that such a translation should be easily intelligible to ordinary readers, and that if any emendation of the Hebrew were deemed to be necessary, these should 'incline to the conservative side'. Individual groups of scholars would be responsible for the historical books, the legal literature, the poetical books, and the prophetic books. It was decided that frequent meetings of these groups would not be necessary but specimen chapters could be prepared and circulated in advance amongst members of each group and these would then be considered at the next Meeting of the Society. However, no sooner had the criteria for the new translation been decided than the Society learned that a new translation of the Old Testament on the lines contemplated had already been prepared 'by a well-known scholar' and would shortly be ready for publication. When the new translation by

James Moffatt appeared, in two volumes, in 1924, the Society decided to abandon the project, at least for the time being, but to keep it under review.

c. *Volumes Sponsored by the Society*
In the early 1920s the idea was mooted of co-operating with SPCK to contribute volumes to a projected series entitled 'Texts for Students', and it was decided that studies on the book of Ruth (which was assigned to A.R.S. Kennedy) and Amos (assigned to T.H. Robinson) should open the series. As Robinson observed in his Secretary's report in January 1921: 'If this Society had done nothing else, it would have justified itself by thus bringing so much of the scholarship of the country into touch with the practical needs of the day'. SPCK agreed to publish the volume on Amos on two conditions: first, the Society must guarantee the sale of 1,000 copies and, second, the Society must offer a monetary guarantee of £20. The volume on Amos appeared in 1923 and by 1933 it had sold 1,085 copies; the volume on Ruth appeared in 1928 and by 1933 it had sold 1,130 copies.

At the Meeting of the Society in July 1920 one newly enrolled member contributed a monetary gift to establish a Publications Fund, and during a Meeting of the Society in the following year it was resolved to use money from the Fund to produce volumes by members of the Society, so that their research could be made available to a wider public. At the Winter Meeting 1922 it was reported that the Publications Fund stood at £50, and it was decided that a subvention from the Fund be made towards the publication of an Aramaic Grammar, which was in the process of being prepared by W.B. Stevenson. The Grammar, published by the Clarendon Press, appeared in 1924, and over 200 copies were sold within a few months of its publication. At about the same time the Committee recommended that a volume of essays be prepared by members of the Society designed to survey the current state and progress of research in various fields of Old Testament study, and it was agreed that if financial guarantees were to be required by the Press for its publication, such guarantees would be granted by the Society 'provided that the sum were not too large'. The volume, edited by A.S. Peake, appeared in 1925 under the title *The People and the Book*, and by 1935 it had sold in excess of 4,000 copies. In order to celebrate the 21st anniversary of the Society's foundation it was decided to publish another volume on similar lines; this was published by the Clarendon Press under the title *Record and Revelation*, and was edited by H. Wheeler Robinson. A further volume of essays outlining the present position of Old Testament studies was commissioned to mark the Jubilee Meeting of the Society; this volume appeared under the title *The Old Testament and Modern Study* and was edited by H.H. Rowley. To mark its 40th anniversary the Society arranged for the publication of a volume of extra-biblical texts in English translation illustrating the Old Testament, and D. Winton Thomas was appointed as editor. The volume appeared under the title *Documents from Old Testament Times* (1958), and the Society was so pleased with the way the book had been produced that a letter was sent to the publishers, Messrs Thomas Nelson and Sons, commending them for 'the excellence of the production of the book and the remarkably low price'. A further volume, entitled *Archaeology and Old Testament Study*, also edited by D. Winton Thomas, appeared in 1967 to celebrate the Jubilee year of the Society's foundation.

In 1974 Henton Davies expressed the hope that the Diamond Jubilee of the Society would be marked by a volume discussing aspects of the theological message of the Old Testament, and the Committee agreed to commission such a volume and appointed G.W. Anderson as its editor. It was expected that the volume would be published in time for the Summer Meeting 1975, so that it would coincide with the 50th anniversary of the publication of *The People and the Book*. In 1976, however, it was reported that there had been a delay in publication, occasioned partly by defaulting contributors, and partly by the fact that one chapter had to be reduced from 30,000 to 9,000 words! The volume, outlining research in various branches of Old Testament study, eventually appeared in 1979 under the title *Tradition and Interpretation,* and it was to prove so popular that a quarter of a century later Oxford University Press included it in its new 'print-on-demand' programme, thus making it available to a new generation of biblical scholars. Ten years after the publication of *Tradition and Interpretation* the Society sponsored another volume, this time exploring insights gained from a cross-disciplinary approach to the Old Testament. The volume, edited by R.E. Clements, appeared under the title *The World of Ancient Israel: Sociological, Anthropological and Political Perspectives*, and contained 18 contributions by members of the Society. At the Winter Meeting 1991 it was reported that the hardback version of the book was out of print, having sold more than a thousand copies, and that a Japanese translation was being prepared.

It was at the Winter Meeting of the Society in 1988 that David Clines reported on a proposal to produce a new Hebrew Dictionary which would not be confined to Biblical Hebrew but would cover material down to the Qumran writings. He suggested—possibly more in hope than expectation—that the project would be completed in five years. The Society was asked to indicate its support for the venture by making a grant towards the initial expense of producing the Dictionary, and members were encouraged to become involved in various aspects of the work. The project was welcomed by the Society and the sum of £500 was given to assist with the early stages of its preparation. It was agreed that the project would be deemed as being carried out under the auspices of the Society. At the next Meeting of the Society, in the summer of 1988, it was reported that £100,000 had been promised for the project, and that work would start on it in September, four research assistants having been appointed to begin on the massive undertaking. At the Summer Meeting 1990 Clines reported that the Aleph volume (which represented 10% of the completed work) was due to appear in the New Year. It was at the Winter Meeting 1994 that the Committee welcomed the first volume of the *Dictionary of Classical Hebrew*, and Sheffield Academic Press presented the Society with an archive copy of the first volume of the Dictionary in recognition of its initial sponsorship of the project.

Over the years the Society has sponsored three series of monographs, the first of which, entitled 'Old Testament Studies', was published by T. & T. Clark and appeared between 1935 and 1956. A second series, published by Cambridge University Press, appeared between 1970 and 1984, and a third series, published by Ashgate and edited by Margaret Barker, was officially launched at the Winter Meeting 2005, the final volume appearing in 2013. A fourth series, to be published by Cambridge University Press and edited by Lena-Sofia Tiemeyer, is due to appear from 2017 onwards. During the Winter Meeting 1984 it was recommended that the Society should be associated with a series of Old Testament Guides, to be edited by R.N. Whybray, and published by Sheffield Academic Press. The series proved extremely popular and covered every book in the Old Testament. Twenty years later, a new series of Old Testament Guides was commissioned, published by Sheffield Phoenix Press (and subsequently by Bloomsbury Publishing), and edited by Adrian Curtis.

d. *The SOTS 'Wiki'*

As part of the centenary celebrations, it was decided to develop a SOTS Wiki. The aim was to provide a reliable source of information about the Old Testament for the lay reader on the Web, written by SOTS members and based on sound critical scholarship. As a wiki, it was not intended to be static but to be regularly corrected and developed by any person registered to do so, thus enabling it to be continuously kept up to date. The idea was developed by James Aitken and Stuart Weeks, and Walter Houston was appointed as its editor, with a grant to enable him to employ student editorial assistants. The work is ongoing under the direction of these three members together with Jonathan Stökl. At January 2016 there was a page on most of the books of the Old Testament, and a number of supplementary pages on a variety of topics. It is hoped eventually to have complete coverage of the books of the Hebrew canon and Apocrypha, together with a hundred or so pages on related topics.

Of all the Society's publications, however, one in particular deserves special mention, since it has proved an indispensable tool for those engaged in the study of the Old Testament. This, of course, is the Society's *Book List*.

e. *The Book List*

It was during the 13th Summer Meeting of the Society in July 1931 that the idea of issuing a *Book List* was first mooted. A fairly bland list of publications by members had been included in the Minutes of all the previous Meetings since the inception of the Society, but it was now decided to issue, in addition, a short list, on an annual basis, of the most important books dealing with the Old Testament which had been published during the previous year 'with brief notes as to their value'. A *Book List* committee was established, and various scholars were allocated responsibility for particular areas of research according to their expertise: G.R. Driver (Philology), H. Wheeler Robinson (Theology), T.H. Robinson and W.O.E. Oesterley (History), etc. The first issue of the *Book List* appeared in 1933 and contained brief notices relating to some 36 books listed under various appropriate sub-headings (Archaeology; Exegesis; History of Israel; Philology; Religion of Israel; etc.).

From the outset it was deemed desirable that the *Book List* be made available as widely as possible, and the Society was delighted to receive letters from the London Library and Dr Williams' Library expressing a willingness to receive copies of the List and even to purchase some of the volumes recommended therein. Individual members of the Society were encouraged to persuade their local libraries to do likewise. In 1968 the possibility was considered of increasing the *Book List*'s circulation of approximately 1,250 per annum, and in the following year it was agreed to send out a leaflet explaining the nature of the publication to Universities, Theological Colleges and Colleges of Education as well as to 'interested individuals throughout the world'. Although this measure brought the List to the attention of a much wider readership, some members felt that there was scope to extend its circulation even further, and in the early 1990s discussions took place with Scholars Press regarding the possibility of publicising the *Book List* in North America, where the largest potential market was to be found. An agreement was reached whereby Scholars Press would advertise the *Book List* in its catalogue, in return for which it would retain a percentage of the revenue from the sales. The agreement would be for a period of three years in the first instance, to be followed by a review. At the Winter Meeting 1993 it was reported that the new arrangement with Scholars Press was well in place and that sales of the *Book List* had shown an encouraging up-turn; thus, in the following year the Society had little hesitation in agreeing that the arrangement with Scholars Press should be renewed for a further period.

Over the years the cost of producing the *Book List* has often proved contentious, and the Society has always sought to abide by the principle that the *Book List* should finance itself, and that members should not be made to subsidise its cost to non-members. Various proposals were made at Meetings of the Society as to how to reduce the cost of producing the *Book List*. One suggestion was to ask reviewers to pay the postage for the books they received to review; another was to apply to the British Academy for a grant to defray the expense involved in its production. In the event, the application to the Academy proved successful and generous grants were received towards its publication throughout much of the 1980s.

By the end of the 1980s, however, further grants from the British Academy were no longer forthcoming, and in 1997 it was noted that publication of the *Book List* was once again beginning to drain the Society's resources. The Committee thus had little hesitation in welcoming an offer made by Sheffield Academic Press to print the *Book List* on behalf of the Society at no cost to members on condition that it be published each year as issue 5 of the *Journal for the Study of the Old Testament* and circulated to subscribers to the Journal. The principle was endorsed that, as from 1998, the printing of the *Book List* would be transferred from W.S. Maney & Son to Sheffield Academic Press, an arrangement which undoubtedly involved substantial savings for the Society. It was made clear, however, that editorial control of the *Book List* would remain firmly in the hands of the *Book List* editor, and that the Society would retain the copyright. In 1998 it was decided that the rest of the Society's printing, notably the Bulletin and the printing and circulation of conference details, be transferred from Maney's to Sheffield Academic Press. Thus it was that the long-standing relation with W.S. Maney & Son Ltd of Leeds came to an end after more than half a century. Appropriately enough, in 1996 it was agreed to make Mr Stanley Maney an Honorary Life Member of the Society in recognition of the huge debt owed by the Society over the years to him and his staff.

As has already been indicated, the first issue of the *Book List*, published in 1933, contained some 36 short notices; recent volumes of the List, on the other hand, have contained review-notices covering between 400 and 500 volumes. In his *Short History* of the Society covering the period 1917–92, John Rogerson rightly notes that 'there is no doubt that *Book List* Editors and Sales Secretaries have devoted time and energy to the *Book List* beyond the call of duty', and that the Society is 'more deeply indebted to them than anyone can realize'. In a strongly worded letter to the Society, dated 11th July 1999, Lester Grabbe, the retiring editor of the *Book List*, pleaded that any future editor should be given adequate clerical and administrative support by the Society. He had devoted 'practically the entirety of each December and January to the *Book List* for the past seven years', adding 'I do not think the sheer volume of ordering, receiving, and cataloguing 400–500 books, writing to reviewers, packaging up, posting the books, receiving and editing the reviews…has been grasped by everyone'. He thus proposed that the Society contribute £2,000 a year towards the cost of providing the editor with the necessary clerical assistance, since 'no other journal of such influence and value to scholarship is as poorly resourced as the *Book List*'. His suggestion received general support from the Committee, and his successor agreed to accept the role on condition that he received the required assistance in 'the more mechanical aspects of the post'. A proposal was approved by the Business Meeting that an annual amount of £2,000 should be paid to provide the editor with the necessary administrative assistance. While there can be no doubt that such assistance has relieved the *Book List* editor over recent years of some of the administrative burdens involved, the work remains a huge task, and in 2007 John Day noted that in his own experience the work of *Book List* editor had occupied 'hundreds of hours' each year, even *with* the help of an assistant, although he admitted that it did have its plus side, 'enabling one to have the pick of the reviews'.

9. *Financial Matters*

The original subscription to the Society was set at five shillings per annum, and by the end of 1917 the accounts of the Society showed a balance of £5 4s 11d, most of which had been invested in War Loan Certificates. Already in August of the following year a notice had to be sent out to members drawing attention to the fact that 'there are still several subscriptions outstanding'. At the first Meeting of the Society following the War, however, it was noted that its finances were 'in a fairly good condition', which was perhaps not surprising, given that 'expenditure has been very small during the last thirty months’. It was at a Meeting of the Society held in July 1920 that the Society decided to appoint a Treasurer. In the Summer Meeting of 1926, however, attention had to be drawn once again to the fact that the subscription of some members was still outstanding, and it was resolved that any member who was more than three years in arrears would be deemed to have resigned from the Society.

At the 15th Winter Meeting held in 1933 warm tributes were paid to F.B. Rockstro, who was retiring as Treasurer after ten years of service, and it was noted that the financial position of the Society had steadily improved during the previous decade, due in no small measure to the efficiency and patience with which he had performed his office. The total assets of the Society now stood at £372, and five years later, at the ‘coming of age’ Meeting of the Society to celebrate 21 years since its inception, the total assets of the Society amounted to £436. Members had been encouraged during the previous year to pay their subscriptions by Banker’s Order, though only 16 had opted to do so. An appeal was made by the Treasurer for more members to pay their subscriptions in this way, and by the following summer the number paying by Banker’s Order had doubled to 32.

During the years of the Second World War the total assets of the Society stood at approximately £500. The policy during these years was not to ask for subscriptions, but to welcome them if they were paid. By the end of the War, however, the Society was in a more precarious situation, financially, and the Treasurer was authorized to cash War Savings Certificates, not exceeding the value of £200, to prevent an overdraft at the bank. The Committee proposed a motion to the Winter Meeting 1947 that the membership fee be raised to ten shillings per annum, and the possibility was considered of establishing a Life Membership of the Society by commutation of fees. The motion was passed, and it was agreed that ‘members of five years’ standing should have the option of paying a life subscription of six guineas, which should be reduced by one guinea for each five year period of membership’. Members of 35 years’ standing would be permitted to become Life Members without further financial obligation to the Society.

It is clear that various factors had contributed to the Society’s parlous financial situation during this period. One factor was that an increasing number of members had booked a room at a Meeting but, owing to illness or some other unforeseen circumstance, had been prevented from attending, thus rendering the Society liable for payment of the room. It was therefore decided that a booking fee of five shillings be charged to members who had booked a room but who had later been unable to attend.

A more significant factor contributing to the dire financial position of the Society, however, was that no fewer than 53 members had failed to pay their subscriptions, and it was decided to name and shame the culprits (two of whom, embarrassingly, were later to be elected Presidents of the Society!).

Various ingenious methods were suggested during this period as to how to keep the Society on a sound financial footing. One suggestion made at the Winter Meeting 1950 was that the cigars remaining from the Jubilee Dinner held on the Thursday evening should be auctioned, an expedient which managed to raise the princely sum of £2 for the Society's coffers! The following year it became necessary to raise the subscription to one guinea per annum and, in order to make further savings, it was decided that, as from January 1952, the size of the Annual Bulletin which was sent out to members should be reduced. This Bulletin was the first to appear without the list of members' publications. Furthermore, a plea was made to those who had compounded for Life Membership to make a voluntary contribution to the newly established 'Life Membership Fund'; clearly, the Society had no further claim on them, but if they felt they would like to make a supplementary payment, the Treasurer would 'be pleased to hear from them'.

By the 28th Winter Meeting of the Society, held during 30th December 1952–1st January 1953, its finances appeared much healthier: its assets had now exceeded £1,000 for the first time, due partly to the increased subscription, and partly to an increase in sales of the *Book List*. Members were reminded that it was now possible to pay their subscriptions under Deed of Covenant for seven years, provided that they paid Income Tax at the standard rate. Subscriptions paid in this way were worth almost double to the Society, and the amount of tax refunded would be credited to the Publications Fund.

The Bulletin for 1974, however, noted that rising costs were severely impacting on the financial position of the Society. Postal charges had increased, adding to the bill for sending books to reviewers for the *Book List*, and the *Book List* itself had been affected by a 40% increase in the cost of paper. Continuing inflation meant that subscriptions would have to rise sooner than expected, and the failure of some members to pay their dues merely added to the difficult financial situation. Not surprisingly, a long discussion followed the Treasurer's report to the Committee at the Winter Meeting 1975, and various suggestions were made as to how to keep the Society's costs down and to ensure its financial stability. Some argued that the *Book List* in future should be paid for by members, rather than given gratis to those who had paid a subscription. One member even suggested that the papers read at Meetings of the Society could be taped and sold to those who had been unable to attend! It is perhaps worth noting that the financial difficulties encountered by the Society during this period were by no means unique, for similar problems were experienced by other learned societies, who were themselves compelled to take drastic measures in order to reduce their costs. The subscription was raised to £12 in 1980, and this measure undoubtedly helped to establish the Society on a firm financial footing. Indeed, by the mid-1980s the finances of the Society were, once again, in a reasonably healthy state. This was partly due to the fact that some members had given generous donations to the Society, and partly due to the fact that grants had been received throughout much of the decade from the British Academy toward the publication of the *Book List*. By 1987 the Society's assets stood at over £20,000.

The Society was acutely aware of the fact that the cost of attending its Meetings was such that some who might wish to attend were unable to do so. To this end, a Bursary Fund was established to assist members with such expenses, and the Society encouraged its members to draw upon this wherever appropriate. The Fund was designed primarily for members of the parochial clergy and others who did not hold academic posts. A subgroup was set up to look at the cost of membership and especially the possibility of applying differential rates, and it suggested that a two-tier system might be the simplest solution: one for salaried members and the other for graduate students and retired members. However, since the cost of attending a Meeting represented considerably greater outlay than membership subscription, it was decided that notice should be given, both in the programme and in the Bulletin, that the Society was keen for the Bursary Fund to be drawn upon wherever and whenever appropriate. There can be no doubt that the establishment of the Bursary Fund and the decision to permit a lower subscription rate has contributed greatly to the success of the Society in recent years by enabling it to recruit a steady stream of doctoral and post-doctoral students as members. The current age profile of its members is a tribute to the wisdom of the Society in implementing these measures.

The Society's Committee over the years managed to devise ingenious ways of saving unnecessary expenditure for its members. In 2003, for example, some difficulty with the sound had been experienced by a number of members who had attended Meetings in the New Common Room at the Manor House in Birmingham, and the Committee was asked to look into the possibility that the Society might invest in its own public address system for use at future Meetings. The Minutes for that year note that, in view of the likely cost that would be incurred, 'the Committee was minded to seek, rather, a rearrangement in the seating at Manor House for the next Winter Meeting'. The problem was thus solved, and no further complaints were heard regarding the quality of the sound at the Manor House in Birmingham!

10. *Conclusion*

The Society for Old Testament Study (fondly known as SOTS to its regular members) was established as a fellowship of those interested in the study of the Old Testament as an academic discipline and who wished to give and receive the support that comes from sharing common aims and interests. There can be no doubt that the service of the Society to Old Testament scholarship over the past century has been immense, and as H.H. Rowley observed in his Introduction to the *Festschrift* presented to one of its founder members, Theodore H. Robinson, the 'fellowship it has promoted amongst Protestant, Roman Catholic and Jewish scholars, and the stimulus it has provided by the papers read at its meetings would alone have justified its formation'. In his Secretary's Report presented to the Winter Meeting of the Society in January 1921, when the Society had been in existence for a mere four years, T.H. Robinson made the following observation: 'We are not working merely for today or for this year; we hope that the full value of this Society will be manifested in later generations in an increased interest and more complete co-ordination of Old Testament Studies in this country'. His words may serve as a fitting memorial to the work of the Society during the last hundred years, whilst at the same time encapsulating its aspirations for the years to come.

OVERLEAF: The following pages reproduce the pages in the Society's 'Presidential Bible' (see above, p. 42) on which the successive Presidents of the Society have signed their names at the time of their installation as President.

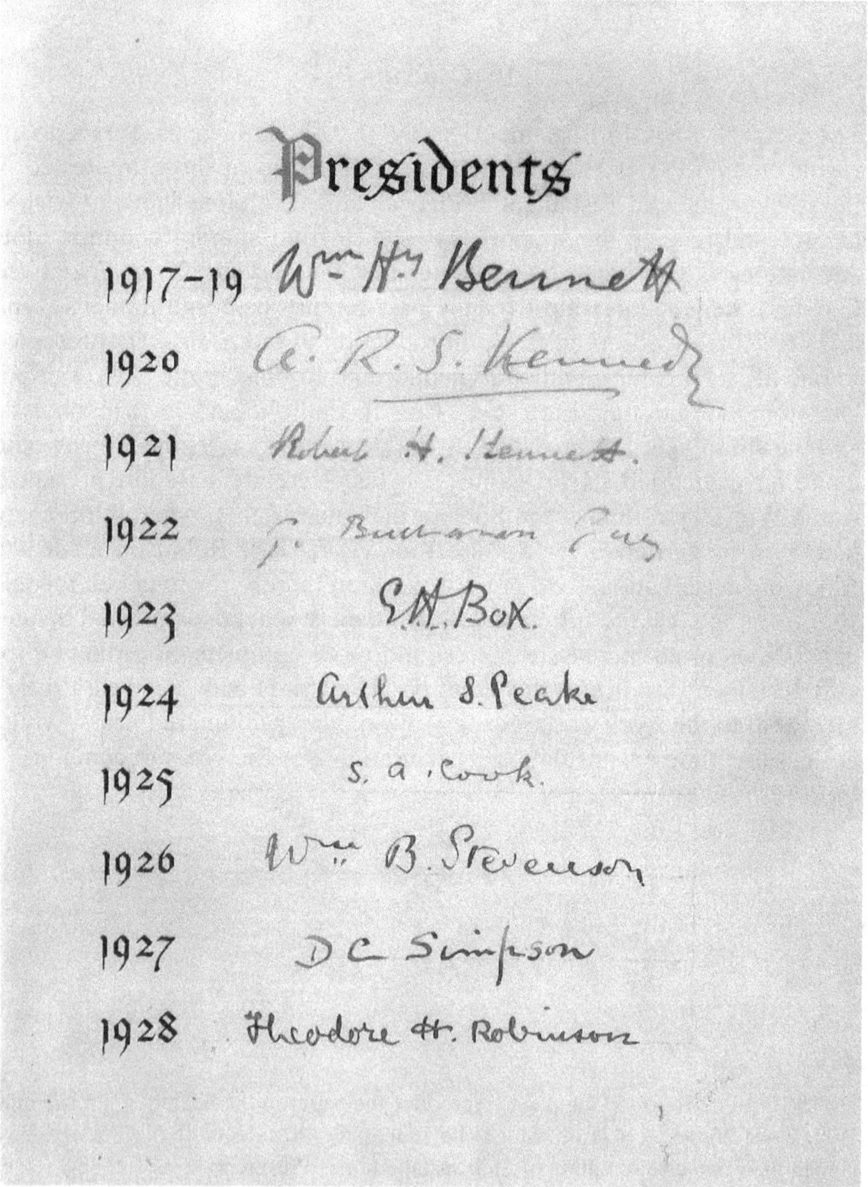

Presidents

1917–19 Wm Hy Bennett

1920 A. R. S. Kennedy

1921 Robert H. Kennett.

1922 G. Buchanan Gray

1923 G.H. Box.

1924 Arthur S. Peake

1925 S. A. Cook.

1926 Wm B. Stevenson

1927 D C Simpson

1928 Theodore H. Robinson

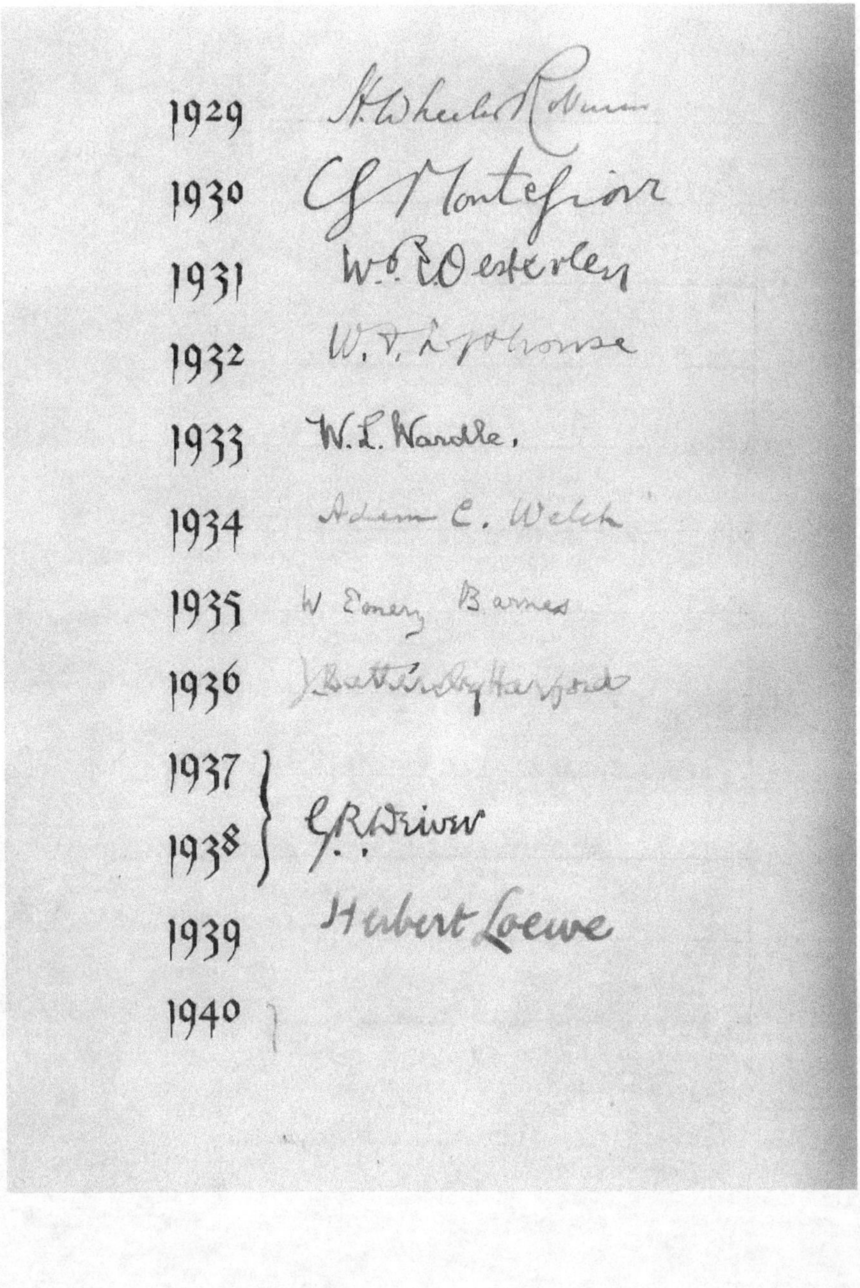
1929
1930 C G Montefiore
1931 W. O. E. Oesterley
1932 W. F. Lofthouse
1933 W. L. Wardle.
1934 Adam C. Welch
1935 W Emery Barnes
1936
1937
1938 G R Driver
1939 Herbert Loewe
1940

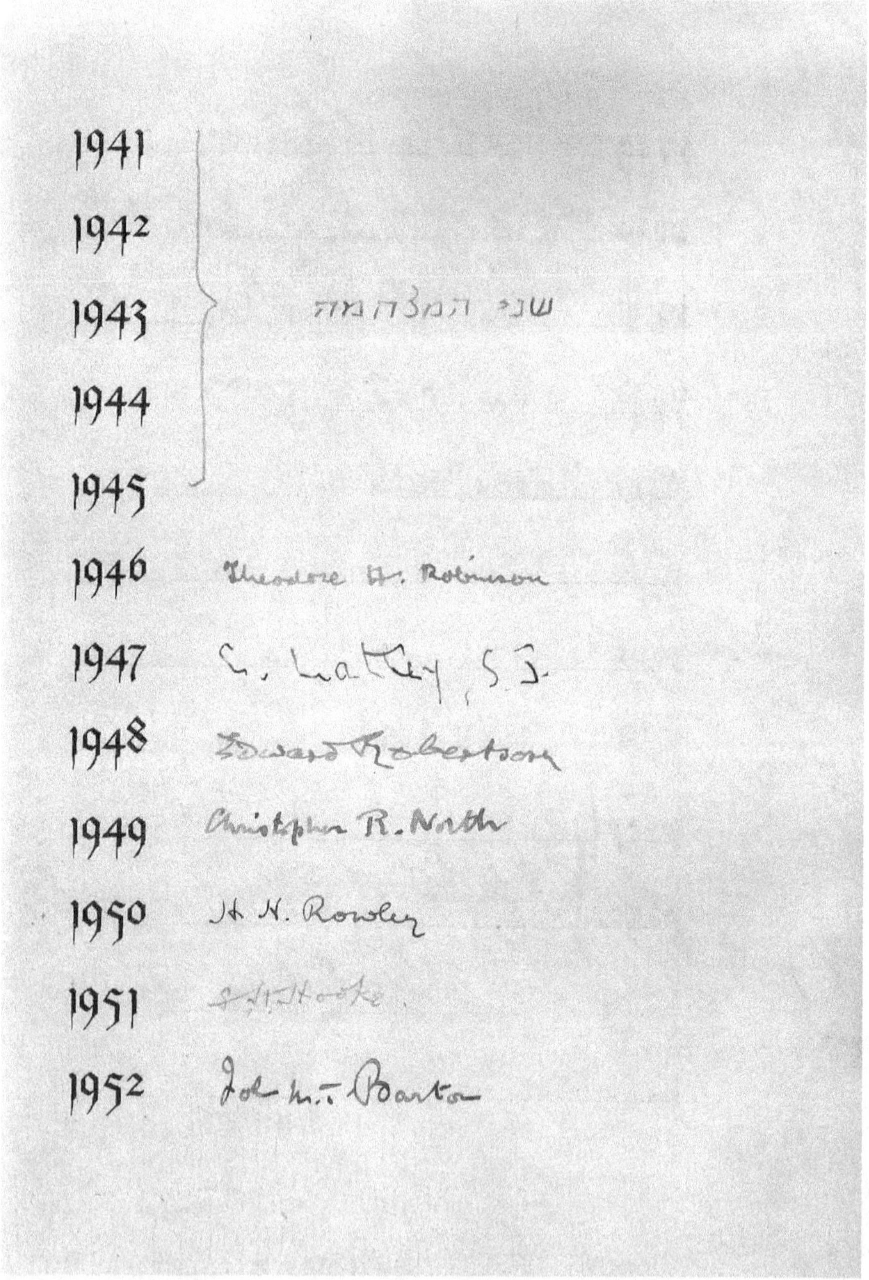
1941
1942
1943 שני המלחמה
1944
1945
1946 Theodore H. Robinson
1947 C. Lattey, S.J.
1948 Edward Robertson
1949 Christopher R. North
1950 H. H. Rowley
1951 S. H. Hooke
1952 John M. T. Barton

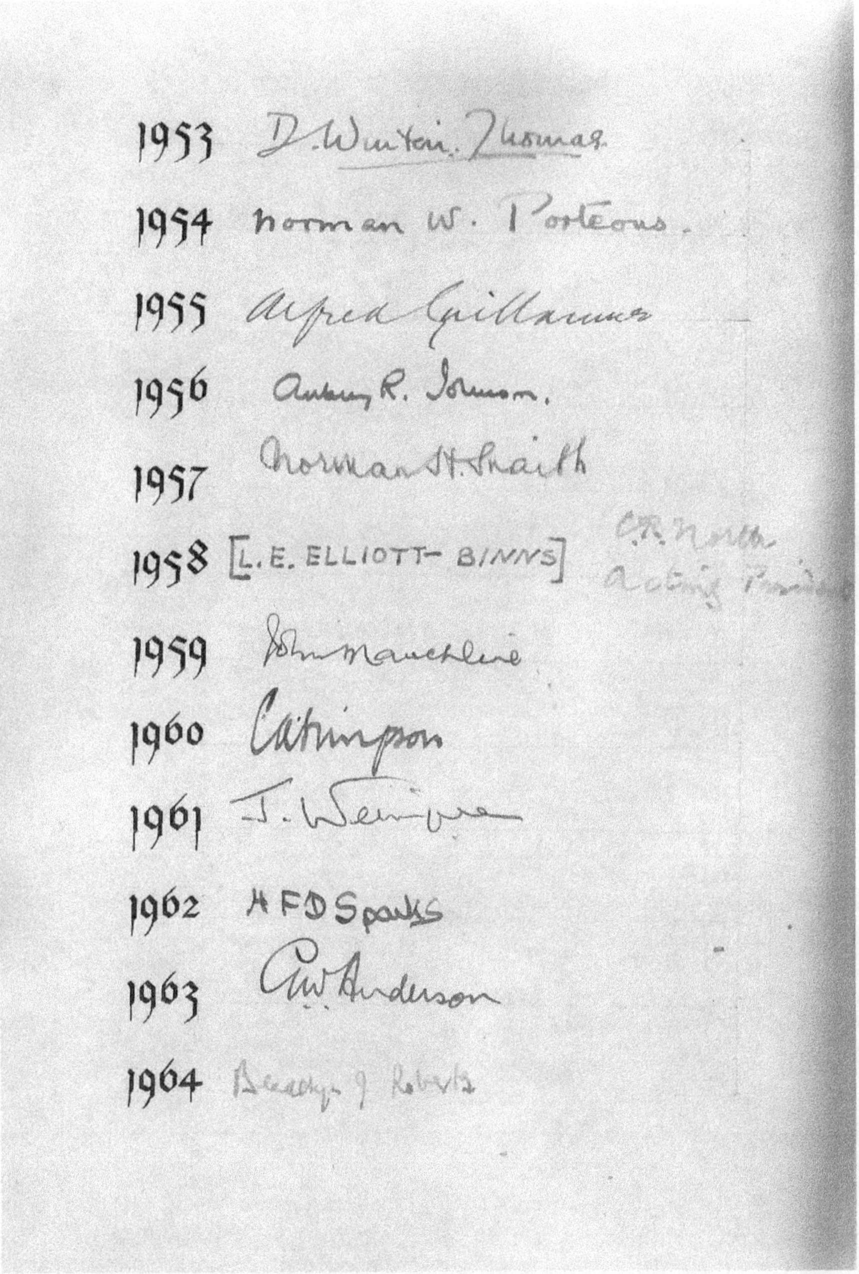
1953 D. Winton Thomas
1954 Norman W. Porteous.
1955 Alfred Guillaume
1956 Aubrey R. Johnson.
1957 Norman H. Snaith
1958 [L.E. ELLIOTT-BINNS] C.R. North Acting President
1959 John Mauchline
1960 C A Simpson
1961 J. Weingreen
1962 H F D Sparks
1963 G W Anderson
1964 Bleddyn J Roberts

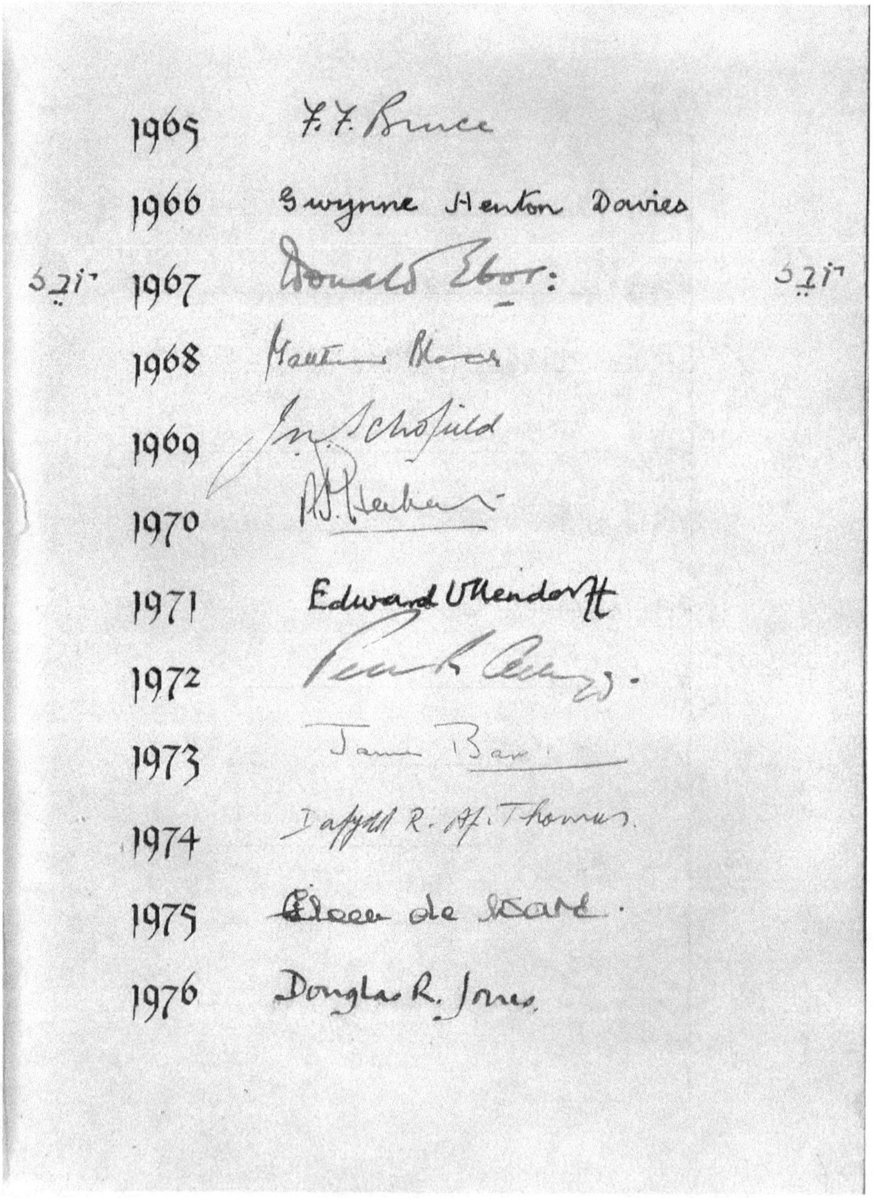
1965 F. F. Bruce
1966 Gwynne Henton Davies
1967 Donald Ebor:
1968 Matthew Black
1969 J. N. Schofield
1970 A. S. Herbert
1971 Edward Ullendorff
1972 Peter R. Ackroyd
1973 James Barr
1974 Dafydd R. Ap-Thomas
1975 [illegible] de Boer
1976 Douglas R. Jones

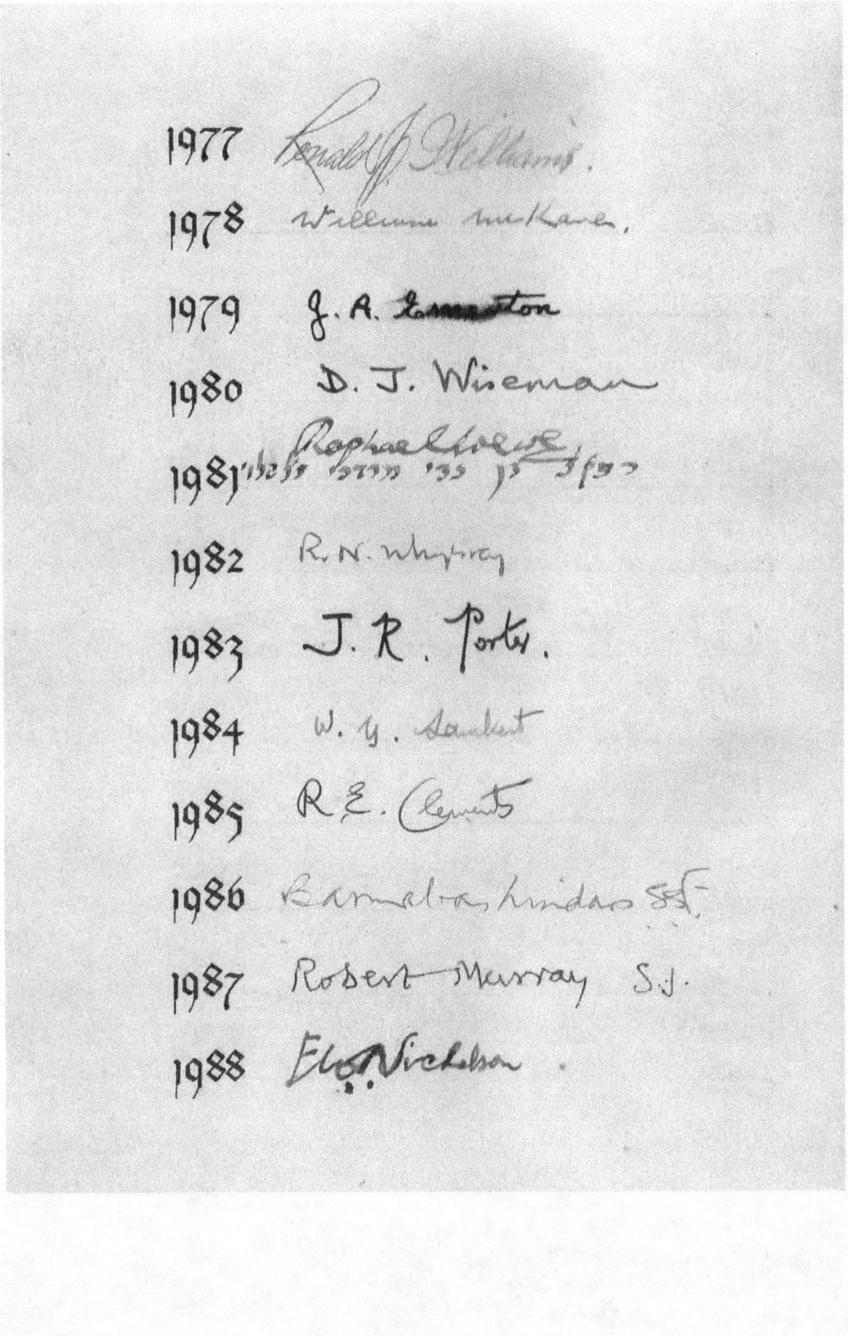

1977 Ronald J. Williams.

1978 William McKane.

1979 J. A. Emerton

1980 D. J. Wiseman

1981 Raphael Loewe [illegible]

1982 R. N. Whybray

1983 J. R. Porter.

1984 W. G. Lambert

1985 R. E. Clements

1986 Barnabas Lindars SSF.

1987 Robert Murray S.J.

1988 E. W. Nicholson.

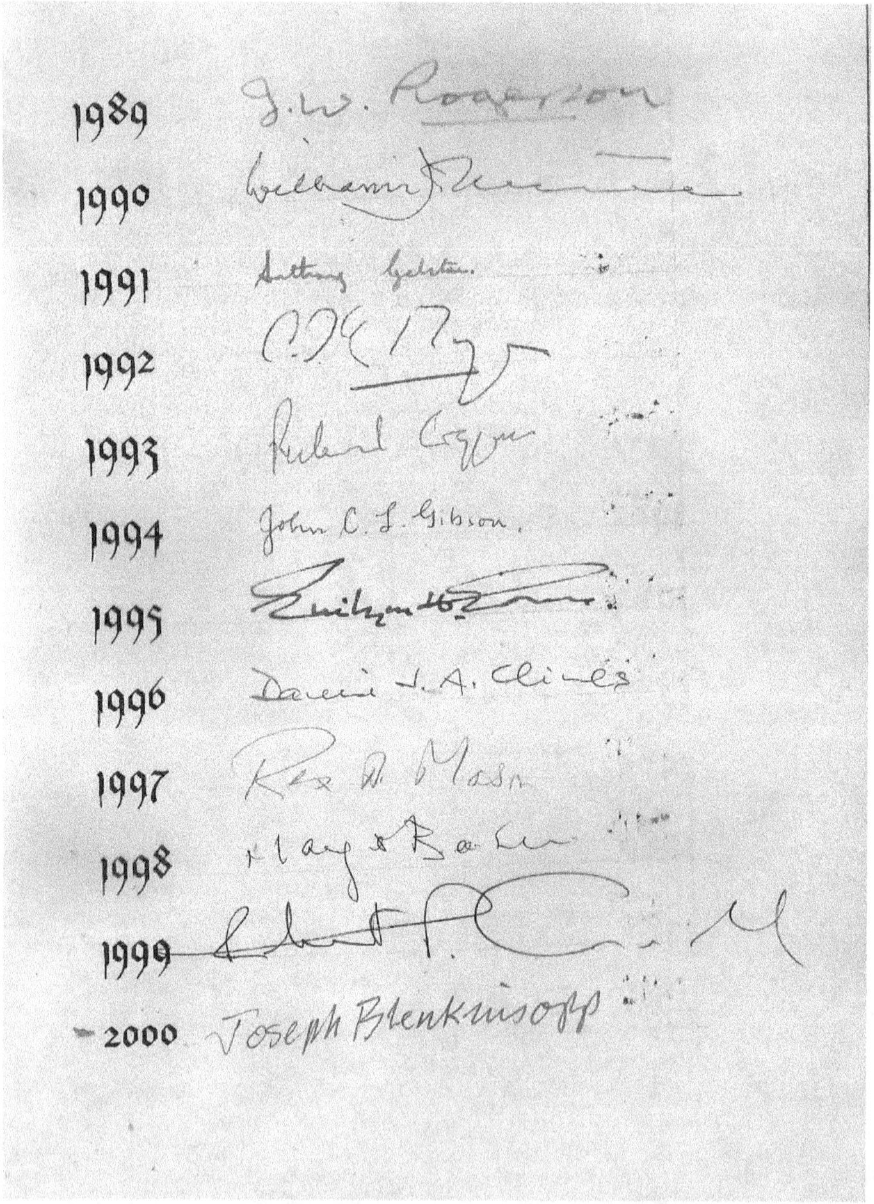
1989 J.W. Rogerson
1990
1991 Anthony Gelston
1992
1993 Richard Coggins
1994 John C.L. Gibson.
1995
1996 David J.A. Clines
1997 Rex A. Mason
1998 Margaret Barker
1999
2000 Joseph Blenkinsopp

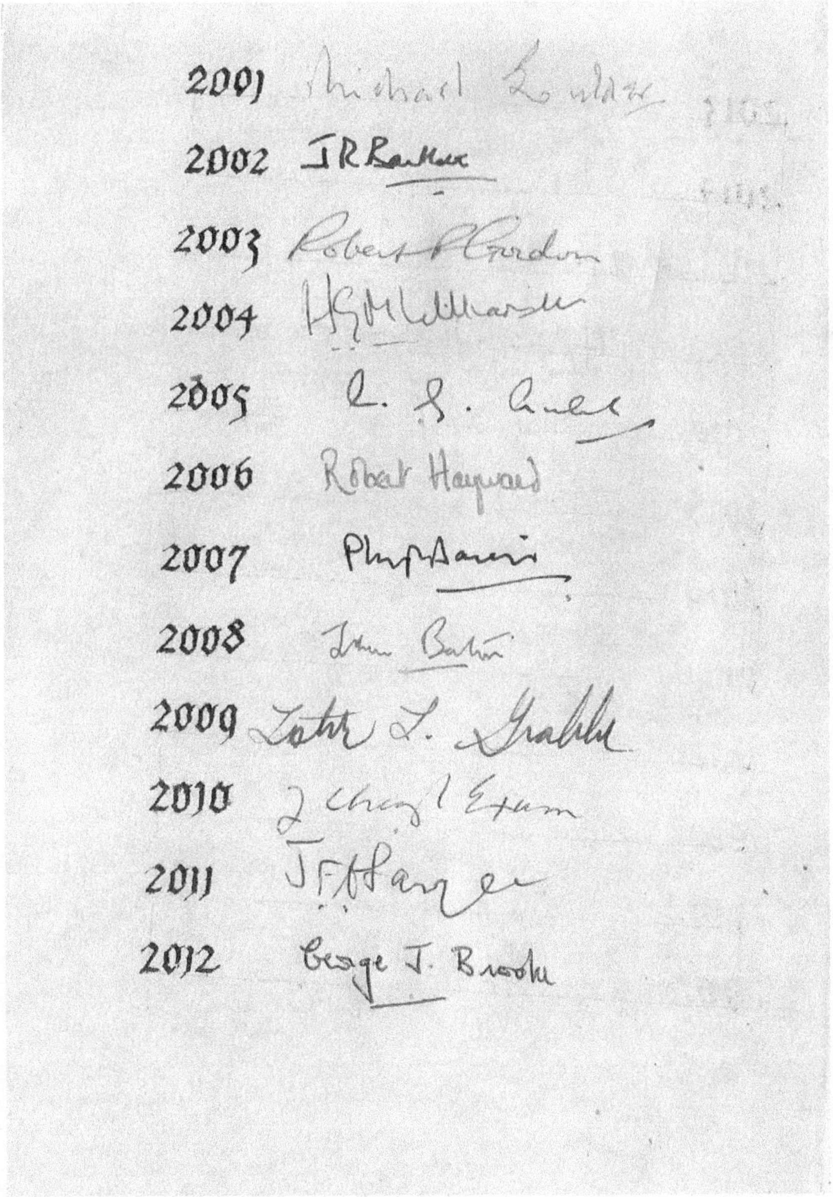

2001 [illegible]
2002 J R Bartlett
2003 [illegible]
2004 [illegible]
2005 [illegible]
2006 Robert Hayward
2007 Philip Davies
2008 John Barton
2009 Lester L. Grabbe
2010 J. Cheryl Exum
2011 J F Healey
2012 George J. Brooke

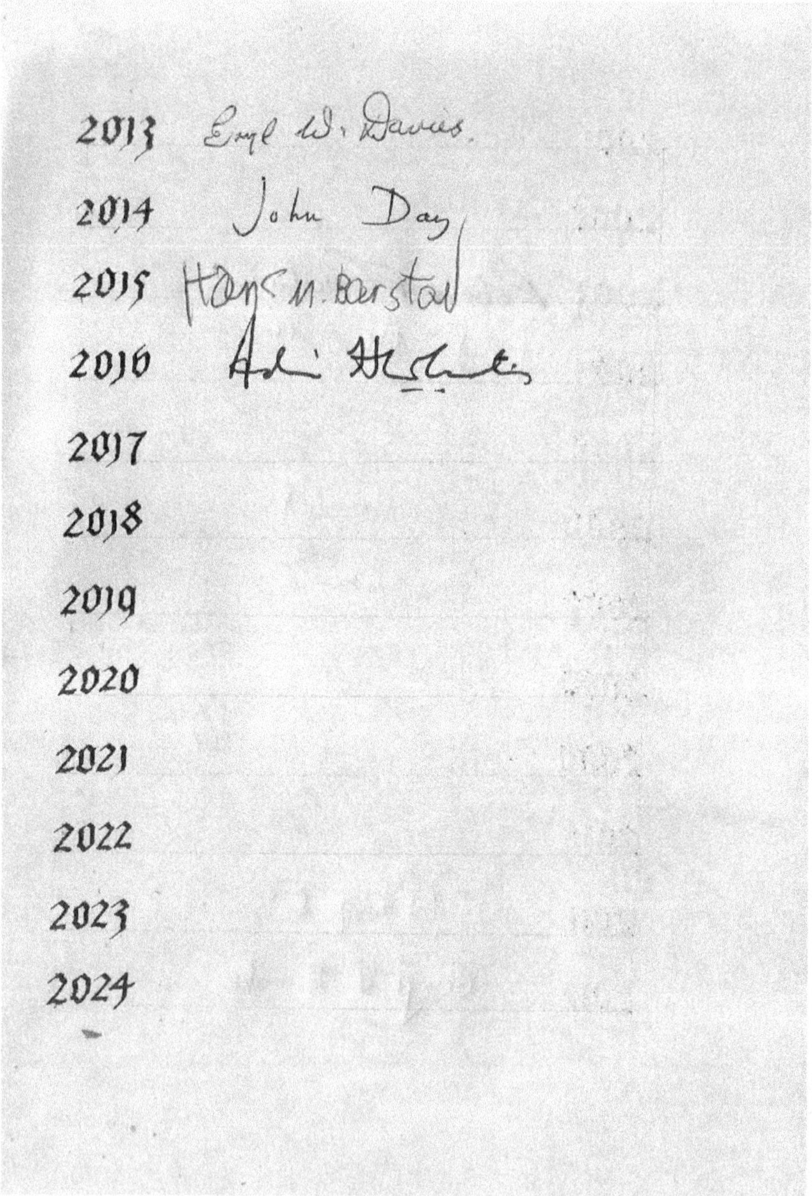
2013 Eryl W. Davies.
2014 John Day
2015 Hans M. Barstad
2016 [illegible]
2017
2018
2019
2020
2021
2022
2023
2024

A Timeline of SOTS

A chronological record of the meetings, officers, publications, and selected other diverse activities of the Society for Old Testament Study during its first 100 years, from the Inaugural Meeting held in January 1917 to the celebration of its Centenary in 2017.

(Note: Presidents of the Society are cited in terms of the academic post which they held during or prior to their presidential year and of a publication for which they were renowned at that time. No account is taken of retirements from the cited post by the time of the presidential year, or of subsequent moves to other posts or of subsequent publications for which an individual might have received greater renown in later times.)

Compiled by
John Jarick

■ **The Inaugural Meeting** of the Society for Old Testament Study was held at King's College, LONDON, on 3rd January 1917. The meeting elected as **President**, WILLIAM BENNETT (Professor of Old Testament Exegesis at New College, London, and author of *The Value of the Old Testament for the Religion of Today*), and as **Secretary**, THEODORE ROBINSON (Lecturer in Semitic Languages at University College, Cardiff). There were thirty original members, and the initial assets of the Society were eleven Savings Certificates and seven pounds in cash.

1917 **1918**

■ **In 1918** the newly formed Society was not in a position to hold any further meetings after the inaugural meeting of 1917, not least on account of the continuation of the 'Great War'. But a solid foundation had been laid upon which SOTS could flourish in the years ahead, given that 'the Society was formed for the promotion of the study of the OT, and seeks to include in its membership all persons who in recognized institutions are concerned with instruction in OT studies, and all persons who are properly qualified to pursue their interest in the OT' (as it was phrased in the Society's *Short History, 1917–1950*).

■ **The Second Meeting** of the Society was held at Dalton Hall, MANCHESTER, on 16th–18th July 1919. A presidential address was given by WILLIAM BENNETT (who had been elected as the inaugural President in 1917) on 'The Work and Activities of the Society'. Among the topics discussed at the meeting were proposals for a journal devoted to OT studies, and for a new translation of the OT. (In due course the proposed journal proved to be beyond the Society's resources, and the proposed translation was also put aside, despite considerable preparation, because the Moffatt translation was about to appear.)

1919

1920

■ **The President for 1920** was ARCHIBALD KENNEDY, Professor of Hebrew and Semitic Languages at Edinburgh, who gave a presidential address on 'The Beginnings of Hebrew Study amongst Christians, with special reference to Scotland'.

■ **A Winter Meeting** was held at King's College Hostel, LONDON, on 30th December 1919–1st January 1920.

■ **A Summer Meeting** was held at Coates Hall, EDINBURGH, on 20th–22nd July.

■ **In 1920** the Society decided to produce a series of ***Texts for Students*** and translations of OT books into colloquial English for use in schools.

1921

■ **The President for 1921** was ROBERT KENNETT, Regius Professor of Hebrew at Cambridge and author of *Deuteronomy and the Decalogue*. The title of the presidential address is not recorded.

■ **The Winter Meeting** was held at King's College Hostel, LONDON, on 4th–6th January.

■ **The Summer Meeting** was held at Cheshunt College, CAMBRIDGE, on 19th–21st July.

■ **In 1921** the Society's first **Treasurer** (JOHN MCCLURE) took office; and it was resolved that steps be taken to consider the preparation of a new critical edition of the Masoretic Text.

1922

■ **The President for 1922** was BUCHANAN GRAY, Professor of Hebrew and Old Testament at Mansfield College, Oxford, and author of *Forms of Hebrew Poetry*, who gave a presidential address on 'The Horizons of Old Testament Scholarship'.

■ **The Winter Meeting** was held at King's College Hostel, LONDON, on 3rd–5th January.

■ **The Summer Meeting** was held at Keble College, OXFORD, on 18th–20th July.

■ **In 1922** a new **Treasurer** (FRANK ROCKSTRO) took office; and it was decided 'to suspend the new translation of the OT' (but yet 'to keep the project constantly in view').

■ **The President for 1923** was GEORGE BOX, Samuel Davidson Professor of OT at King's College London and author of *The Book of Isaiah*, who gave a presidential address on 'The Liturgical Factor in Some Recent Old Testament Criticism'.
■ **The Winter Meeting** was held at King's College Hostel, LONDON, on 2nd–4th January.
■ **The Summer Meeting** was held at University House, BIRMINGHAM, on 17th–19th July.
■ **In 1923** the membership of the Society passed 100; and a donation was made to the *Zeitschrift für die alttestamentliche Wissenschaft* on account of its financial straits.

1923

■ **The President for 1924** was ARTHUR PEAKE, Rylands Professor of Biblical Criticism and Exegesis at Manchester and author of *The Problem of Suffering in the OT*, who gave a presidential address on 'The Present Position of OT Criticism'.
■ **The Winter Meeting** was held at King's College Hostel, LONDON, on 1st–3rd January.
■ **The Summer Meeting** was held at Dalton Hall, MANCHESTER, on 15th–17th July.
■ **In 1924** the Society adopted qualifications for membership, among them that new members be engaged in teaching the OT and have a degree or diploma that included study of Hebrew.

1924

■ **The President for 1925** was STANLEY COOK, Lecturer in Hebrew at Cambridge and author of *The Laws of Moses and the Code of Hammurabi*, who gave a presidential address on 'The Trend of OT Studies'.
■ **The Winter Meeting** was held at King's College Hostel, LONDON, on 30th December 1924–1st January 1925.
■ **The Summer Meeting** was held at Cheshunt College, CAMBRIDGE, on 14th–16th July.
■ **In 1925** the Society's first volume of collected essays, ***The People and the Book*** (edited by ARTHUR PEAKE), was published.

1925

■ **The President for 1926** was WILLIAM STEVENSON, Professor of Hebrew & Semitic Languages at Glasgow and author of *Grammar of Palestinian Jewish Aramaic*, who gave a presidential address on 'The Ancient Legal Codes of the Nearer East'.
■ **The Winter Meeting** was held at King's College Hostel, LONDON, on 5th–7th January.
■ **The Summer Meeting** was held at Queen Margaret Hall, GLASGOW, on 13th–15th July.
■ **In 1926** the Society produced a ***Scripture Bibliography*** for use in schools (4000 copies at a price of 6d per copy, published by Nisbet & Company).

1926

■ **The President for 1927** was DAVID SIMPSON, Oriel Professor of the Interpretation of Holy Scripture at Oxford and author of *Pentateuchal Criticism*, who gave a presidential address on '1 Esdras 3:1–5:6'.
■ **The Winter Meeting** was held at King's College Hostel, LONDON, on 28th–30th December 1926.
■ **The Summer Meeting** was held at Keble College, OXFORD, on 27th–30th September.
■ **In 1927** CHRISTOPHER NORTH took office as joint **Secretary**, and the category of **Honorary Membership** was introduced.

1927 **1928** **1929** **1930**

■ **The President for 1928** was THEODORE ROBINSON, Professor of Semitic Languages at University College, Cardiff, and author of *Prophecy and the Prophets in Ancient Israel*, who gave a presidential address on 'Some Remarks on Hebrew Grammar' (later published as a booklet by Oxford University Press on the Society's behalf, under the title *The Genius of Hebrew Grammar*).
■ **The Winter Meeting** was held at King's College Hostel, LONDON, on 27th–29th December 1927.
■ **The Summer Meeting** was held at St Michael's College, CARDIFF, on 24th–26th July.

■ **The President for 1929** was WHEELER ROBINSON, Principal of Regent's Park College, Oxford, and author of *The Cross of Job*, who gave a presidential address on 'The Unity of the Old Testament in Israel's Consciousness of Election'.
■ **The Winter Meeting** was held at King's College Hostel, LONDON, on 1st–3rd January.
■ **The Summer Meeting** was held at Keble College, OXFORD, on 16th–18th July.
■ **In 1929** WILLIAM OESTERLEY and THEODORE ROBINSON were tasked with producing ***A History of Israel*** (published in 1932).

■ **The President for 1930** was CLAUDE MONTEFIORE, Jewish theologian and Reform leader, and author of *The Old Testament and After*, who gave a presidential address on 'The Achievement of the OT'.
■ **The Winter Meeting** was held at King's College Hostel, LONDON, on 31st December 1929–2nd January 1930.
■ **The Summer Meeting** was held at High Leigh, HODDESDON, on 22nd–24th July.
■ **In 1930** the admission to membership of scholars who were not resident in the British Isles was approved; and Exam Boards were asked to include the Bible as an exam subject.

■ **The President for 1931** was WILLIAM OESTERLEY, Professor of Hebrew and OT Exegesis at King's College, London, and author of *The Doctrine of the Last Things, Jewish and Christian*, who gave a presidential address on 'The Date of Zechariah 9–14'.
■ **The Winter Meeting** was held at King's College Hostel, LONDON, on 30th December 1930–1st January 1931.
■ **The Summer Meeting** was held at Rankin Hall, LIVERPOOL, on 21st–23rd July.
■ **In 1931** arrangements were made to issue to members an annual list of selected books in the field of OT studies.

■ **The President for 1934** was ADAM WELCH, Professor of Hebrew and OT Exegesis at Edinburgh and author of *The Code of Deuteronomy: A New Theory of Its Origin*, who gave a presidential address on 'The Attitude and Aim of the Chronicler'.
■ **The Winter Meeting** was held at King's College Hostel, LONDON, on 2nd–4th January.
■ **The Summer Meeting** was held at Carlyle Hotel, EDINBURGH, on 17th–19th July.
■ **In 1934** the Society expressed alarm at plans in Palestine to alter the level of the Sea of Galilee in the interests of a large electrical installation.

1931 **1932** **1933** **1934**

■ **The President for 1932** was WILLIAM LOFTHOUSE, Principal of Handsworth College, Birmingham, and author of *Israel after the Exile*, who gave a presidential address on '*Hen* and *Hesedh* in the Old Testament'.
■ **The Winter Meeting** was held at King's College Hostel, LONDON, on 5th–7th January.
■ **The Summer Meeting** was held at Handsworth College, BIRMINGHAM, on 12th–14th July.
■ **In 1932** the idea emerged of obtaining a **'presidential' Hebrew Bible**, and ARCHIBALD KENNEDY presented one the following year.

■ **The President for 1933** was WILLIAM WARDLE, Principal of Hartley College, Manchester, and author of *Israel and Babylon*, who gave a presidential address on 'Notes on the Structure and Exegesis of the Book of Job'.
■ **The Winter Meeting** was held at King's College Hostel, LONDON, on 3rd–5th January.
■ **The Summer Meeting** was held at Lancashire Independent College, MANCHESTER, on 11th–13th July.
■ **In 1933** a new **Treasurer** (BERNARD PICKERING) took office; and the ***Book List*** was produced for the first time (ed. THEODORE ROBINSON).

1935

■ **The President for 1935** was Emery Barnes, Hulsean Professor of Divinity at Cambridge and author of *The Psalms* in the Westminster Commentaries series, who gave a presidential address on 'The Old Testament in Greek'.
■ **The Winter Meeting** was held at King's College Hostel, London, on 1st–3rd January.
■ **The Summer Meeting** was held at Cheshunt College, Cambridge, on 16th–18th July.
■ **In 1935** the first volume in the SOTS-sponsored series of **'Old Testament Studies'** (*The Ras Shamra Tablets* by James Jack) was published.

1936

■ **The President for 1936** was Battersby Harford, Canon of Ripon Cathedral and author of *Studies in the Book of Ezekiel*, who gave a presidential address on 'The Origin and Growth of Religion'.
■ **The Winter Meeting** was held at Westminster College, London, on 1st–3rd January.
■ **The Summer Meeting** was held at St Margaret's Training College, Ripon, on 14th–16th July.
■ **In 1936** the second volume in the SOTS-sponsored series of **'Old Testament Studies'** (*Problems of the Hebrew Verbal System* by Godfrey Driver) was published.

1937

■ **The President for 1937** was Godfrey Driver, Reader in Comparative Semitic Philology at the University of Oxford and author of *Problems of the Hebrew Verbal System*. No presidential address was given on account of the president being ill.
■ **The Winter Meeting** was held at King's College Hostel, London, on 29th–31st December 1936.
■ **The Summer Meeting** was held at Richmond College, Surrey, on 13th–15th July.
■ **In 1937** the Society produced a second edition of its ***Scripture Bibliography*** for use in schools.

1938

■ **In 1938** no new President took office; rather, Godfrey Driver, who had been ill in 1937, was reappointed for a further year, and delivered a presidential address on 'Hebrew Lexicography'.
■ **The Winter Meeting** was held at King's College Theological Hall, London, on 28th–30th December 1937.
■ **The Summer Meeting** (designated the 'Coming of Age Meeting') was held at Keble College, Oxford, on 20th–23rd September.
■ **In 1938** the volume ***Record and Revelation: Essays on the Old Testament*** (ed. Wheeler Robinson) was published.

■ **The President for 1939** was HERBERT LOEWE, Reader in Rabbinics at Cambridge and author of *The Petrie-Hirschfeld Papyri*, who gave a presidential address on 'Mosaic Religion'.
■ **The Winter Meeting** was held at King's College Theological Hall, LONDON, on 3rd–5th January.
■ **The Summer Meeting** was held at Queen's College, CAMBRIDGE, on 18th–20th July.
■ **In 1939** a new **Treasurer** (AUGUSTINE FARRER) took office; and the President of that year commissioned a *shittim*-wood casket for the protection of the Society's 'presidential' Bomberg Bible.

1939 **1940** **1941** **1942**

■ **In 1940** no new President took office on account of the death of the President-elect, GEORGE COOKE, Regius Professor of Hebrew at Oxford and author of *Ezekiel* in the ICC series. In these circumstances HERBERT LOEWE, the President for 1939, was asked to continue in office for a further year. Thereafter as World War II proceeded the activities of the Society were largely in abeyance, and WHEELER ROBINSON, who had been President in 1929, was appointed as **Acting President** of the Society for the duration of the war.

■ **In 1941** and for the remainder of the war years no meetings were held. Nevertheless an annual Bulletin was sent to members giving such news as was available. The Bulletin for 1941 includes the note that 'the title Acting President is intended to distinguish the office from that of the usual presidency', and accordingly that the Society is 'not establishing a precedent for a second election to the presidency in normal times'. It further notes that 'it is not possible at the moment to make plans for future meetings; we must wait on events'.

■ **In 1942** the Bulletin sent out to members reported that 'the Committee has carefully considered whether we should attempt to hold a meeting this year, and has decided that in view of all the difficulties and uncertainties it is not yet possible to carry it through successfully; our course may be clearer next year.' It further noted that 'the policy of not asking for subscriptions, but welcoming them if they come, will be continued' (a policy of no longer sending out the previously customary bills for subscription until meetings are resumed had been announced in the previous year's Bulletin).

■ **In 1943** the Bulletin sent out to members reported that 'the Committee has once more given full and careful consideration to the advisability of holding a Summer Meeting this year, and has regretfully decided against it; apart from the uncertainties of the coming months, our membership is very scattered, and from all we can gather it is probable that few members would be able to attend a meeting'. Again it was noted that 'the policy of not asking for subscriptions, but of welcoming them if they come, is continued' (some members were paying by Banker's Order, and others continued to remit directly to the Treasurer).

■ **The President for 1946** was THEODORE ROBINSON, who had also been President in 1928. His presidential address for 1946 was on 'Retrospect and Prospect in OT Studies'.

■ **A Winter Meeting** was held at Regent's Park College, OXFORD, on 1st–3rd January.

■ **A Summer Meeting** was held at Aberdare Hall, CARDIFF, on 9th–13th September.

■ **In 1946** a new **Secretary** (HENTON DAVIES) and a new **Treasurer** (LEONARD BROCKINGTON) took office, together with HAROLD ROWLEY in the new office of **Foreign Secretary** (dealing with the honorary members of the Society).

1943 1944 1945 1946

■ **In 1944** no new Bulletin was issued. Later, the first postwar report of the Secretaries (CHRISTOPHER NORTH and THEODORE ROBINSON) stated matters as follows: 'During the war Bulletins have been sent out to members, the last in March '43, since when there has been nothing to report. The question whether we should attempt to hold a meeting has from time to time been discussed between the officers, but the difficulties have always seemed insuperable.' At the end of the war years the number of members was 170, and the new Treasurer (LEONARD BROCKINGTON) reported that funds stood at £614.

■ **In 1945** a booklet of *European Scholars and Publications chiefly relating to the Old Testament during the War Years* was prepared by HAROLD ROWLEY, who was also elected as ***Book List*** **Editor** to prepare the annual *Book List* from 1946 onwards. The booklet on the war years included information on the deaths, relocations or appointments of various scholars, and on the continuation or interruption of various journals, as well as a list of books which had been published during those years; the founding in 1939 of a Dutch Old Testament Society, which met in secret during the war, was noted with admiration.

1947

■ **The President for 1947** was Cuthbert Lattey, Professor of Scripture at Heythrop College, Oxfordshire, and general editor of *The Westminster Version of the Sacred Scriptures*, who gave a presidential address on 'Biblical Stocktaking'.
■ **The Winter Meeting** was held at Wills Hall, Bristol, on 31st December 1946–2nd January 1947.
■ **The Summer Meeting** was held at Keble College, Oxford, on 22nd–24th July.
■ **In 1947** the membership fee was raised to 10 shillings per year, and a new category of life membership was introduced.

1948

■ **The President for 1948** was Edward Robertson, Professor of Semitic Languages and Literatures at Manchester and author of *The Old Testament Problem*, who gave a presidential address (at the Summer Meeting) on 'The Plot of the Book of Ruth'.
■ **No Winter Meeting** was held, on account of the fuel crisis of the 1947–48 winter.
■ **A Summer Meeting** was held at Hulme Hall, Manchester, on 7th–10th September.
■ **In 1948** the Society resolved to consider the question of eligibility for membership of non-British subjects.

1949

■ **The President for 1949** was Christopher North, Professor of Hebrew and OT Studies at Bangor and author of *The Suffering Servant in Deutero-Isaiah*, who gave a presidential address on 'Old Testament Theology and the History of Hebrew Religion'.
■ **The Winter Meeting** was held at King's College Hostel, London, on 4th–6th January.
■ **The Summer Meeting** (designated the 'Silver Jubilee of Summer Meetings') was held at the George Hostel, Bangor, on 19th–22nd July.
■ **In 1949** the category of **Associate** (i.e. overseas) **Membership** was introduced.

1950

■ **The President for 1950** was Harold Rowley, Professor of Hebrew Language & Literature at Manchester and author of *The Relevance of Apocalyptic*, who gave an address on 'The Unity of the Book of Daniel'.
■ **The Winter Meeting** (designated the 'Silver Jubilee of Winter Meetings') was held at King's College Hostel, London, on 3rd–6th January.
■ **The Summer Meeting** was held at The Castle, Durham, on 18th–21st July.
■ **In 1950** ***Studies in OT Prophecy*** (for Theodore Robinson) and ***SOTS: A Short History, 1917–1950*** (by Henton Davies) were published.

■ **The President for 1951** was Samuel Hooke, Samuel Davidson Professor of OT at King's College London and author of *The Origins of Early Semitic Ritual*, who gave a presidential address on 'The Theory and Practice of Substitution'.
■ **The Winter Meeting** was held at King's College Hostel, London, on 2nd–4th January.
■ **The Summer Meeting** was held at Norwich Training College, Keswick, Norfolk, on 17th–20th July.
■ **In 1951** the volume ***The Old Testament and Modern Study*** (edited by Harold Rowley) was published.

■ **The President for 1954** was Norman Porteous, Professor of Hebrew and Semitic Languages at the University of Edinburgh and author of 'Towards a Theology of the Old Testament' in the *Scottish Journal of Theology*, who gave a presidential address on 'The Old Testament and Some Theological Categories'.
■ **The Winter Meeting** was held at King's College Hostel, London, on 5th–7th January.
■ **The Summer Meeting** was held at Playfair Hostel, Edinburgh, on 13th–16th July.
■ **In 1954** the first **Hospitality Secretary** (Arthur Herbert) took office.

1951 1952 1953 1954

■ **The President for 1952** was John Barton, Consultor of the Pontifical Biblical Commission, who gave a presidential address on 'The Dominican School of St Etienne, Jerusalem, and Old Testament Studies'.
■ **The Winter Meeting** was held at King's College Hostel, London, on 1st–3rd January.
■ **The Summer Meeting** was held at Florence Boot Hall, Nottingham, on 15th–18th July.
■ **In 1952** a new **Treasurer** (Christopher North) took office, and a **special meeting** was held at the Pontifical Biblical Institute in Rome on 6th–13th April.

■ **The President for 1953** was Winton Thomas, Regius Professor of Hebrew at the University of Cambridge and author of *The Recovery of the Ancient Hebrew Language*, who gave a presidential address on 'A Consideration of Some Unusual Ways of Expressing the Superlative in Hebrew'.
■ **The Winter Meeting** was held at King's College Hostel, London, on 30th December 1952–1st January 1953.
■ **The Summer Meeting** was held at St Catharine's College, Cambridge, on 21st–24th July.
■ **In 1953** a **Publications Sales Secretary** (Dafydd Ap-Thomas) took office.

■ **The President for 1955** was ALFRED GUILLAUME, Professor of Arabic at SOAS, University of London, and author of *Prophecy and Divination among the Hebrews and Other Semites*, who gave a presidential address on 'The Horizon of OT Studies'.
■ **The Winter Meeting** was held at King's College Hostel, LONDON, on 5th–7th January.
■ **The Summer Meeting** was held at Woodbrooke College, Selly Oak, BIRMINGHAM, on 12th–15th July.
■ **In 1955** the practice of sending out an annual Bulletin (succeeding earlier occasional Bulletins) was begun.

1955

■ **The President for 1956** was AUBREY JOHNSON, Professor of Semitic Languages at Cardiff and author of *The Cultic Prophet in Ancient Israel*, who gave a presidential address on '"Holy Spirit" in the Thought of Ancient Israel'.
■ **The Winter Meeting** was held at King's College Hostel, LONDON, on 4th–6th January.
■ **The Summer Meeting** was held at Aberdare Hall, CARDIFF, on 17th–20th July.
■ **In 1956** the third and final volume in the SOTS-sponsored series of '**Old Testament Studies**' (*Canaanite Myths and Legends* by GODFREY DRIVER) was published.

1956

■ **The President for 1957** was NORMAN SNAITH, Principal of Headingley College, Leeds, and author of *The Distinctive Ideas of the Old Testament*, who gave a presidential address on 'Sacrifices in the Old Testament'.
■ **The Winter Meeting** was held at King's College Hostel, LONDON, on 1st–3rd January.
■ **The Summer Meeting** was held at St John's College, YORK, on 23rd–26th July.
■ **In 1957** a new ***Book List* Editor** (GEORGE ANDERSON) took office, and ***Documents from OT Times*** (ed. WINTON THOMAS) was prepared for publication in 1958.

1957

■ **The President for 1958** was LEONARD ELLIOTT-BINNS, Canon and Treasurer of Truro Cathedral and author of *From Moses to Elisha*. The presidential address (not presented because of illness) was on 'The Old Testament and Other Studies'.
■ **The Winter Meeting** was held at King's College Hostel, LONDON, on 1st–3rd January.
■ **The Summer Meeting** was held at Hope Hall, EXETER, on 15th–18th July.
■ **In 1958** a new **Treasurer** (ARTHUR HERBERT) and a new **Hospitality Secretary** (PETER ACKROYD) both took office.

1958

■ **The President for 1959** was John Mauchline, Professor of Old Testament Language and Literature at the University of Glasgow and author of *Isaiah 1–39* in the TBC series, who gave a presidential address on 'The Essentials of Old Testament Theology'.
■ **The Winter Meeting** was held at King's College Hostel, London, on 1st–3rd January.
■ **The Summer Meeting** was held at Jordanhill Training College, Glasgow, on 21st–24th July.
■ **In 1959** an **IOSOT Congress** was held in Oxford under the presidency of Godfrey Driver.

1959

1960

■ **The President for 1960** was Cuthbert Simpson, Dean of Christ Church, Oxford, and author of *Revelation and Response in the Old Testament*, who gave a presidential address on 'An Enquiry into the Biblical Theology of History'.
■ **The Winter Meeting** was held at King's College Hostel, London, on 5th–7th January. The meeting included a visit to the London Planetarium for a session on 'Stars of the Bible'.
■ **The Summer Meeting** was held at Christ Church, Oxford, on 19th–22nd July.
■ **In 1960** it was resolved that 'the number of ordinary members should not exceed 350'.

1961

■ **The President for 1961** was Jacob Weingreen, Professor of Hebrew at Trinity College, Dublin, and author of *A Practical Grammar for Classical Hebrew*, who gave a presidential address on 'The Continuity of Tradition from Old Testament to Early Rabbinic Times'.
■ **The Winter Meeting** was held at King's College Hostel, London, on 4th–6th January.
■ **The Summer Meeting** was held at Trinity Hall, Dublin, on 18th–21st July.
■ **In 1961** a new **Secretary** (Dafydd Ap-Thomas) and a new **Foreign Secretary** (Henton Davies) took office.

1962

■ **The President for 1962** was Hedley Sparks, Oriel Professor of the Interpretation of Holy Scripture at Oxford and author of *The Old Testament in the Christian Church*, who gave a presidential address on 'The Bible and Tradition'.
■ **The Winter Meeting** was held at King's College Hostel, London, on 3rd–5th January.
■ **The Summer Meeting** was held at King Alfred's College, Winchester, on 17th–20th July.
■ **In 1962** a new **Hospitality Secretary** (Islwyn Blythin) took office, and meanwhile a new **Publications Sales Secretary** (George Farr) had taken office the previous year.

■ **The President for 1963** was GEORGE ANDERSON, Professor of Old Testament Literature and Theology at the University of Edinburgh and author of *A Critical Introduction to the Old Testament*, who gave a presidential address on 'Israel's Creed: Sung Not Signed'.
■ **The Winter Meeting** was held at King's College Hostel, LONDON, on 2nd–4th January.
■ **The Summer Meeting** was held at Grey College, DURHAM, on 16th–19th July.
■ **In 1963** the volume ***Promise and Fulfilment*** (edited by FREDERICK BRUCE) was presented to SAMUEL HOOKE on his 90th birthday.

1963 1964 1965 1966

■ **The President for 1964** was BLEDDYN ROBERTS, Professor of Hebrew and Biblical Studies in the University of Wales at Bangor, and author of *The OT Text and Versions*, who gave a presidential address on 'The Hebrew Bible since 1937'.
■ **The Winter Meeting** was held at King's College Hostel, LONDON, on 1st–3rd January, and included a presentation on 'Excavations at Jerusalem' by KATHLEEN KENYON.
■ **The Summer Meeting** was held at Plas Gwyn Hostel, BANGOR, on 21st–24th July.
■ **In 1964** a new **Foreign Secretary** (GEORGE ANDERSON) took office.

■ **The President for 1965** was FREDERICK BRUCE, Rylands Professor of Biblical Criticism and Exegesis at Manchester and author of *Israel and the Nations*, who gave an address on 'Josephus and Daniel'.
■ **The Winter Meeting** was held at King's College Hostel, LONDON, on 6th–8th January.
■ **The Summer Meeting** was held at Ashburne Hall, MANCHESTER, on 20th–23rd July.
■ **In 1965** membership of the Society passed 400 as its half-centenary approached, and meanwhile it sent its warmest felicitations to the Palestine Exploration Fund on that organisation's centenary.

■ **The President for 1966** was HENTON DAVIES, Principal of Regent's Park College, Oxford, and author of *Exodus* in the Torch Bible Commentary series, who gave a presidential address on 'The Ark of the Covenant'.
■ **The Winter Meeting** was held at King's College Hostel, LONDON, on 5th–7th January.
■ **The Summer Meeting** was held at Neuadd Gilbertson, SWANSEA, on 19th–22nd July.
■ **In 1966** an **archaeological study tour** of Palestine was held in August and September; and ***SOTS: A Short History, 1917–1967*** was compiled by DAFYDD AP-THOMAS for distribution in the Jubilee Year.

■ **The President for 1967** was DONALD COGGAN, Archbishop of York, who gave an address (though not a paper as such) to the Jubilee Dinner at the start of the Winter Meeting.
■ **The Winter Meeting** was held at King's College Hostel, LONDON, on 4th–6th January, and began with a Jubilee Dinner in the Ballroom of the St Ermin's Hotel, Westminster.
■ **The Summer Meeting** was held at St John's College, YORK, on 18th–21st July.
■ **In 1967** a new ***Book List* Editor** (PETER ACKROYD) took office, and ***Archaeology and OT Study*** (ed. WINTON THOMAS) was published.

■ **The President for 1970** was ARTHUR HERBERT, Professor of OT at Selly Oak Colleges, Birmingham, and author of *Worship in Ancient Israel*, who gave an address on 'An Aspect of the Vocation of Israel'.
■ **The Winter Meeting** was held at Hughes-Parry Hall, LONDON, on 31st December 1969–2nd January 1970.
■ **The Summer Meeting** was held at Selly Oak Colleges, BIRMINGHAM, on 21st–24th July.
■ **In 1970** a new **Treasurer** (CLIVE THEXTON) and a new **Hospitality Secretary** (ERNEST NICHOLSON) took office; and a **Meeting with OTW** was held in ZEIST on 1st–4th September.

1967 1968 1969 1970

■ **The President for 1968** was MATTHEW BLACK, Principal of St Mary's College in the University of St Andrews and author of *An Aramaic Approach to the Gospels and Acts*, who gave a presidential address on 'Aramaic Studies and the Language of Jesus'.
■ **The Winter Meeting** was held at King's College Hostel, LONDON, on 3rd–5th January.
■ **The Summer Meeting** was held at St Salvator's Hall, ST ANDREWS, on 16th–19th July.
■ **In 1968** an agreement was made with Cambridge University Press for a new **SOTS Monograph Series** to be edited by JOHN EMERTON.

■ **The President for 1969** was JOHN SCHOFIELD, Lecturer in Hebrew and OT Studies at Cambridge and author of *Introducing OT Theology*, who gave a presidential address on 'The Medium and Message of Second Isaiah'.
■ **The Winter Meeting** was held at King's College Hostel, LONDON, on 1st–3rd January.
■ **The Summer Meeting** was held at Newnham College, CAMBRIDGE, on 22nd–25th July.
■ In 1969 a new **Publications Sales Secretary** (RICHARD COGGINS) was elected, to take effect with the following year's edition of the *Book List*.

■ **The President for 1971** was EDWARD ULLENDORFF, Professor of Ethiopian Studies at the School of Oriental and African Studies, University of London, and author of *The Semitic Languages of Ethiopia*, who gave a presidential address on 'Is Biblical Hebrew a Language?'
■ **The Winter Meeting** was held at Mansfield College, OXFORD, on 6th–8th January.
■ **The Summer Meeting** was held at International Hall, LONDON, on 20th–23rd July (with the papers being read in the Reading Room of SOAS, and with a visit to the Royal Library at Windsor Castle).

1971

■ **The President for 1972** was PETER ACKROYD, Samuel Davidson Professor of OT at King's College London and author of *Exile and Restoration*, who gave a presidential address on 'Theological Geography'.
■ **The Winter Meeting** was held at Halliday Hall, LONDON, on 5th–7th January.
■ **The Summer Meeting** was held at Eliot College, CANTERBURY, on 18th–21st July.
■ **In 1972** a new **Secretary** (JOHN ROGERSON) took office; and a **special meeting** was held in LOS ANGELES, as part of the International Congress of Learned Societies in the Field of Religion.

1972

■ **The President for 1973** was JAMES BARR, Professor of Semitic Languages at Manchester and author of *The Semantics of Biblical Language*, who gave a presidential address on 'Etymology and the OT'.
■ **The Winter Meeting** (a **Joint Meeting with OTW**) was held at Halliday Hall, LONDON, on 3rd–6th January.
■ **The Summer Meeting** was held at Hulme Hall, MANCHESTER, on 24th–27th July.
■ **In 1973** a new **Treasurer** (EVA PINTHUS) and **Hospitality Secretary** (JOHN MCKAY) took office; and ***Peoples of OT Times*** (ed. DONALD WISEMAN) was published.

1973

■ **The President for 1974** was DAFYDD AP-THOMAS, Senior Lecturer in Hebrew at Bangor and author of *A Primer of Old Testament Text Criticism*, who gave an address on 'Hebrew Studies in the British Isles'.
■ **The Winter Meeting** was held at Halliday Hall, LONDON, on 2nd–4th January.
■ **The 50th Summer Meeting** was held at Neuadd Rathbone, BANGOR, on 23rd–26th July.
■ **In 1974** a new **Foreign Secretary** (RONALD CLEMENTS) and a new ***Book List*** **Editor** (NORMAN WHYBRAY) took office; and an **IOSOT Congress** was held in EDINBURGH under the presidency of GEORGE ANDERSON.

1974

■ **The President for 1975** was EILEEN DE WARD, independent scholar and author of 'Mourning Customs in 1 and 2 Samuel' in the *Journal of Jewish Studies*, who gave a presidential address on 'Trial by Ordeal in the Old Testament'.
■ **The 50th Winter Meeting** was held at Halliday Hall, LONDON, on 1st–3rd January.
■ **The Summer Meeting** was held at Lady Margaret Hall, OXFORD, on 22nd–25th July.
■ **In 1975** the decision was taken that in future the *Book List* should be paid for by members and should not be paid out of membership dues.

■ **The President for 1978** was WILLIAM MCKANE, Professor of Hebrew and Oriental Languages at St Andrews and author of *Prophets and Wise Men*, who gave a presidential address on 'The Construction of Jeremiah, Chapter 19'.
■ **The Winter Meeting** was held at Halliday Hall, LONDON, on 4th–6th January.
■ **The Summer Meeting** was held at St Salvator's Hall, ST ANDREWS, on 18th–21st July.
■ **In 1978** a new **Publications Sales Secretary** (ROBIN DUCKWORTH) took office, and a new **Hospitality Secretary** (GARETH LLOYD JONES) was elected, to take office in 1979.

1975 1976 1977 1978

■ **The President for 1976** was DOUGLAS JONES, Lightfoot Prof. of Divinity at Durham and author of *Haggai, Zechariah & Malachi* in the TBC series, who gave an address on 'The Language Tradition of the OT'.
■ **The Winter Meeting** was held at Halliday Hall, LONDON, on 17th–19th December 1975.
■ **The Summer Meeting** was held at Collingwood College, DURHAM, on 20th–23rd July.
■ **In 1976** a new **Hospitality Secretary** (GRAHAM DAVIES) and **Publications Sales Secretary** (ANDREW MAYES) took office; and a **Joint Meeting with OTW** was held in LEUVEN on 30th August–2nd September.

■ **The President for 1977** was RONALD WILLIAMS, Professor of Near Eastern Studies at the University of Toronto and author of *Hebrew Syntax: An Outline*, who gave a presidential address on '"Canonical" Editions in Egypt and Israel'.
■ **The Winter Meeting** was held at Halliday Hall, LONDON, on 20th–22nd December 1976.
■ **The Summer Meeting** was held at St John's College, CAMBRIDGE, on 19th–22nd July.
■ **In 1977** a new **Secretary** (DAVID CLINES) took office; and the *Book List* began to cost members £1.50.

■ **The President for 1979** was JOHN EMERTON, Regius Professor of Hebrew at Cambridge and author of *The Peshitta of the Wisdom of Solomon*, who gave a presidential address on 'The Promises to the Patriarchs in the Book of Genesis'.
■ **The Winter Meeting** was held at Halliday Hall, LONDON, on 3rd–5th January.
■ **The Summer Meeting** (a **Joint Meeting with OTW**) was held at St John's College, CAMBRIDGE, on 16th–19th July.
■ **In 1979** an **archaeological study tour** of Palestine was held, and ***Tradition and Interpretation*** (ed. GEORGE ANDERSON) was published.

■ **The President for 1982** was NORMAN WHYBRAY, Professor of Hebrew and OT Studies at the University of Hull and author of *The Intellectual Tradition in the OT*, who gave a presidential address on 'OT Theology: A Non-Existent Beast?'
■ **The Winter Meeting** was held at Halliday Hall, LONDON, on 6th–8th January.
■ **The Summer Meeting** was held at The Lawns, University of HULL, on 19th–22nd July.
■ **In 1982** a new **Foreign Secretary** (WILLIAM MCKANE) and a new **Hospitality Secretary** (JOHN HEALEY) took office; and a **Joint Meeting with OTW** was held in ZEIST on 1st–3rd September.

1979 1980 1981 1982

■ **The President for 1980** was DONALD WISEMAN, Professor of Assyriology at the University of London and author of *The Vassal Treaties of Esarhaddon*, who gave a presidential address on '"Is It Peace?": Covenant and Diplomacy'.
■ **The Winter Meeting** was held at Halliday Hall, LONDON, on 2nd–4th January.
■ **The Summer Meeting** was held at Halifax Hall, SHEFFIELD, on 21st–24th July.
■ **In 1980** the rule on life membership was amended so that only those who had been members for thirty years *and* had retired from their employment were eligible.

■ **The President for 1981** was RAPHAEL LOEWE, Goldsmid Professor of Hebrew at University College London and author of *The Medieval Christian Hebraists of England*, who gave a presidential address on '"Salvation" is Not of the Jews'.
■ **The Winter Meeting** was held at Halliday Hall, LONDON, on 17th–18th December 1980.
■ **The Summer Meeting** was held at St John's College, CAMBRIDGE, on 21st–24th July.
■ **In 1981** a new **Treasurer** (RICHARD COGGINS), ***Book List* Editor** (MICHAEL KNIBB) and **Publications Sales Secretary** (MERVYN RICHARDSON) all took office.

■ **The President for 1983** was ROY PORTER, Professor of Theology at the University of Exeter and author of *Moses and Monarchy*, who gave a presidential address on 'The Deuteronomic Redaction of the Prophets: Some Reflections'.
■ **The Winter Meeting** was held at Halliday Hall, LONDON, on 5th–7th January.
■ **The Summer Meeting** was held at Lopes Hall, EXETER, on 19th–22nd July.
■ **In 1983** a new **Secretary** (ADRIAN CURTIS) took office, and the first volume in a series of **Old Testament Guides** (edited by NORMAN WHYBRAY) was published.

1983 1984 1985 1986

■ **The President for 1984** was WILFRED LAMBERT, Professor of Assyriology at the University of Birmingham and author of *Babylonian Wisdom Literature*, who gave a presidential address on 'Ebla and Hebrew'.
■ **The Winter Meeting** was held at Halliday Hall, LONDON, on 4th–6th January.
■ **The Summer Meeting** was held at Manor House, BIRMINGHAM, on 17th–19th July.
■ **In 1984** the Society made representations to the educational authorities concerning the diminution of language teaching in schools which was affecting the number of students able to study Hebrew.

■ **The President for 1985** was RONALD CLEMENTS, Samuel Davidson Professor of OT at King's College London and author of *OT Theology: A Fresh Approach*, who gave an address on 'Prophecy and Midrash: A Reconsideration of Isaiah 10:16-34'.
■ **The Winter Meeting** was held at Halliday Hall, LONDON, on 2nd–4th January.
■ **The Summer Meeting** (a **Joint Meeting with OTW**) was held at Fitzwilliam College, CAMBRIDGE, on 16th–19th July.
■ **In 1985** a new **Hospitality Secretary** (WALTER HOUSTON) took office.

■ **The President for 1986** was BARNABAS LINDARS, Rylands Professor of Biblical Criticism and Exegesis at Manchester and author of *The Gospel of John* in the NCBC series, who gave an address on 'Additions to the Old Greek Text of Judges'.
■ **The Winter Meeting** was held at Halliday Hall, LONDON, on 18th–20th December 1985.
■ **The Summer Meeting** was held at Hulme Hall, MANCHESTER, on 15th–17th July.
■ **In 1986** a cooperation with the Association of Centres of Advanced Theological Education was approved, leading to **OT workshops** at an ACATE consultation the following year..

■ **The President for 1987** was ROBERT MURRAY, Lecturer in Theology at Heythrop College, London, and author of *Symbols of Church and Kingdom*, who gave a presidential address on 'The Cosmic Covenant'.
■ **The Winter Meeting** was held at Halliday Hall, LONDON, on 17th–19th December 1986.
■ **The Summer Meeting** was held at Eliot College, CANTERBURY, on 14th–17th July.
■ In 1987 a new **Treasurer** (ROBERT HAYWARD), a new **Foreign Secretary** (PETER ACKROYD), and a new ***Book List* Editor** (GRAEME AULD) all took office.

1987 **1988** **1989** **1990**

■ **The President for 1988** was ERNEST NICHOLSON, Oriel Professor of the Interpretation of Holy Scripture at Oxford and author of *Deuteronomy and Tradition*, who gave a presidential address on '"Desacralization" in Deuteronomy and Its Significance'.
■ **The Winter Meeting** was held at Halliday Hall, LONDON, on 5th–7th January.
■ **The Summer Meeting** was held at Lady Margaret Hall, OXFORD, on 19th–22nd July.
■ **In 1988** a new **Hospitality Secretary** (CAROL SMITH) took office, and a **Joint Meeting with OTW** was held at ELSPEET on 29th–31st August.

■ **The President for 1989** was JOHN ROGERSON, Professor of Biblical Studies at the University of Sheffield and author of *Anthropology and the OT*, who gave a presidential address on '"*Mah Enosh*" (Psalm 8:5): The Central Question of Old Testament Theology?'
■ **The Winter Meeting** was held at Halliday Hall, LONDON, on 4th–6th January.
■ **The Summer Meeting** was held at Halifax Hall, SHEFFIELD, on 18th–20th July.
■ **In 1989** a new **Secretary** (PAUL JOYCE) took office, and ***The World of Ancient Israel*** (edited by RONALD CLEMENTS) was published.

■ **The President for 1990** was WILLIAM JOHNSTONE, Professor of Hebrew and Semitic Languages at Aberdeen and author of *Exodus* in the OT Guides series, who gave a presidential address on '*'Ish lepi 'oklo*: The Two Theological Versions of the Passover Pericope in Exodus'.
■ **The Winter Meeting** was held at Halliday Hall, LONDON, on 3rd–5th January.
■ **The Summer Meeting** was held at Crombie-Johnston Hall, ABERDEEN, on 16th–19th July.
■ **In 1990** a new **Foreign Secretary** (JOHN ROGERSON) took office; and a rise in the membership dues to £18 per annum was approved.

■ **The President for 1991** was Anthony Gelston, Reader in Theology at the University of Durham and author of *The Peshitta of the Twelve Prophets*, who gave a presidential address on 'Universalism in Second Isaiah'.

■ **The Winter Meeting** was held at Wellington Hall, London, on 2nd–4th January.

■ **The Summer Meeting** (a **Joint Meeting with OTW**) was held at Grey College, Durham, on 16th–19th July, under the theme 'Texts and Versions' (and with a shared session with the British Association of Jewish Studies on the interpretation of Genesis 1–3).

1991

■ **The President for 1992** was Andrew Mayes, Professor of Hebrew at Trinity College Dublin and author of *The OT in Sociological Perspective*, who gave a presidential address on 'On Describing the Purpose of Deuteronomy'.

■ **The Winter Meeting** was held at Halifax Hall, Sheffield, on 17th–19th December 1991.

■ **The Summer Meeting** was held at Trinity College, Dublin, on 13th–16th July.

■ **In 1992** (the Society's 75th Anniversary Year) the booklet ***SOTS: A Short History, 1917–1992*** (by John Rogerson) was published.

1992

■ **The President for 1993** was Richard Coggins, Senior Lecturer in Old Testament at King's College London and author of *Samaritans and Jews: The Origins of Samaritanism Reconsidered*, who gave a presidential address on 'The Society in the Remainder of the Century'.

■ **The Winter Meeting** was held at Queen Elizabeth Hall, London, on 5th–7th January.

■ **The Summer Meeting** was held at St Luke's Campus, Exeter, on 19th–21st July.

■ **In 1993** a new ***Book List* Editor** (Lester Grabbe) and a new **Publications Sales Secretary** (Keith Whitelam) took office.

1993

■ **The President for 1994** was John Gibson, Professor of Hebrew and Semitic Languages at Edinburgh and author of the revised edition of *Canaanite Myths and Legends*, who gave a presidential address on 'The *Vav* Consecutive'.

■ **The Winter Meeting** was held at Queen Elizabeth Hall, London, on 4th–6th January.

■ **The Summer Meeting** was held at Pollock Halls, Edinburgh, on 18th–21st July.

■ **In 1994** a **Joint Meeting with OTW** was held at the Theological University of Kampen on 28th–31st August, under the theme 'Synchronic or Diachronic? Method in OT Exegesis'.

1994

■ **The President for 1995** was GWILYM JONES, Professor of Religious Studies at Bangor and author of *1 & 2 Kings* in the NCBC series, who gave a presidential address on 'Bible Translation: Some Second Thoughts'.
■ **The Winter Meeting** was held at Manchester College, OXFORD, on 3rd–5th January.
■ **The Summer Meeting** was held at Neuadd Rathbone, BANGOR, on 10th–13th July.
■ In 1995 a new **Secretary** (KATHARINE DELL) and a new **Treasurer** (JOHN HEALEY) took office; and an **IOSOT Congress** was held in CAMBRIDGE under the presidency of JOHN EMERTON.

■ **The President for 1998** was MARGARET BARKER, independent scholar and author of *The Older Testament*, who gave a presidential address on 'The Veil of the Temple'.
■ **The Winter Meeting** was held at St Catharine's College, CAMBRIDGE, on 5th–7th January.
■ **The Summer Meeting** was held at Florence Boot Hall, NOTTINGHAM, on 20th–23rd July.
■ In 1998 a new **Hospitality Secretary** (JANET TOLLINGTON) took office, together with PHILIP JENSON in the new role of **Information Officer** and JOHN ROGERSON in the new role of **Archivist**.

1995 1996 1997 1998

■ **The President for 1996** was DAVID CLINES, Professor of Biblical Studies at the University of Sheffield and author of *The Theme of the Pentateuch*, who gave a presidential address on 'The Pyramid & the Net: OT Studies in a Postmodern Age'.
■ **The Winter Meeting** was held at University House, BIRMINGHAM, on 3rd–5th January.
■ **The Summer Meeting** was held at Halifax Hall, SHEFFIELD, on 16th–19th July.
■ **In 1996** a new **Hospitality Secretary** (DERYN GUEST) and the first **Membership Secretary** (HEATHER MCKAY) both took office.

■ **The President for 1997** was REX MASON, Fellow and Tutor in OT at Regent's Park College, Oxford, and author of *OT Pictures of God*, who gave a presidential address on 'Henry Wheeler Robinson Revisited'.
■ **The Winter Meeting** was held at University House, BIRMINGHAM, on 6th–8th January.
■ **The Summer Meeting** (a **Joint Meeting with OTW**) was held at Wadham College, OXFORD, on 22nd–25th July.
■ **In 1997** a new **Treasurer** (PETER ADDINALL) and a new **Foreign Secretary** (GRAEME AULD) both took office; and it was agreed that the *Book List* would become part of *JSOT*.

1999

■ **The President for 1999** was ROBERT CARROLL, Professor of Hebrew and Semitic Studies at the University of Glasgow and author of *Jeremiah* in the Old Testament Library series, who gave a presidential address on 'Beyond Kerygma and Kritik: A Future for Hebrew Bible Studies in the Institutions of Our Learning?'.
■ **The Winter Meeting** was held at University House, BIRMINGHAM, on 4th–6th January.
■ **The Summer Meeting** was held at Kelvin Conference Centre, GLASGOW, on 19th–22nd July, under the theme 'Academy, Bible and Church'.

2000

■ **The President for 2000** was JOSEPH BLENKINSOPP, Professor of OT at Notre Dame and author of *Prophecy and Canon*, who gave an address on 'The Prophetic Biography of Isaiah'.
■ **The Winter Meeting** was held at St Catharine's College, CAMBRIDGE, on 4th–6th January.
■ **The Summer Meeting** was held at St Catherine's College, OXFORD, on 24th–27th July.
■ **In 2000** a new **Secretary** (JOHN JARICK) and ***Book List* Editor** (GEORGE BROOKE) took office; a **Joint Meeting with OTW** was held in SOESTERBERG on 27th–30th August; and ***Text in Context*** (ed. ANDREW MAYES) was published.

2001

■ **The President for 2001** was MICHAEL GOULDER, Professor of Biblical Studies at the University of Birmingham and author of *Midrash and Lection in Matthew*, who gave a presidential address on 'Behold My Servant Jehoiachin'.
■ **The Winter Meeting** was held at Devonshire Hall, LEEDS, on 3rd–5th January.
■ **The Summer Meeting** was held at Chamberlain Hall, BIRMINGHAM, on 16th–19th July, under the theme 'The Pentateuch'.
■ **In 2001** the Society embarked on a new **SOTS Monograph Series**, edited by MARGARET BARKER.

2002

■ **The President for 2002** was JOHN BARTLETT, Principal of Church of Ireland Theological College, Dublin, and author of *Edom and the Edomites*, who gave a presidential address on 'Between Scylla and Charybdis: The Problem of Israelite Historiography'.
■ **The Winter Meeting** was held at Halifax Hall, SHEFFIELD, on 2nd–4th January.
■ **The Summer Meeting** was held at Trinity College, DUBLIN, on 22nd–25th July.
■ **In 2002** arrangements were made for members to be able to pay their annual subs by credit card, a scheme intended to help members from outside the UK.

■ **The President for 2003** was ROBERT GORDON, Regius Professor of Hebrew at Cambridge and author of *Studies in the Targum to the 12 Prophets*, who gave a presidential address on '"Comparativism" and the God of Israel'.
■ **The Winter Meeting** was held at Manor House, BIRMINGHAM, on 6th–8th January, under the theme 'The Hebrew Bible against its Ancient Near Eastern Background'.
■ **The Summer Meeting** (a **Joint Meeting with OTW**) was held at St Catharine's College, CAMBRIDGE, on 21st–23rd July, and continued the theme of the Winter Meeting.

■ **The President for 2006** was ROBERT HAYWARD, Professor of Hebrew and Old Testament at the University of Durham and author of *The Targum of Jeremiah*, who gave a presidential address on 'Targum, *Biblia Hebraica Quinta*, and Jewish Biblical Interpretation'.
■ **The Winter Meeting** was held at Manor House, BIRMINGHAM, on 4th–6th January.
■ **The Summer Meeting** was held at University College, DURHAM, on 17th–20th July.
■ **In 2006** a new **Membership Secretary** (DEBORAH ROOKE) took office, and a **Joint Meeting with OTW** was held in APELDOORN on 21st–24th August.

2003 **2004** **2005** **2006**

■ **The President for 2004** was HUGH WILLIAMSON, Regius Professor of Hebrew at Oxford and author of *The Book Called Isaiah*, who gave a presidential address on 'Do We Still Need Commentaries?'
■ **The Winter Meeting** was held at Manor House, BIRMINGHAM, on 5th–7th January.
■ **The Summer Meeting** was held at St Catherine's College, OXFORD, on 19th–22nd July.
■ **In 2004** a new **Treasurer** (JANET TOLLINGTON), a new **Hospitality Secretary** (ELIZABETH HARPER), and a new **Archivist** (EDWARD BALL) all took office.

■ **The President for 2005** was GRAEME AULD, Professor of Old Testament at the University of Edinburgh and author of *Kings without Privilege: David and Moses in the Story of the Bible's Kings*, who gave a presidential address on 'Voices from the Past'.
■ **The Winter Meeting** was held at Manor House, BIRMINGHAM, on 5th–7th January.
■ **The Summer Meeting** was held at Pollock Halls, EDINBURGH, on 18th–21st July.
■ **In 2005** a new **Foreign Secretary** (DAVID CLINES) took office, in a role that was shortly to be renamed 'Secretary for Honorary Members'.

■ **The President for 2007** was PHILIP DAVIES, Professor of Biblical Studies at Sheffield and author of *In Search of 'Ancient Israel'*, who gave an address on '"Apocalyptic": An Otherworldly Tour through the Hebrew Bible (and Beyond)'.
■ **The Winter Meeting** was held at the University of CHESTER, on 3rd–5th January.
■ **The Summer Meeting** was held at Tapton Hall, SHEFFIELD, on 9th–12th July.
■ **In 2007** a new **Information Officer** (JAMES AITKEN) and ***Book List* Editor** (JOHN DAY) took office, and a new series of **OT Guides** (edited by ADRIAN CURTIS) was commissioned.

■ **The President for 2010** was CHERYL EXUM, Professor of Biblical Studies at Sheffield and author of *Fragmented Women: Feminist (Sub)versions of Biblical Narratives*, who gave a presidential address on 'The Arts and the Exegete'.
■ **The Winter Meeting** was held at Fitzwilliam College, CAMBRIDGE, on 5th–7th January, under the theme 'The Bible and Culture'.
■ **The Summer Meeting** was held at the University of SHEFFIELD on 19th–23rd July, and continued the earlier theme.
■ **In 2010** a new **Secretary** (FRANCESCA STAVRAKO-POULOU) took office.

2007 **2008** **2009** **2010**

■ **The President for 2008** was JOHN BARTON, Oriel & Laing Professor of the Interpretation of Holy Scripture at Oxford and author of *Reading the OT: Method in Biblical Study*, who gave a presidential address on 'Prophecy and Theodicy'.
■ **The Winter Meeting** was held at the University of CHESTER on 2nd–4th January.
■ **The Summer Meeting** was held at Wadham College, OXFORD, on 21st–24th July.
■ **In 2008** a new **Membership Secretary** (VIVIENNE ROWETT) was elected, to take office the following year, and a new ***Book List* Editor** (DEBORAH ROOKE), for the 2010 edition.

■ **The President for 2009** was LESTER GRABBE, Professor of Hebrew Bible & Early Judaism at the University of Hull and author of *A History of Jews and Judaism in the Second Temple Period*, who gave a presidential address on 'The Case of the Corrupting Consensus'.
■ **The Winter Meeting** was held at Fitzwilliam College, CAMBRIDGE, on 5th–7th January.
■ **The Summer Meeting** (a **Joint Meeting with OTW**) was held at the University of LINCOLN on 27th–29th July, under the theme 'History of Ancient Israel: Between Evidence and Ideology'.

■ **The President for 2011** was JOHN SAWYER, Professor of Biblical Studies and Judaism at the University of Lancaster and author of *The Fifth Gospel: Isaiah in the History of Christianity*, who gave a presidential address on 'The Divine *hinneni* ("Here I am") in the Book of Isaiah'.
■ **The Winter Meeting** was held at Collingwood College, DURHAM, on 4th–6th January.
■ **The Summer Meeting** was held at St Hilda's College, OXFORD, on 18th–21st July, and included a day of papers and other events held jointly with the British Association for Jewish Studies.

2011

■ **The President for 2012** was GEORGE BROOKE, Rylands Professor of Biblical Criticism and Exegesis at Manchester and author of *The Dead Sea Scrolls and the New Testament*, who gave a presidential address on 'The Scribal Aesthetics of the Dead Sea Scrolls'.
■ **The Winter Meeting** was held at Collingwood College, DURHAM, on 3rd–5th January.
■ **The Summer Meeting** was held at Hulme Hall, MANCHESTER, on 16th–19th July.
■ **In 2012** a new **Archivist** (ERYL DAVIES) took office, and a **Joint Meeting with OTW** was held in AMSTERDAM on 22nd–26th July.

2012

■ **The President for 2013** was ERYL DAVIES, Reader in OT at Bangor University and author of *The Immoral Bible*, who gave a presidential address on 'Ideology and Constructions of the History of Israel'.
■ **The Winter Meeting** was held at Fitzwilliam College, CAMBRIDGE, on 2nd–4th January.
■ **The Summer Meeting** was held at Neuadd Reichel, BANGOR, on 22nd–25th July.
■ **In 2013** a new **Secretary** (HILARY MARLOW), **Treasurer** (ALASTAIR HUNTER), **Secretary for Honorary Members** (LESTER GRABBE), and **Hospitality Secretary** (JAMES PATRICK) all took office.

2013

■ **The President for 2014** was JOHN DAY, Professor of OT Studies at Oxford and author of *Yahweh and the Gods and Goddesses of Canaan*, who gave a presidential address on 'Problems in the Interpretation of the Story of the Garden of Eden'.
■ **The Winter Meeting** was held at Collingwood College, DURHAM, on 6th–8th January.
■ **The Summer Meeting** was held at St Hilda's College, OXFORD, on 21st–24th July.
■ **In 2014** a new **Information Officer** (JONATHAN STÖKL) took office, and *Archaeology & OT Study and Peoples of OT Times* became available 'print-on-demand' from OUP.

2014

■ **The President for 2015** was HANS BARSTAD, Professor of Hebrew & OT Studies at the University of Edinburgh and author of *The Myth of the Empty Land*, and the presidential address was on 'The Bible in the University: SOTS and the Academy'.
■ **The Winter Meeting** was held at Fitzwilliam College, CAMBRIDGE, on 5th–7th January.
■ **The Summer Meeting** (a **Joint Meeting with OTW**) was held at Pollock Halls, EDINBURGH, on 20th–23rd July.
■ **In 2015** a new **Secretary** (DAVID SHEPHERD) took office, and the membership fee was raised to £30.

■ As the Society moves into its second century, some words of THEODORE ROBINSON in the *Short History* of 1950 may again be apposite: '[The founders] knew that such a Society was really needed, but we could not foresee what shape it would ultimately take. We had, however, sense enough to allow it to grow as conditions demanded, with the result that it is today a much greater and more influential organization than we ever thought possible. May it continue to advance, and to grow even stronger and more efficient in its task of spreading the knowledge of Scripture.'

2015 2016 2017 →

■ **The President for 2016** was ADRIAN CURTIS, Senior Lecturer in Hebrew Bible Studies at the University of Manchester and author of *Psalms* in the EC series, who gave a presidential address on 'From *People and Book* to *Text in Context*: Volumes that Speak Volumes'.
■ **The Winter Meeting** was held at Collingwood College, DURHAM, on 4th–6th January.
■ **The Summer Meeting** was held at Hulme Hall, MANCHESTER, on 25th–28th July.
■ **In 2016** arrangements were in hand for a new **Monographs Series** (edited by LENA-SOFIA TIEMEYER) and a **'SOTS Wiki'** (edited by WALTER HOUSTON).

■ **The President for 2017** is PAUL JOYCE, Samuel Davidson Professor of Old Testament/ Hebrew Bible at King's College London and author of *Ezekiel* in the LHBOTS series, and the presidential address is on 'The Way of the Future? Into Our Second Century'.
■ **The Winter Meeting** (the **Centennial Meeting**) is scheduled for Cripps Hall, NOTTINGHAM, on 3rd–5th January.
■ **The Summer Meeting** is scheduled for King's College, LONDON, on 17th–20th July.
■ **In 2017** a new **Membership Secretary** (JANET TOLLINGTON) and a new ***Book List* Editor** (JOHN JARICK) take office.

A Century of SOTS Papers

David J.A. Clines

Over the past century, the Society has heard 1448 papers, delivered by 687 readers, at 195 Meetings.[1] In order to analyse the papers, I first had to compile a list of them. The SOTS website has included, since its creation in the late 1990s, a list (with abstracts) of papers read at Meetings from that time onwards.[2] That was the foundation of my list, but for the earlier years (1917–1989) I asked the Society's Archivist, Professor Eryl Davies of Bangor, where the archives of the Society are held, to engage

1. There have usually been two Meetings each year, one in the summer, normally in the home town of the President, the other in early January or late December, often in London. In some years there were fewer. Because of the First World War, and its aftermath, there was only one Meeting in 1917, none in 1918, and one in 1919. For six years of World War II (1940–1945 inclusive) there was no Meeting. In January 1948 there was no Winter Meeting. There have also been additional Meetings: From 1970 onward, there has been every three years a joint Meeting with the Dutch–Flemish Oudtestamentisch Werkgezelschap (OTW), the venue alternating between the UK and the Netherlands or Belgium; when SOTS is the host, the joint Meeting is also SOTS's regular Summer Meeting, and when OTW is the host, it forms an additional SOTS Meeting. There have been eight such additional Meetings. In April 1952 there was an extra Meeting held in Rome at the Pontifical Biblical Institute, and in September 1954 SOTS participated in the VIes Journées Bibliques in Louvain. In September 1972 SOTS was one of the societies participating in the International Congress of Learned Societies in the Field of Religion held in the Century Plaza Hotel, Los Angeles. The papers at these extra Meetings have been included in the present survey (in the case of the Los Angeles Meeting, only the papers given by SOTS members).

2. That service to the Society was begun by the first SOTS Information Officer, Dr Philip Jenson, who created the first SOTS website, and it was continued by his successor, Dr James Aitken, during the years when the website was at www.sots.ac.uk. The Society's current Information Officer, Dr Jonathan Stökl, maintains and updates such information on the current (at the time of going to press) webpage sots1917.org (though the Society may return to the previous web address in due course).

a postgraduate student to photocopy the programmes (or, failing that, the Minutes) of Meetings for me. Gareth Hugh Evans-Jones did that, and I then created PDFs of them and sent them to Nathan French, a postgraduate student in Aberdeen, to type up the materials into an Excel spreadsheet.[3]

On that spreadsheet is now recorded the year of the Meeting, the month, the location, the title and name of the paper reader, the person's gender, their home town, the title of the paper, and an abstract of it when it is available.[4] I added the country in the case of overseas readers and of members in the UK and the Republic of Ireland,[5] and I analysed the subjects of the papers. In all, there are now 25 elements of data about each paper, c. 35,000 bits of data all told. I also divided the list into 20-year periods, so as to track changes that had occurred in the course of the century.

The data on that spreadsheet are now available to members and other interested persons on the Society's website.[6]

3. I am very grateful to these people for their assistance, and also to SOTS itself in the person of the Treasurer, Dr Alastair Hunter, for meeting the cost of the secretarial time.

4. Professor John Day kindly assisted me in discovering the home town of a number of paper readers, especially from the early years of the Society (programmes did not always state where the reader was from).

5. When the Society was formed in 1917 the whole of Ireland was part of the United Kingdom, and SOTS has therefore (in my understanding) always included members from the Republic of Ireland, even in the years before the distinction between members and associate (overseas) members, instituted in 1949, was abolished in 1996. Citizens of the British Commonwealth countries, as British subjects (until 1983), must always have been eligible for membership. However, a note in the Report of the Winter Meeting for 1927 contains the decision, following an enquiry from a Canadian scholar, that 'the rules governing the admission of ordinary members should be so interpreted as to allow scholars resident abroad to become members'; this decision appears to have been strangely unaware that the Canadian, as a British subject, must have already been eligible for membership, while at the same time apparently opening the door to ordinary membership on the part of scholars of every country. The Report of the Winter Meeting of 1950 refers to 'new rules relating to the Associate Membership of non-British citizens which were passed at the last meeting (Bangor, July 1949)', but I have not been able to discover what those rules were. Professor John Rogerson wrote in his history of the Society (www.sots.ac.uk/historyofsots.html, 1992), 'A later modification [after 1949] added citizens of the Irish Republic to those eligible for Ordinary membership'—which creates a further complication. In 1967 Professor F.F. Bruce noted that 'ordinary membership is limited to British citizens, together with citizens of the Commonwealth and of the Republic of Ireland' ('The Society for Old Testament Study, 1917–1967', *ExpT* 78 [1967], pp. 147-48 [147]). I leave to others to investigate the changing status of various nationalities in the eyes of SOTS.

6. The website is currently sots1917.org (but see n. 2).

In the first chart one can see how the numbers of papers given to the Society have increased over the years, from 127 in the first period of 20 years to 424 in the most recent 20 years:[7]

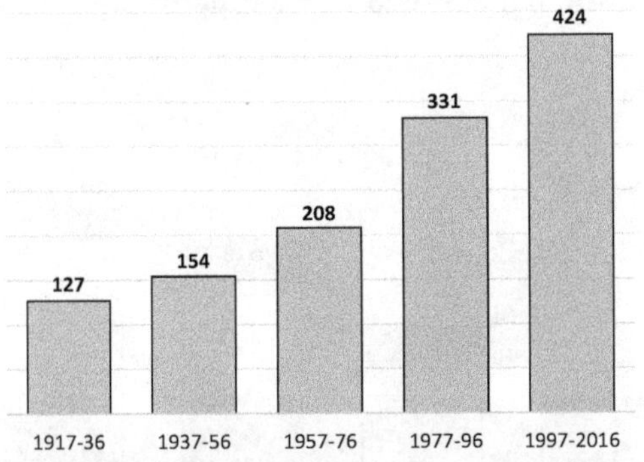

Chart 1. *Number of Papers by 20-Year Periods*

1. *Readers of Papers*

Who have been the readers of papers to SOTS? There are various ways of answering the question.

a. *Home and Overseas*

A first, and quite striking, answer is available from an analysis of the countries from which the paper readers have come. Though the Society is clearly a British society, it is noteworthy how many papers have been given by overseas speakers, 22.3%, in fact, or rather more than 1 in 5. Chart 2 shows the figures quite dramatically:

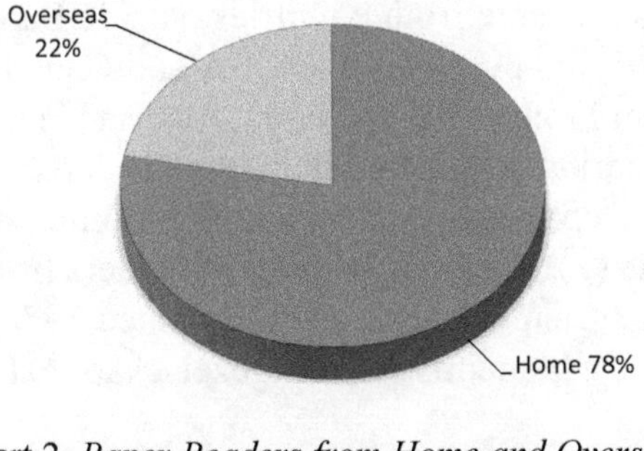

Chart 2. *Paper Readers from Home and Overseas*

7. When a Winter Meeting was held in December, I have attributed it to the following year. Panels and discussions count as a paper unless the participants are mentioned, in which case they each are regarded as reading a paper. I have counted 58 such items, variously described as discussions, panels, symposia and fora.

The proportion of overseas paper readers has increased over the years. In the chart below, the century of SOTS papers is divided into periods of 20 years, and the number of papers given by overseas visitors is shown as a percentage of all the papers read in each period:

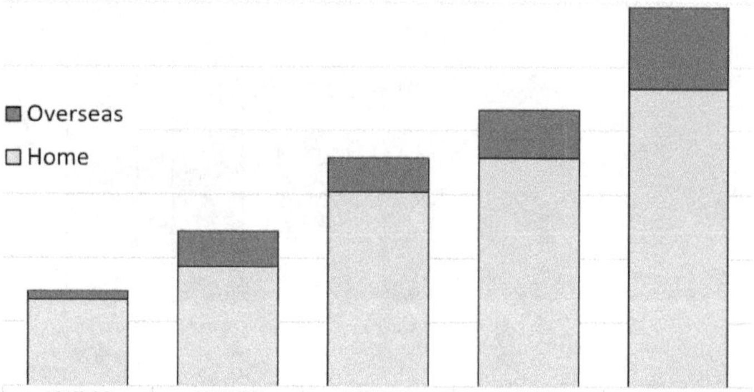

	1917-36	1937-56	1957-76	1977-96	1997-2016
Overseas % of All	9.6%	29.4%	17.4%	21.0%	27.3%
Overseas Papers	13	55	53	75	127
All Papers	135	187	304	357	466

Chart 3. *Paper Readers from Overseas, by 20-Year Periods*

The surprise here is that the highest percentage of overseas paper readers take place in the second 20-year period (1937–56), when almost one in three of the papers given were from foreign visitors.

The next chart shows the 13 top-scoring countries from which overseas readers have come; 24 overseas countries in all have been represented. 27% of overseas readers have been from the Netherlands, 20% from the USA, 11% from Germany and 6% from Israel. Only 16 of the 324 paper readers from overseas came from countries outside Europe (if we include Israel in Europe for this purpose), the USA and Canada. Notable are the small numbers from France (9), Spain (1), Austria (1) and Eastern Europe (1). Even more remarkable is the total absence of Japan, Singapore, Korea and all of Africa except South Africa, and the minimal presence of South Africa (1) and India (2), The high number of readers from the Netherlands is largely due to the triennial joint meetings since 1970 of SOTS and the Dutch–Flemish Oudtestamentisch Werkgezelschap (OTW).

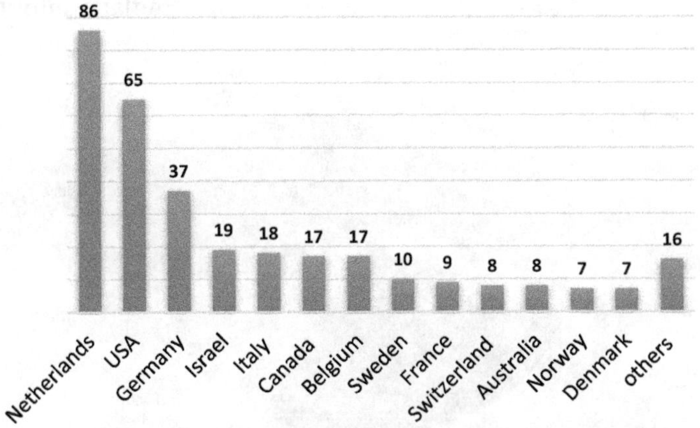

Chart 4. *Paper Readers from Overseas, by Country*

b. *SOTS Home Countries*
We can see next how the constituent home countries of SOTS are represented. The one surprising feature of this chart is the small percentage of paper readers from Wales. The importance of scholars from Wales in the foundation and earlier years of the Society has been often remarked upon; they have obviously been punching above their weight when we look at the actual numbers.

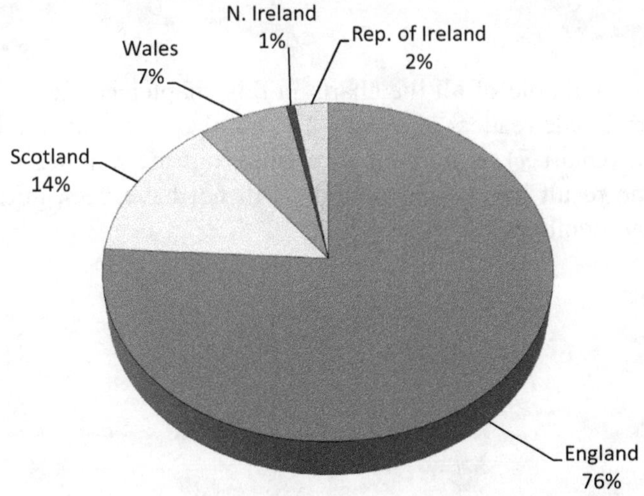

Chart 5. *Paper Readers from the SOTS Home Countries*

The next chart breaks up the 76% segment for England into its major parts:

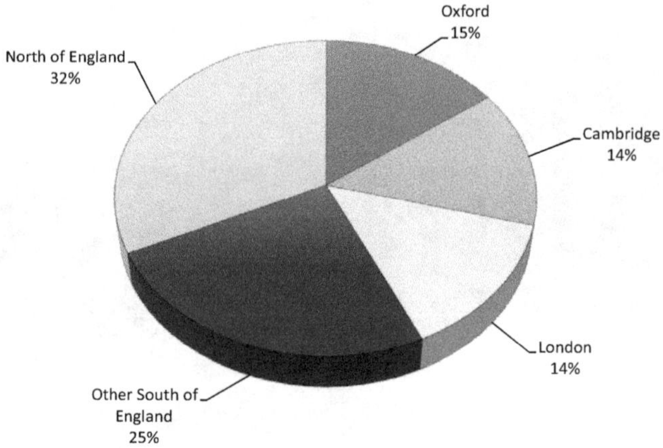

Chart 6. *Paper Readers from England*

The distribution of paper readers among the regions of England corresponds more or less to the distribution of the population, with a balance in favour of the North, which has 23.7% of the population (and 32% of SOTS papers). London has 12.9% of the population (and 14% of SOTS papers), while the South, including Oxford and Cambridge, accounts for 76.3% of the population and 68% of the paper readers.

c. *Gender*

The most remarkable of all the charts in this chapter is one showing the numbers of female readers of papers. The number of female readers, 12% of the total (Chart 7), is nothing surprising, but the number in Chart 8, showing the result by 20-year periods, will not have been guessed at, I suppose, by members.

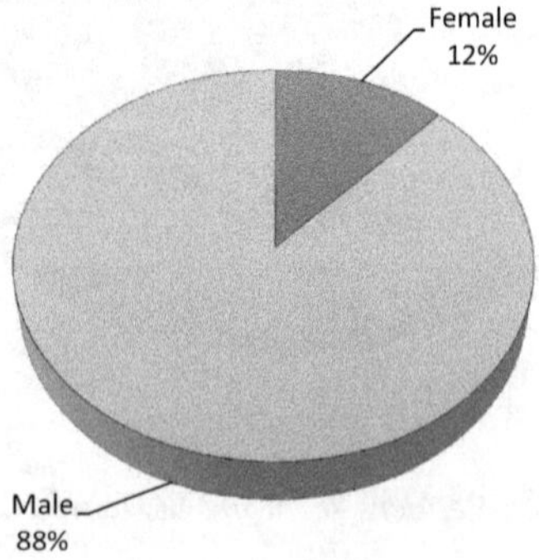

Chart 7. *Gender of Paper Readers*

In the first three 20-year periods, there were almost no female readers; only in the fourth (1977–96) was there a significant increase (to 10.9%). It is in the latest 20-year period (1997–2016) that an extraordinary surge has occurred: to 29.5% of the papers read. If we divide this period into two decades, the advancement of women's participation has been even more striking: in the first decade of that period the figure was 21.3%, but in the last decade (2007–2016) it has grown to 31.3%, almost one in three of paper readers. The SOTS participation rate outperforms the Society of Biblical Literature (23.9% in 2014), though that figure is not strictly comparable since it is a percentage of members rather than of paper readers.[8]

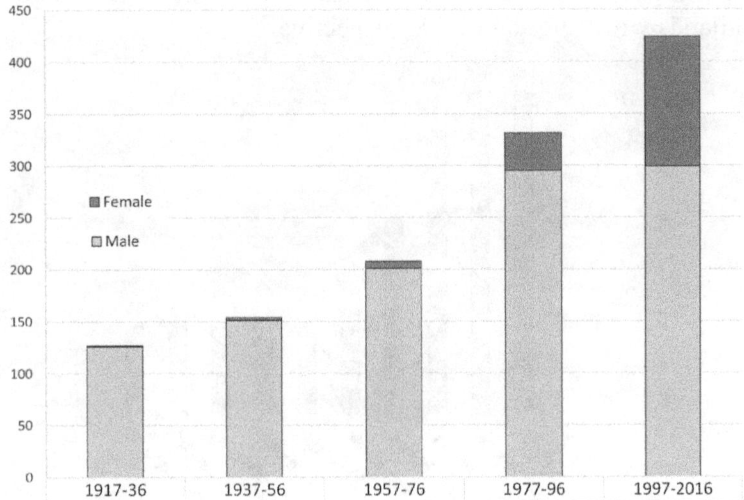

	1917-36	1937-56	1957-76	1977-96	1997-2016
Female % of All	0.8%	1.9%	3.4%	10.9%	29.5%
Female	1	3	7	36	125
Male	126	151	201	295	299

Chart 8. *Paper Readers by 20-Year Periods, Male and Female*

8. www.sbl-site.org/assets/pdfs/memberProfileReport2014.pdf. By way of comparison, I had found the highest proportion of women readers at any SBL International Meeting from 1983 to 1998 to be 23.5% ('From Salamanca to Cracow: What Has [and Has Not] Happened at SBL International Meetings', in *On the Way to the Postmodern: Old Testament Essays, 1967–1998*, I [JSOTSup, 292; Sheffield: Sheffield Academic Press, 1998], pp. 158-93 [172]). At IOSOT Congresses from 1953 to 1998, the highest proportion was 24% ('From Copenhagen to Oslo: What Has [and Has Not] Happened at Congresses of the IOSOT', in *On the Way to the Postmodern*, I, pp. 194-221 [214]).

d. *Location*

The next chart examines the most common places cited as the home town of paper readers. The nomenclature is somewhat fuzzy: it could refer to a reader's institution or to their residence. But it is the only information we have about where readers come from, and by and large the information seems both plausible and interesting.

The chart shows the number of paper readers from the 10 highest-scoring locations. Four of the places are in the southern half of England, three in the north, two in Scotland, and one in Wales. Oxford, Cambridge and London are, not surprisingly, the highest scoring, with 28.1% of the total; then come Manchester, Sheffield and Durham with 13.2%, Edinburgh and Glasgow with 7.0%, then Bangor in Wales and Birmingham in the Midlands with 2.9% and 2.8% respectively.

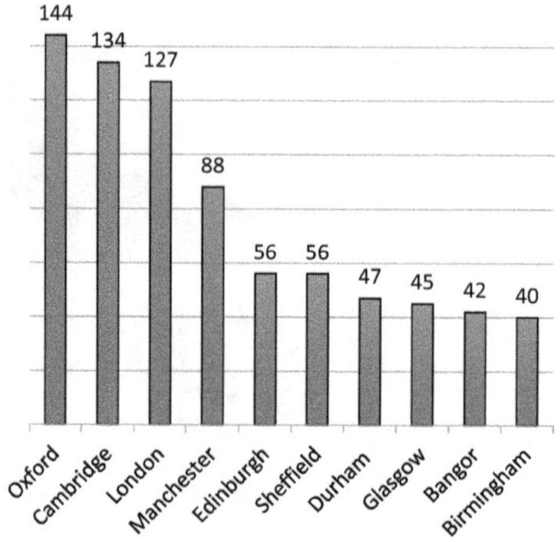

Chart 9. *The Ten Highest-Scoring Locations 1917–2016*

A second version of the chart (Chart 10) analyses the figures for the same places by 20-year periods. The most striking feature here is the increase in the last period (1997–2016) in the representation of Oxford, Cambridge, Manchester and Durham: they show about double the number of paper readers compared with their score for the previous period (in 1997–2016 Oxford gave as many papers as all five Scottish universities put together). Noteworthy also are the increase in the figures for Sheffield (only four papers prior to 1977)[9] and the elevated figures for Bangor in

9. The writer cannot refrain from mentioning his discovery that the first President of the Society, Principal W.H. Bennett (1855–1920), had a connection with Sheffield.

1957–96. I suspect that the large increase in numbers in the last decade reflects the opening up of membership to graduate students (the Society treats all members alike and does not identify which paper readers are graduate students; so I cannot extract figures for them).

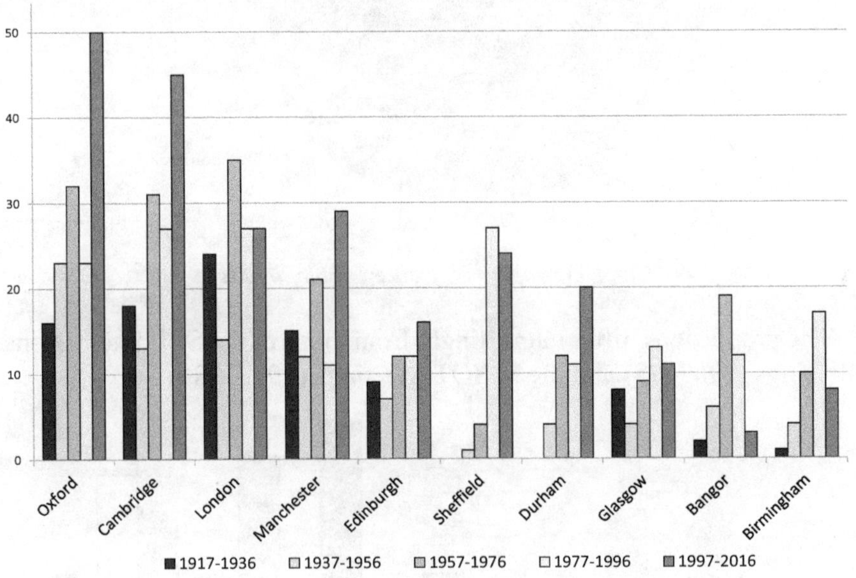

Chart 10. *The Ten Highest-Scoring Locations by 20-Year Periods*

2. *Papers*

The questions of interest here are: Which have been the areas paper readers have most often been interested in, and have those areas changed over the years?

If we take papers on some particular book or passage of the Hebrew Bible, and divide the Hebrew Bible into Pentateuch, Historical Books, Prophets and Writings, we arrive at this result:

In 1919 he was Principal of the Lancashire Independent College, Manchester, but had at one time been Lecturer in Hebrew at Firth College, Sheffield (one of the constituent colleges that became the University of Sheffield in 1905).

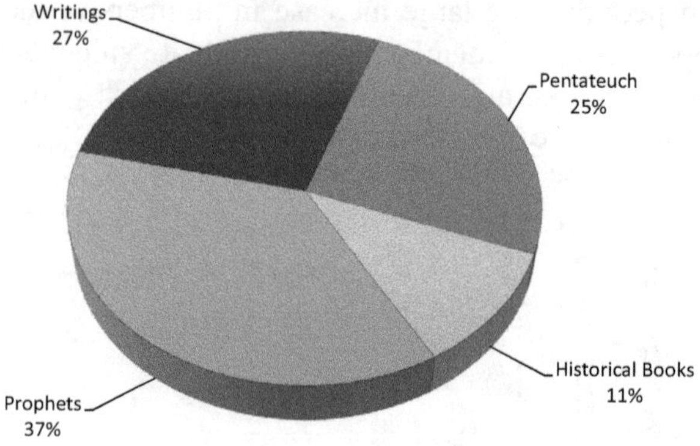

Chart 11. *Papers on Hebrew Bible, by Area*

The proportions differ interestingly from those of the SBL International Meetings (1983–98) and the IOSOT Meetings (1953–98):

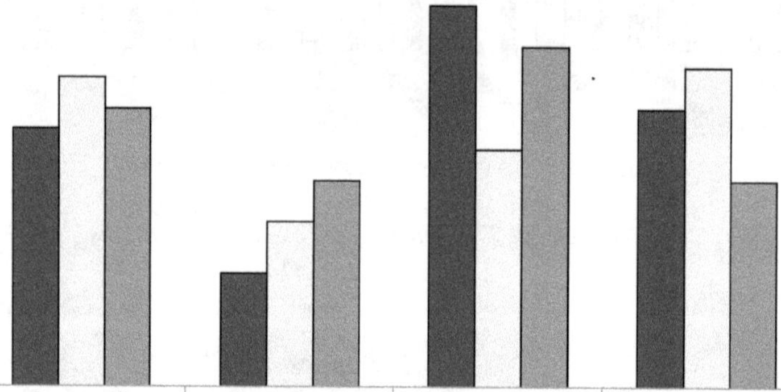

	Pentateuch	Historical Books	Prophets	Writings
■ SOTS	25	11	37	27
□ SBL	30	16	23	31
■ IOSOT	27	20	33	20

Chart 12. *Papers on Hebrew Bible, by Area, SOTS Compared with SBL and IOSOT*

In each case, the Historical Books have attracted the least attention. At SOTS and at IOSOT, the Prophets and the Pentateuch have been the highest scoring, whereas at SBL it has been the Writings and the Pentateuch. The attraction of SOTS to the Prophets (should we call it an affinity?) has been one of its most distinctive features.

But that observation needs to be qualified by the next chart, which shows changes of emphasis at SOTS over the years:

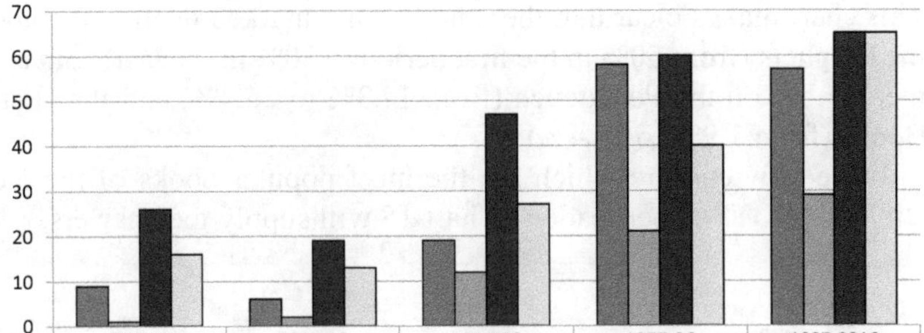

	1917-36	1937-56	1957-76	1977-96	1997-2016
Pentateuch	9	6	19	58	57
Historical	1	2	12	21	29
Prophets	26	19	47	60	65
Writings	16	13	27	40	65

Chart 13. *Number of Papers in Hebrew Bible Areas, by 20-Year Periods*

It is only in recent decades that the Historical Books have attracted much interest, and that the Pentateuch has become more prominent. The Prophets seem to have declined in popularity in the last forty years, but we need to consider a further chart, which shows the attention given to the four areas of the Hebrew Bible as a percentage of the papers in all four areas:

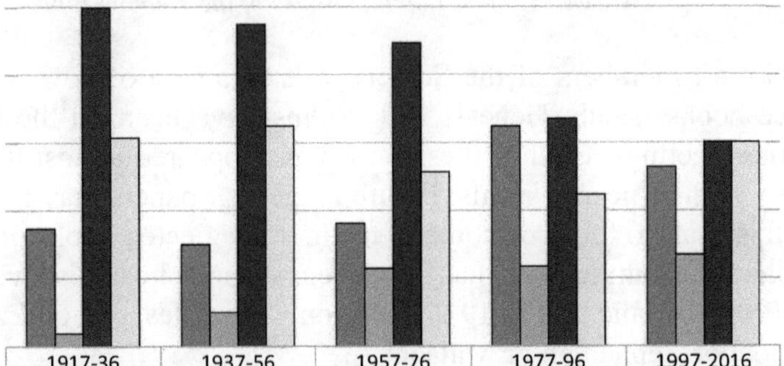

	1917-36	1937-56	1957-76	1977-96	1997-2016
Pentateuch	17.3	15.0	18.1	32.4	26.4
Historical	1.9	5.0	11.4	11.7	13.4
Prophets	50.0	47.5	44.8	33.5	30.1
Writings	30.8	32.5	25.7	22.3	30.1

Chart 14. *Percentage of Papers in Hebrew Bible Areas, by 20-Year Periods*

This chart makes clear that there has been a marked decline in papers on the Prophets (from 50% in the first period to 30% in the last), and a rise in the number on the Pentateuch (from 17.3% to 26.4%) and the Historical Books (from 1.9% to 13.4%).

If we now enquire which are the most popular books of the Hebrew Bible for SOTS paper readers, Chart 15 will supply the answers:

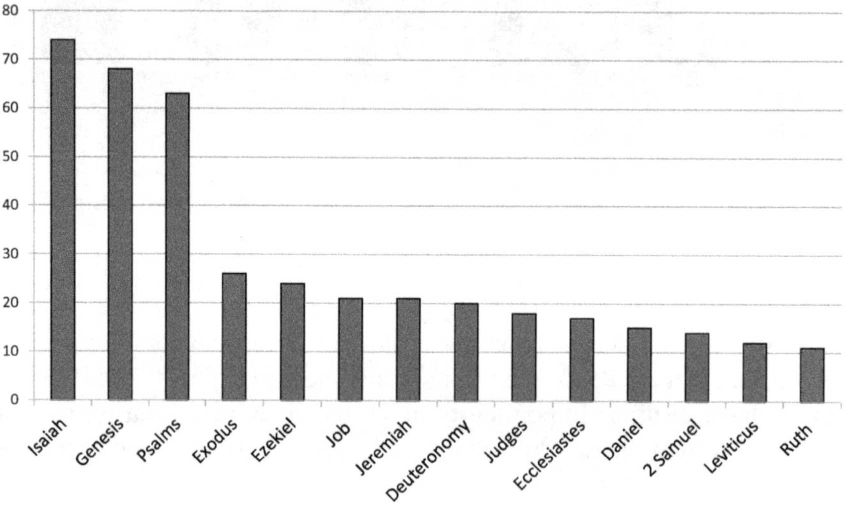

Chart 15. *Most Popular Books of the Hebrew Bible*

Not all members of the Society will be aware of how prominent the three books Isaiah, Genesis and Psalms have been on the programmes of the Meetings; each of these books has appeared almost three times as often as their nearest rivals. Future readers of papers may be encouraged by this chart to focus on some of the more neglected books of the Hebrew Bible; for example, there has only been, as far as I can discover, one paper on Proverbs (and that in 1926), four on Chronicles, one on Ezra and none on Joel or Zephaniah or Malachi.

Turning now to the whole collection of papers, we might consider the areas that have attracted the most interest. In addition to the groups of biblical books, I have identified 10 areas (appearing in the chart in a clockwise direction after the four main Hebrew Bible areas): Post-Hebrew Bible, Ancient Near East, Archaeology, History, Language, Text and Versions, Religion, Social Life, Theology and General, represented in this chart:

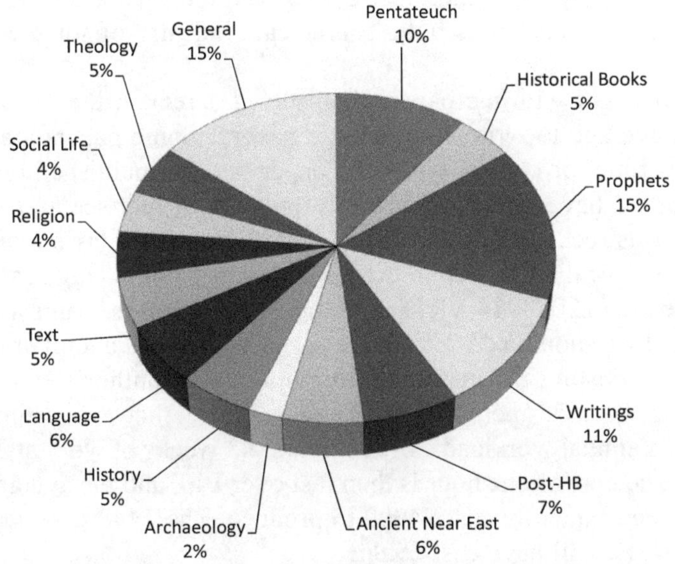

Chart 16. *Main Areas of Papers*

The chart shows that 41% of the papers were devoted to particular Hebrew Bible books or passages in them. Some 15% were concerned with topics strictly outside the scope of Hebrew Bible studies (Ancient Near East, archaeology and post-biblical texts, including Qumran), no doubt because SOTS members have always felt their Meetings should educate them on subjects beyond their own professional expertise. The six other areas (History, Language, Text and Versions, Religion, Social Life, Theology) show a close degree of parity. The 'General' division includes papers not otherwise classifiable.

By way of comparison, the IOSOT Congresses of 1953–98 showed 14% devoted to language and text, 6% to theology, 10% to sociology, 9% to history and archaeology. SBL International Meetings of 1983–1998 had 13% theology, 8% language and text, 7% sociology, 9% history and archaeology.

3. *Economics*

Quite a different question will next occupy us: What has it cost to create and deliver and listen to these 1448 SOTS papers over the last 100 years? A full appreciation of the history of SOTS papers should take into account the economics of preparing the papers, of staging the events at which the papers have been presented, and of the value of the time that members have devoted to Meetings. Even a notional reckoning of the expenses of these 1448 papers signals that SOTS has not been a leisure activity for some few idle scholars but a small-scale industry of some economic significance.

We can begin with the papers themselves. I reckon that it takes 100 hours on average to write an academic paper.[10] Some papers are written in far less time, of course, but if the paper is to be published (and most SOTS papers have been subsequently published) that seems a realistic figure. Let us reckon the cost of the author's time in today's money, and regard the typical author as an academic earning the average salary of a UK academic in 2013–14, viz. £48,460.[11] Salary is not the same as cost, of course, and we should add 25% to the salary to arrive at a total of what the academic is costing the institution to employ. The author's employment then costs £60,575 per annum. Then suppose that we estimate the academic's annual workload as 1500 hours (43 weeks of work at 35 hours a week). The cost of one hour is then just over £40, and the average paper will have consequently cost £4000 to produce. The 1448 papers, then, at today's prices, will have cost £5.8m.

Let us turn to the audience. We do not have good records of the attendance at Meetings over the century,[12] but we know that by the 1950s attendance was often over 100, as it is today. Let us, however, be cautious about the numbers and suppose that the average number of members attending over the course of the century was 50. The number of papers per Meeting has been 1448 papers divided by 195 Meetings, i.e. 7.4. A member attending to 7.4 papers would be at work for 11 hours, not counting meal times (which will have been largely occupied with shop talk, and so could have been not unreasonably added in). In any event, again at today's prices, 50 persons at £40 per hour for 11 hours would be £22,000, and for the 195 Meetings in the century the cost of members' time would be £4.3m.

There is also the cost of the accommodation and meals at the Meeting. In a recent year (2012), the Society paid some £32,000 to the venues for the two Meetings for room and board for its members. If we suppose that, on average over the century, the number of members present was half the number at those Meetings, and the cost of the venue was therefore half,

10. This paper has taken 119.8 hours to write, including the 36 hours for gathering the data.

11. www.timeshighereducation.com/features/times-higher-education-pay-survey-2015/2019360.article.

12. In January 1949 the attendance of 67 was said to be a record, though in September 1946 there had been 80 including 36 visitors. In January 1950 there were 99 members present.

we would arrive at a figure of £8000 for each conference. At that rate, which is to say, at today's prices, the 195 Meetings would have cost the participants some £1.56m.

We should not omit the cost and the time of travel to the Meetings. We might suppose an average travel time of two hours each way at a cost of, say, £50 return. If we calculate the travel of 50 members to each of the 195 Meetings at £50 + £160 for four hours of their time, we can add another £2.05m to the bill.

I will leave out of account the marginal costs of academics to their institutions, that is, the costs, above the employment costs, of adding one person to the academic staff. That would mean, simply put, the total cost of running a university divided by the number of staff, and would include the cost of the administration, the support of staff, the library and the maintenance of the buildings, etc. Such costs in UK universities are roughly equivalent to the salary and direct overheads costs of staff, and if applied to the present calculation would double the per hour cost of an academic's time.

Leaving that matter aside, the total bill for a century of SOTS, then, is of this order:

Preparation of papers	£5.8m
Participants' time	£4.3m
Accommodation and meals	£1.56m
Travel (incl. time)	£2.05m
Total	£13.7m

For that, we have had 1448 papers, at an average cost of £9,461.

Finally, looking to the future, we may attempt a recalculation of the economics of SOTS papers on the basis not of the past 100 years but of the past 10 years (with their 23 Meetings). So doing we may get a sense of the scale of the SOTS business in its current form, and imagine what it will cost to run for the next century. The key differences from the figures used above for the past century are these, for each Meeting: (1) Average number of papers: 12.5. (2) Hours of papers: 19. (3) Accommodation and meals: £16,000. (4) Number of participants: 120.

Preparation of papers	£11.5m
Participants' time	£21m
Accommodation and meals	£3.7m
Travel (incl. time)	£5.8m
Total	£42m

Cost per paper: £14,609 (the perceptive reader will see that there are economies of scale in having larger and longer Meetings). Another 100 years of SOTS papers at the present rate would cost £42m, more than three times the cost of the first century of papers at today's prices. Each Meeting would be costing £182,600. All the figures would, of course, be much more if we took into account the full cost to their employers of the academics reading the papers.

4. *Observations*

One of the most important facts about SOTS papers is that they are all plenary papers. There are no parallel sessions, and every paper reader expects to address all the members present at a Meeting (which is to say, about one quarter of the total membership). All paper readers must therefore decide, in choosing a topic, not only upon a subject within their own competence, but also upon a subject they imagine would be beneficial and interesting to their audience as a whole. Some paper readers, indeed, may be obliged to give their paper in the one very narrow area they are comfortable in, but, even so, the SOTS arena is very different from that of most large conferences, where specialists speak unto specialists and eager listeners must carefully chart a course among sessions that keep within the realm of what they may find intelligible. The plenary audience for SOTS papers, it must be allowed, has not deterred some readers from delivering papers on esoteric themes.

I believe that the SOTS plenary audience is part of the reason for the omission from SOTS programmes of topics one might have expected to crop up. But there is also at play the famed British tendency to empiricism and distaste for theory. What are the topics that have not figured on the SOTS programmes? I cannot of course assert that a particular topic has never been raised at a SOTS Meeting, since my evidence consists solely of the titles of papers and the abstracts of 800 of them. Nevertheless, that evidence amounts to some 125,000 words (which is the length of an average monograph), and it is not unreasonable to suggest that the following terms, which occur rarely or never in that corpus (number of occurrences in brackets), are not likely to have been very prominent in the course of the 100 years of SOTS papers:

Wittgenstein (0)
Derrida (0)
Foucault (0)
reader response (0)
indeterminacy (0)

formalism (0)
Marx (0)
textuality (1)
intertextuality (1)
cultural criticism (0)
(literary) characterization (3)
ideological criticism (0)
postcolonial (2 papers)[13]
deconstruction (2 papers)
psychoanalytic (1)
materialist criticism (2 papers)
structuralism (2)
poststructuralism (0)
rhetorical criticism (1)

Only in two areas that I can readily identify has SOTS moved on in the last 20 years, intellectually speaking. Feminism (in 6 papers) and gender issues (masculinity in 4 papers), and the study of the reception of the Bible (30 papers) have emerged as new themes. None of these areas has been thought to pose any threat, one might suppose, to the continuing dominance of historical criticism. It has not been the SOTS way to expose itself to modern movements of thought about textuality and about meaning in general. When compared with the range of topics currently appearing in international congresses the SOTS menu might seem to some a bit anti-intellectual; certainly, if there is one thing that SOTS might well aspire to for its second century it would be to expand its horizons to include a wider world of thought beyond its traditional specialisms.

13. 'Papers' after a number means that the topic was treated quite extensively and not just mentioned in the paper.

Summer Meeting 1967, the 50th Anniversary Year of the Society. The photograph is taken after a garden party at Bishopthorpe (the Archbishop of York's residence), with Archbishop Donald Coggan (President of SOTS) in the centre of the front row.

From *People and Book* to *Text in Context*: Volumes that Speak Volumes

Adrian Curtis

1. *Introduction*

Some years ago, when required to produce at fairly short notice an MA module on 'Approaches and Methods in the Study of the Hebrew Bible', I hit upon the idea of basing it around the series of SOTS volumes which had been published over the years, in particular those which aimed to give an overview of the state of the discipline at the time of publication (or shortly before). Students were invited to pick a broad area, such as history, religion, critical approaches or literary approaches, and to read the successive essays observing changes in approach and emphasis. I have to say, *en passant*, that it worked better with some students than others, perhaps not surprisingly. Some students found the first volume, published in 1925, to be too modern and radical, and struggled to get beyond it! Fortunately others were able to see something of the changes and developments to which I firmly believe these volumes bear witness.

For the purposes of the present survey, for reasons of space, I propose to concentrate on the five volumes which sought to offer a broad overview of aspects of the study of the Hebrew Bible, namely *The People and the Book* (ed. A.S. Peake; Oxford: Clarendon Press, 1925), *Record and Revelation* (ed. H.W. Robinson; Oxford: Clarendon Press, 1938), *The Old Testament and Modern Study* (ed. H.H. Rowley; Oxford: Clarendon Press, 1951), *Tradition and Interpretation* (ed. G.W. Anderson; Oxford: Clarendon Press, 1979), and *Text in Context* (ed. A.D.H. Mayes; Oxford: Oxford University Press, 2000). They cover the bulk of the twentieth century, with three-quarters of a century between the dates of publication of the first and the last. But the Society also commissioned four other volumes devoted to specific topics: the first two were edited by the same person, D.W. Thomas, namely *Documents from Old Testament*

Times (London: Thomas Nelson & Sons, 1958), and the Jubilee Volume marking the Society's 50th Anniversary, *Archaeology and Old Testament Study* (Oxford: Clarendon Press, 1967); relatively shortly after that came *Peoples of Old Testament Times* (ed. D.J. Wiseman; Oxford: Clarendon Press, 1973), and subsequently in 1989 the volume edited by R.E. Clements (*The World of Ancient Israel: Sociological, Anthropological and Political Perspectives* [Cambridge: Cambridge University Press, 1989]) which was somewhat wider in focus but still narrower than the five overview volumes. Although not concentrating on these in this essay here, it is relevant to reflect on what they indicate about the Society's interests and the issues which were felt to be important for wider dissemination—perhaps a more rounded appreciation of archaeology and the ancient Near Eastern context than was being provided in some 'popular' works and an appropriate appreciation of the importance of the application of the social sciences to biblical study.

2. *Some General Comments*

One thing I do not propose to do in this survey is spend too much time on quoting in detail ideas which today seem very quaint and dated. That would be relatively easy to do, but would definitely not do justice to the earlier volumes. Some of the views *are* dated, but I have no reason to doubt that the contributors were trying to pass on the best of knowledge as it was available to them. The years since the first volume was published have seen some major discoveries and advances—the texts from Ugarit, the Dead Sea Scrolls, new critical editions of the Hebrew Bible and other ancient versions, to mention just a few. It is to be hoped that readers of today will take note of the date of publication and see each volume as a window on to its own time, written by reliable scholars. I recall the pleasure of discovering, during my undergraduate days, the Rowley volume with its potential help for essay writing without, I suspect, appreciating that it was already more than 12 years old. They *are* works of their time, but I have to say that reading or re-reading the essays has left me with the impression that contributors were on the whole not flying their own particular kites, even if one can occasionally hear the distinctive voice of the writer in more recent volumes where the contributor is someone I know, not just a name on a book-spine or in an essay heading. (The earliest encounter with someone I had at least met, even though I did not know him well, and with someone I had heard lecture, was in the 1938 volume and papers by Norman Porteous and H.H. Rowley respectively.)

I have not been able to discover for all of the volumes the extent to which the choice of topics and/or contributors was at the discretion of the editors. But in connection with the 1938 volume, I am grateful to Eryl Davies for locating one piece of relevant information in the Society's Minutes, namely that in 1936 it was agreed to celebrate the 21st anniversary of the founding of the Society by publishing a volume 'on the same lines' as *The People and the Book*; Wheeler Robinson agreed to edit it and the Committee resolved that he should 'be given a free hand'. What is not clear is whether the 'free hand' extended to the choice of contributors or topics or both. (The rather remarkable implication seems to be that a volume agreed upon in 1936 was published just two years later!) With regard to the 2000 volume, I understand from the editor Andrew Mayes that he was given a relatively free hand, but asked to ensure that more recent literary approaches were represented. He engaged in a thorough consultative process with the aim of achieving coherence in the volume as a whole, and of ensuring that both traditional and more recent critical approaches were represented among as comprehensive a selection of contributors as possible.

Before becoming more specific, let me now make just a few general observations which may have relevance in terms of some observable trends. Unsurprisingly, no doubt, the overwhelming majority of contributors were men! In the five overview volumes, we have to wait until the fifth, in 2000, for the first women contributors, Katharine Dell (on 'Wisdom in Israel') and Cheryl Exum (on 'Feminist Study of the Old Testament'). However, in the 1967 Jubilee Volume on Archaeology, Kathleen Kenyon wrote on 'Jericho' and Olga Tufnell on 'Lachish'. And in the 1989 volume, *The World of Ancient Israel*, Grace Emmerson contributed the essay on 'Women in ancient Israel'. I suspect that this imbalance is something that would not even have been noticed, let alone commented on, when lists of contributors were originally drawn up for the earlier volumes. That was the way things were in the subject and in the Society, with the vast majority of teachers and students being men, and with significant numbers having trained, or being trained, as male clergy in various denominations.

One noteworthy feature particularly of some of the earlier volumes is the number of contributors who were not based in Universities but in theological colleges or other institutions. In the Peake volume there are J.E. McFadyen (United Free Church College, Glasgow), W.F. Lofthouse (Handsworth College, Birmingham), H.W. Robinson (Regent's Park College, then in London), H.R. Hall (British Museum) and W.O.E. Oesterley (Rector of St Mary Aldermary, London). By the time of publication, Peake could be presented as Rylands Professor of Biblical Criticism and Exegesis, University of Manchester, but it was in the Primitive Methodist Theological College in Manchester (renamed Hartley College after a major benefactor, Sir William Pickles Hartley of jam fame, in 1906) that he taught my grandfather Hebrew. I often wonder what students like my grandfather, someone with limited formal education but who had worked through his apprenticeship as a printer, made of being taught by the likes of Peake. Unfortunately I was never able to ask him, because he died in 1961, before I went up to Manchester University in 1963 to embark on the Biblical Studies degree, and moved in to what was by then Hartley Victoria College where I lived for five years as a non-ministerial student—and where, since I am being anecdotal, my father trained for the Methodist ministry in the 1930s and was taught by such people as W.L. Wardle, a contributor to the 1938 volume. I know that my father was quite proud that he was taught by some of the same tutors as were the 'Varsity men' as they were apparently known—those taking degrees at the University. (My father did not have matriculation, due to an inability to cope with Latin, so could not take a degree course.) The last time a theological college address is given as the academic home of a contributor is in the 1951 volume, where George Anderson is located at Handsworth College, Birmingham, but for the 1979 volume we find him in the more expected situation of the University of Edinburgh. This observation does prompt the reflection that membership of the Society has not been limited to those currently or previously located in University departments, but has welcomed people from a variety of backgrounds and institutions with a serious scholarly interest in the Old Testament.

Contributors to the five overview volumes were all, to the best of my knowledge, members of the Society. A significant number in each volume were past or future Presidents: 12 in the 1925 volume, 11 in 1938, 8 in 1951, 10 in 1979 and 9 in 2000. Most contributors have been based in the British Isles. It is noted in the 1938 volume that the introduction of Honorary Membership of the Society made possible the inclusion of essays by scholars from overseas: J.A. Montgomery, Johannes Hempel (two essays), Adolphe Lods, and Otto Eissfeldt. Subsequent volumes have also included contributions from scholars based overseas: three in 1951, two in 1979, and five in 2000.

The first two volumes included additional elements. At the end of the Peake volume was an item described, in terms somewhat reminiscent of Psalm 151 in the LXX, as 'outside the scheme of the volume' (p. xix). Entitled 'The Horizons of Old Testament Study', it was the 1922

Presidential Address of G. Buchanan Gray, to whom the volume as a whole was dedicated. This was not published by Gray before his death, but prepared for publication in this volume by T.H. Robinson. Two comments struck me as I read it. One was his conclusion that 'We stand in very serious need of a new edition of the Hebrew Lexicon' (p. 472) and the rider, 'I am not suggesting that our society should add to its other ambitions the editing of a new dictionary; but it may certainly serve to define and articulate the need' (p. 473). He speculates as to whether something less bulky and expensive than that of Brown, Driver and Briggs was required. Perhaps he would have approved of an eight-volume lexicon with a one-volume 'concise' edition, such as we now have in the *Dictionary of Classical Hebrew*. And in terms of the Society's horizons, he at least mentioned the possibility of 'enlarging the scope of our Society and of any publications it may ultimately undertake either so as to become a society of Semitic studies on the one hand or of Biblical study on the other' (p. 476). I am aware, of course, of subsequent debates over the Society's name, but not of such a broadening of its range of interest.

In the 1938 volume, there was a list of recent commentaries, published since 1925. The joint winners, numerically speaking, were Psalms and Isaiah with 12 each, with none listed for 1 Samuel, 1 Kings or 2 Chronicles. I suspect it would be unwise to draw any conclusions from this! There was also a brief appendix, describing the founding of the Society and its history to date, by the then secretary, T.H. Robinson.

3. *Peake 1925*

Some of the overview volumes do suggest that they had a more specific aim. In the Introduction to the Peake volume, it was indicated that 'The goal of our study is to understand the religion' of ancient Israel (p. xvi). This aim is reflected in the fact that there were three essays on religion and one on cultic matters ('Worship and Ritual'). The three essays on religion were arranged chronologically, implying what today may seem a surprising confidence in the possibility of doing this. There was claimed to be a growing interest at the time in psychology, hence an essay on 'Hebrew Psychology' by Wheeler Robinson—a subject which made its one and only appearance in this first volume.

A feature of the first volume, which continued into the second, was the inclusion of essays explicitly relating to Judaism/Jewish interpretation and the New Testament/Christianity. In the Introduction to the first volume we read that 'In recent years the value of the Jewish interpretation of the Old Testament has been much more generously recognized' (p. xix), and, perhaps implying the expectation of a predominantly non-Jewish readership, that the essay will make 'a truer valuation of Jewish exegesis possible to many readers'. Interestingly, in the essay itself, it was noted that Jewish and Christian students of the Hebrew Bible used the same works (p. 403) and that 'In most...respects modern Jewish exegesis is identical with Christian' (p. 407), though there were exceptions, e.g. Jews were agreed that the Suffering Servant was not Jesus (p. 410). With reference to the essay on the Old Testament's value for studying the New, the editor commented: 'That the Old Testament deserves loving study for its own sake and amply repays it is a conviction in which the writers of this volume are united. But they recognize with equal conviction that it is the indispensible approach to the right interpretation of the New Testament' (p. xix).

As already indicated, it is not my intention to spend a lot of time reporting ideas which now seem very dated. I have already made the point that the essays must be read as products of their time. But it may be relevant to illustrate how views have changed over the time-span involved. In the essay on 'Israel and the Surrounding Nations', H.R. Hall commented with regard to the equation of the Exodus with the expulsion of the Hyksos, 'personally I think the view of Josephus more probable than the guess of the moderns' (p. 10). He went on to say, 'the probability that the Khabiru of Akhenaten's day were the Hebrews of Joshua's seems to me to be great' (p. 14), and referred to the absolute philological equivalence of the names. Amraphel was 'probably the historical king Hammurabi, of the Amorite dynasty of Babylon' (p. 18). The modern reader will perhaps be able to feel more at home with the cautionary comment by S.A. Cook ('The Religious Environment of Israel') regarding objects reputed to have been features of Solomon's Temple: 'parallels can be found in the ancient world. But it does not follow that each object meant for Israel what its parallel did for Mesopotamia, Egypt, &c' (p. 45). He also warned against the assumption that so-called primitive traits were necessarily early (p. 55). In the essay on 'Methods of Higher Criticism', T.H. Robinson made this interesting comment on the reaction of some to an engagement with critical approaches: 'Confronted with evolutionary theory they might conceivably have reconciled Gen. i with Darwin, but they could not reconcile Gen. i with Gen. ii' (pp. 152-53).

Mention has already been made of the volume's stated emphasis on religion, and the inclusion of three essays arranged according to successive chronological periods. A noteworthy feature of the first of these was a comparison of the figure of Moses with that of Mohammed, but one of the conclusions made less comfortable reading: ‘The gaze of Islam… was really manward; …the gaze of Mosaism was Godward…’ (p. 238). It was perhaps in the essay on ‘Worship and Ritual’ that confidence in the possibility of undertaking a historical reconstruction was particularly striking, and today surprising. For example, features of pre-Mosaic religion were noted, and reference was made to the situation ‘during the lifetime of Moses’ (p. 336). The second of the essays on Religion (dealing with the period from David to the return from Exile) did note the problems with the Old Testament sources, but commented, ‘We may nevertheless be thankful that the period in which Old Testament religion touched its loftiest point and fashioned its most splendid achievement is that in which the history is most fully known’ (p. 256). The final comment to be mentioned from the first volume is another piece of praise for the Old Testament (albeit doubtless open to challenge). In the essay on ‘The Contribution of the Old Testament to Religious Development’ we find the claim that ‘the highest devotional language of the Church is either based upon, or is taken directly from, the Old Testament’ (p. 402).

The volume clearly proved popular. I am again indebted to Eryl Davies for the information (from the Society’s Minutes) that at the Summer Meeting in 1935 it was reported that it had sold 4,000 copies to that date; by comparison, the two-volume *History of Israel* by W.O.E. Oesterley and T.H. Robinson had sold 2,620 to that date.

4. *Robinson 1938*

Publication of the second volume marked the 21st anniversary of the Society’s foundation. The aim of the volume, as indicated in the Introduction, was ‘that of bringing out the contribution of the Old Testament, when critically studied, to both Jewish and Christian *theology*’ (p. vi). In furtherance of this aim, in the arrangement of the contents a distinction was made between the history of the religion of Israel and its theological implications. Four essays were included in a section headed ‘The Religion of Israel’ (on origins, on prophecy, on worship and on ethics), but there was a separate section headed ‘The Theology of the Old Testament’ with two essays by the editor on ‘The Philosophy of Revelation’ and on ‘The Characteristic Doctrines’. The inclusion of an essay dedicated to ethics is noteworthy, since this did not happen again until the 2000 volume. A feature was the attempt to compare Hebrew ethics with other systems such as communism, totalitarianism and individualism which were, perhaps not surprisingly, found wanting. ‘These vast new movements may outgrow their present materialistic, or pseudo-theistic, philosophy, and prove a stage in the moral and material advancement of humanity. But, if not, they are an ethical disaster. It is of supreme importance that the Hebrew and Christian view of human nature should be conserved' (pp. 299-300).

In the essay on the origins of Israelite religion, Adolphe Lods expressed some initial caution with regard to the possibility of knowing about religion prior to the date of the earliest writings in the ninth or at the earliest tenth century. Yet he soon became much more confident! 'It will readily be allowed that tradition has preserved an accurate remembrance of certain great facts in the realm of external events; that, e.g., it is right in portraying the ancestors of Israel as nomads, or when it speaks of a decisive political and religious transformation connected with the person of Moses' (p. 187). He made use of the relatively recently available material from Ras Shamra in describing the religion after the settlement in Canaan, picking up on some early theories which have not on the whole stood the test of more mature reflection. The essay on prophecy, by Norman Porteous, highlighted its importance in no uncertain terms: 'For the appreciation of the uniqueness of Israel's religion there is no source to equal her prophetic writings' (p. 216). Nevertheless, it was stressed that 'it can lead to a grave misapprehension if we fail to realize that these men were Hebrews of the Hebrews, inheritors and not creators of a religious tradition' (p. 217). In an insightful comment, Porteous observed that 'we must recognize that the prophets performed a tremendous service by secularizing religion, that is to say, by refusing to shut God up in the sphere of the sacred and by bringing Him instead right into the secular world of man's daily life' (p. 237).

Whereas one essay was devoted to the history of Israel in the first volume, there were three in the second. These were not so much arranged chronologically as topically, with essays concentrating on the 'Imperial Backgrounds' (highlighting interactions with neighbouring peoples), on 'The Crises' (looking at a series of events, initially largely following the biblical chronology, from the birth of the nation under Moses down to the year 66 CE), and on 'Political and Economic' history. A feature of the first two of these essays seems to me to be a broad acceptance of the underlying historicity of the biblical accounts, the issues being more to do with *when* things happened rather than *whether* they happened. Abraham was accepted as a suitable starting point, but his date was uncertain, and the Amraphel = Hammurabi equation was rejected. Again, the date of the Exodus was felt to be uncertain, though the contributor (W.L. Wardle) preferred the time of Rameses II and Merneptah. In the essay on the crises, by T.H. Robinson, the contrast between nomads and settled farmers and city dwellers was highlighted: 'It is in the clash and interaction of these two theories of human society...that the key to the history of Israel is to be found' (p. 137). Of the important changes evident in the post-exilic period it was suggested, in language which seems at best strange today, that 'Israel had ceased to be a state, and had become a Church' (p. 139)—with a capital 'C'.

The other grouping of several essays into a sub-section was that on 'The Literature of Israel', with two essays by Johannes Hempel (on 'The Forms of Oral Tradition' and on 'The Contents of the Literature') and one on 'Modern Criticism' by Otto Eissfeldt. In the second of his contributions, Hempel made an observation which could in some ways be said to be ahead of its time: 'A decisive factor in the selection which the Canon offers was the religious interest of the Jerusalem community in the Persian and Greek period' (p. 45). Later he commented that 'the literature of the Old Testament reveals the attitude of the post-exilic community in Jerusalem to the fundamental questions about worship of God, history, and individual life' (p. 73). In the essay on modern criticism, it is interesting to note that the Pentateuch (or Hexateuch) was included in the discussion of 'Historical Books'.

Before commenting briefly on points from essays not assigned to groups, it may be worthy of mention that there was no essay on 'textual criticism', deliberately omitted for reasons of space. In the piece on 'New Sources of Knowledge', scepticism over suggestions that Moses wrote down the Decalogue was, it was claimed, reduced by the discovery of an 'archaeological background' in the form of 'early remains of the alphabet in the very desert where the Wanderings of Israel were experienced' (p. 8). There was a reference to 'the Hebraic Ras Shamra texts' (p. 14), reflecting a stage before their common designation as 'Canaanite', with all the attendant problems of the latter phrase. In the essay on the language of the Old Testament, the phrase used of the language of the Ras Shamra texts was a 'strongly Hebraic dialect' (p. 377). And in the essay on archaeology it was suggested that in the story of Keret we probably had 'the Canaanite form of the Hebrew tradition concerning the derivation of the Abraham group from Harran' (p. 354). It is important to remember that these comments were being made less than a decade after the discovery of Ugarit. However, the contributor (S.H. Hooke) felt able to say of the previous years, 'In the main...the result of fresh knowledge gained by the researches of the last decade has been to substantiate the historicity of the background of the patriarchal narratives of Genesis, and of the traditions relating to the Exodus and the settlement in Canaan' (p. 364).

Interestingly the essay on exegesis included a section on how archaeology could help with exegetical matters. But some of the examples chosen were unfortunate. With regard to the fall of Jericho, it was suggested that 'What actually happened has been made clear by archaeology' (p. 421) but the explanation is based on evidence of a fifteenth-century BCE earthquake. The other was the much vaunted injunction not to boil a kid in its mother's milk (Exod. 23.19), a practice for which there was said to be a parallel in the Ugaritic texts. It is true that the contributor (W.O.E. Oesterley) referred to a command to 'seethe a kid in (its mother's) milk' (p. 423), bracketing the words 'its mother's' and presumably thereby indicating an awareness that that key word is not present in the claimed parallel, but there was no questioning of whether the verb means 'seethe' or whether the noun means 'milk'.

Two other comments arising from the second volume: I was intrigued to read in, the essay on 'The Old Testament and Judaism', C.G. Montefiore's suggestion that, for Jews throughout the Christian era, 'God was what He is depicted as being in the best passages and in the highest teachings of the Old Testament; the others were ignored' (p. 433). In the final essay, on 'The Old Testament and Christianity', it is claimed that both Old and New Testaments are record and revelation. I for one wish the writer had stopped there, rather than add the comment that 'the difference is that in the New Testament the final veil is lifted' (p. 479).

5. *Rowley 1951*

Moving on to the 1951 volume, preparation for which was prompted by the 50th Meeting of the Society, the Preface did not suggest any particular focus, such as was the case with the first two. Rather its aim was 'to survey the significant work that has been done during the last thirty years in order to bring out the changes that have come about and the new trends that have appeared' (p. iii). Textual criticism re-appeared, but there was no specific chapter (or chapters) on history. In his Introduction, the editor suggested: 'For the knowledge of Israel's history our main source is, and must continue to be, the Bible, and our acquaintance with its record has not been seriously modified during the period of our survey' (p. xxi). How things were to move on subsequently! Areas where, it was suggested, there were new trends included emphasis on links with neighbouring peoples, re-evaluation of the prophets and of prophetic psychology, interpreting more texts as rituals, recognition of a greater unity in the Old Testament, increased respect for the Masoretic Text, growing awareness of the potential importance of the traditio-historical approach advocated by some Scandinavian scholars, and the application of form-criticism beyond the Psalter to areas such as legal forms. Although the essays were not arranged in named sub-groups, several dealt with aspects of the literature, and two were devoted to archaeology, both written by W.F. Albright.

This was, of course, the first volume to appear since the initial discovery of the Dead Sea Scrolls, a discovery which is mentioned in several of the essays. Not surprisingly W.F. Albright, in the essay on 'The Old Testament and the Archaeology of Palestine', paid attention to the Scrolls and their likely significance, highlighting in particular their importance for textual criticism, and commenting, 'We may rest assured that the consonantal text of the Hebrew Bible, though not infallible, has been preserved with an accuracy perhaps unparalleled in any other ancient Near-Eastern literature' (p. 25). Equally unsurprisingly, D.W. Thomas, in the essay on 'The Textual Criticism of the Old Testament' (a subject which made a return after its omission in 1938), included mention of the Scrolls, though it is more of a surprise, with the benefit of hindsight, that he included them as the 'second new important source of knowledge' after the Lachish ostraca! Particular attention was drawn to the Isaiah Scroll, 'recently published in its entirety' and containing 'numerous variant readings' (p. 240). A.M. Honeyman, in his contribution on 'Semitic Epigraphy and Hebrew Philology', excluded the Scrolls from his general summary, and stated of Hebrew epigraphy in Palestine that 'yields of the last thirty years are...exceedingly meagre'. He commented on 'the sensational discoveries at the cave near 'Ayn Feshkhah above the Dead Sea, which, in so far as they have been published, belong mainly to the chapter on textual criticism' (p. 268). The use of 'cave' in the singular is noteworthy. A perhaps less expected reference to the Scrolls came almost at the beginning of Norman Porteous's contribution on 'Old Testament Theology'. He suggested that 'A lucky find like that of the Dead Sea Scrolls has provided the specialists with problems for years to come' (p. 311). Scrolls scholars would doubtless add an 'Amen' to his comment!

To pick up on some other points from the 1951 volume, Albright opened the first essay with the claim that 'No subject related to biblical research has changed more rapidly and more completely during the thirty years from 1919 to 1949 than Palestinian archaeology' (p. 1). He went on to suggest, in what we now think of as Albrightian terms, regarding the Patriarchal Period: 'by and large there is astonishing similarity between the background provided by archaeology and that presupposed in Genesis' (p. 6). In his second essay, interestingly entitled 'The Old Testament and the Archaeology of the Ancient East' (not Near East), he claimed, 'it must be emphasized that the really great contribution of ancient Eastern archaeology has been in the total picture, which enables us to see the life of the Chosen People against the background of the surrounding world. This is a contribution before which everything else must fade into insignificance' (p. 28).

It was at the end of C.R. North's essay on 'Pentateuchal Criticism' that there was something which definitely took me back to my student days: the two diagrams headed 'The older Sources Hypothesis' and 'The present (tentative) position', the former, basically linear, moving chronologically from oral traditions to R^{JEDP}, and the latter—much reproduced—presenting a rather more complex view of things. I remember finding the latter diagram very helpful, but I cannot help recalling an occasion when, during my term as Secretary of the Society, I was distributing a handout at a SOTS meeting and passed one to an eminent former President of the Society. He leaned towards me and said, *sotto voce*, that he never trusted an argument which included a diagram!

The essay by Norman Snaith on 'The Historical Books' suggested that an ongoing concern at the time was the issue of whether the Pentateuchal sources continued into Joshua, Judges and Samuel. Of Chronicles, Ezra and Nehemiah he felt confident enough to say, 'There is general agreement that all three (four) books were originally one work' (p. 107). Aubrey Johnson's contribution on 'The Psalms' not only started from Gunkel but devoted some 19 pages (almost a quarter of the essay) to a detailed overview of his work, perhaps an indication of its ongoing impact. Baumgartner's treatment of 'The Wisdom Literature' covered an interesting range of material; in a section on Old Testament Apocrypha he dealt not only with Ben Sira and the Wisdom of Solomon, but included Tobit, Baruch, 1 Esdras, 4 Maccabees, the Letter of Aristeas and Pseudo-Phocylides. Subsequently he defended the inclusion of Canticles among the Wisdom literature. A final observation on the 1951 volume takes us back to Norman Porteous on Old Testament theology. Many would sympathise with a remark early in the essay, namely that 'there is no general agreement as to what a theology of the Old Testament should aim at providing' (p. 311). Rather more open to debate may be his final words on the subject: 'A theology of the Old Testament will be worthy of the attention of men today in the measure in which it keeps close to life and does not operate merely at the academic level where thought and action are apt to be divorced' (p. 344).

6. *Three More Specialized Volumes*

The first three volumes appeared with gaps of thirteen years intervening. It was to be another 28 years before the next survey volume was eventually published after, if I recall Business Meetings at the time correctly, some delay beyond the planned date. (In his essay in this centennial collection, Eryl Davies comments on the likely reasons for this delay.)

But three of the more specialized volumes did appear in the interim, two edited by Winton Thomas (*Documents from Old Testament Times* in 1958, and *Archaeology and Old Testament Study* in 1967), and then *Peoples of Old Testament Times*, edited by Donald Wiseman, in 1973. In *Documents from Old Testament Times*, the stated aim was 'to relate each document as closely as possible to the Old Testament, and to bring out relevant points of interest touching history, chronology, archaeology, religion, literature, geography, and so on, in illustration of the Old Testament' (p. v). The longest section is devoted to Cuneiform Documents, mainly from Mesopotamia, but also including texts from Ras Shamra. Other sections present Egyptian, Hebrew, and Aramaic Documents, and a solitary Moabite Document (the Moabite Stone). The Jubilee Volume, *Archaeology and Old Testament Study*, was, we are told, 'not intended primarily for archaeologists…but for those many students of the Old Testament, whether they be teachers of Scripture in schools, or clergy, or others who are not professional scholars, who wish to know what interest and importance particular sites in Palestine and in other countries of the ancient Near East have for them' (p. v). Sites are presented geographically, under the headings Egypt, Mesopotamia, Anatolia (just Boğazköy), Syria and Palestine. Despite the comment that it was necessary to limit the number of sites treated, it is perhaps surprising that Qumran was not included in its own right and received only a couple of passing mentions. (A third, promised by the Index, is certainly not on the indicated page!) The Preface to *Peoples of Old Testament Times* indicated that the idea of the book came from the editor of the two previous volumes, Winton Thomas, and that it was envisaged as 'a third volume to complete the series with its emphasis on the peoples referred to in the Old Testament documents' (p. v). At the end of the Introduction, the editor states, 'The relationship between Israel and Judah and other nations is a major theme in the Old Testament, which is concerned with God and man in all his activities. There is thus a continuing interest for the Hebrews in the other peoples who surrounded them and whose presence was a constant temptation and, at times, a threat to their spiritual and physical existence' (p. xxi). Parts of that last sentence perhaps fit some of the peoples discussed better than others!

7. *Anderson 1978*

There was no explicitly stated 'aim' in the fourth volume, other than perhaps the title given to the Introduction, 'Changing Perspectives in Old Testament Study'. The dust-jacket supported this, claiming that the work was 'a reflection of changing perspectives in Old Testament Study and an appraisal of important changes in method and approach'. But another statement on the dust-jacket that all the essays were 'provided with short bibliographies' was incorrect, since none was provided for those on 'Semitic Philology' or 'Old Testament Historiography'.

Although there were no indicated sub-groups, several essays were devoted to sections of, or types of, literature. Noteworthy is the first (and last) appearance of 'Apocalyptic' as a separate topic. Ernest Nicholson suggested that, since the publication of the 1951 volume, there had been 'a renewed and increasing interest in apocalyptic, and this not only among Old Testament scholars but also among New Testament scholars and systematic theologians' (p. 190). 'Textual Criticism' becomes 'Textual Transmission' or, as expressed more fully in the list of contents, 'The Textual Transmission of the Old Testament (including modern critical editions of the Hebrew Bible)'. By making this change, said the author B.J. Roberts, 'the editor has recognized the change of character that has taken place in the topic during the past few years' (p. 1); he later claimed that 'the study of the text is still the Cinderella of biblical studies' (p. 27). Towards the beginning of the essay, reference was made to new editions, in particular *Biblia Hebraica Stuttgartensia* and the Hebrew University of Jerusalem edition based on the *Aleppo Codex*. In the concluding remarks, Roberts expressed reservations about both editions, highlighting in particular the critical apparatus of *BHS*.

After its absence in 1951, the History of Israel re-appeared with two essays on the Pre-exilic period and on the Exile and Post-exilic periods, and there was an essay on historiography by Roy Porter which concentrated on two 'works', the 'Deuteronomic Historical Work' and the 'Chronistic Historical Work'. With regard to the two essays on the history of Israel, an issue for Peter Ackroyd in the second of them was when the period to be discussed should start and finish. He opted for 587 as preferable to 597 for the starting point and then noted that a 'coverage of the Old Testament period must involve a sufficient extension to include at least all those writings which eventually belong to the canon. This (to include Daniel) takes us to the mid-second century on a minimal canonical view; it takes us a great deal further if account is taken of that massive closely related literary output of the last centuries BC and the first century AD' (p. 321). He raised an important issue regarding the limitations of available sources when he commented (referring specifically to the career of Alexander), 'We must also consider how far events which undoubtedly had far-reaching consequences for the history of the Jewish community were so viewed at the time' (p. 343).

The essay on the Pre-exilic period, by Henri Cazelles, was further subdivided into two sections which seem to me at least to be of rather different nature. That on the pre-monarchic period contained references to ideas which might perhaps be termed speculative at best! For example, we find the suggestion that 'a tribe of Rachel, having Israel as ancester [*sic*], united with a tribe of Leah, or of Zilpah, having Jacob as ancestor; and the two ancestors were then identified with each other' (p. 280). The supporting footnote initially refers the reader to a dictionary article by Cazelles himself! Suggested solutions to problems over routes and indeed the number of Exodus(es) are 'unnecessary if one accepts that what de Vaux calls the "flight Exodus" is the historical Exodus of a small group of Josephite families under the leadership of Moses and that the "expulsion Exodus" recalls the expulsion of the Hyksos as recorded by literary tradition' (pp. 283-84). I am not quite sure how many questions that sentence begs! The treatment of the monarchic period is rather different in nature, largely re-telling the biblical account.

This volume was the first to be able to take account of discussions about covenant, its form and date, arising notably from the work of Mendenhall and his suggestion of affinities with Hittite suzerainty treaties. Several contributions made reference to this, notably those on 'Recent Archaeological Discoveries' by John Gray, on 'Pentateuchal Problems' by Ronald Clements, and on 'The History of Israelite Religion' by Walther Zimmerli. Zimmerli also noted Perlitt's view that the relationship between God and Israel was only later understood as *b^e^rîṯ*. (I understand from Graeme Auld, who translated Zimmerli's paper, that the editor was very impressed by this essay, judging it to be a useful contribution to bridging the gap between Old Testament Theology and the Religion of Israel.) Other points to be noted from those essays include Gray's stress on the importance of the Baal texts from Ras Shamra for the Enthronement Psalms and other texts on the kingship of God in the Old Testament. Ronald Clements ended his essay with the perceptive comment that 'it has proved much more difficult in practice to show the nature and scope of their [i.e. the redactors'] work, than it has been to show what the authors of the individual documents were seeking to achieve' (p. 122).

Some points, now, from other contributions, which highlighted newer trends or re-considered older views. In his essay on ‘Semitic Philology’, James Barr noted that ‘One area which is particularly dependent on the advance of linguistic methods of analysis, and which is in any case growing in importance, is the study of semantics’ (p. 63). The eventual publication of this volume was, of course, some years after his *The Semantics of Biblical Language* (London: Oxford University Press, 1961) had appeared. Closer to the date of an earlier publication was John Eaton’s essay on ‘The Psalms and Israelite Worship’, where echoes of his *Kingship and the Psalms* (Studies in Biblical Theology, Second Series, 32; London: SCM Press, 1976) abound in attempts to reconstruct religious festivals and in the understanding of many psalms of the individual as royal. In the final essay on ‘The Theology and Interpretation of the Old Testament’, F.F. Bruce questioned the use of ‘theology’ in the singular. ‘What is there in common between the theology of Judges and the theology of Second Isaiah? We may reply at once: “A recognition that Yahweh, the righteous God, is Lord of history”—but should we have thought of asking the question, let alone of offering a reply, did it not so happen that Judges and Isaiah 40–55 are included in the same corpus of “sacred” literature?’ (p. 385). He went on to suggest that ‘the attempt should be made to investigate Old Testament theology in its own right and on its own terms, without seeking an interpretative norm outside the Old Testament itself’ (p. 386). An insightful comment on interpretation within the Old Testament was that both prophets and historical books interpret the course of events theologically (p. 405)—an advantage (my comment, not his) of referring to both as *n*^{e}*ḇî’îm*.

8. *A Fourth More Specialized Volume*

At this point, chronologically speaking, the fourth of the more specialized volumes appeared, *The World of Ancient Israel: Sociological, Anthropological and Political Perspectives* (ed. R.E. Clements, 1989). Although somewhat broader in scope than the other three, it did not attempt the wide-ranging overview which was a feature of the five volumes on which this survey is concentrating. It was prompted by a growing interest in the application of the social sciences to biblical study. As the Preface indicated, ‘A primary reason for attempting to deal with the broader issues of a sociological, anthropological or political nature relating to the Old Testament is to be found in the increasing number of scholars who have recognised the valuable insights that are to be gained from doing so' (p. vii). The volume was subdivided into four parts, the first of which ('Introductory Perspectives') included a helpful introduction to the theme of the volume by the editor, and general treatments of anthropology (J.W. Rogerson) and sociology (A.D.H. Mayes). The other sections were devoted to 'Israel', 'Fundamental Institutions', and 'Ideas and Ideals'.

9. *Mayes 2000*

And so to the 2000 volume, whose aim was, we are told in the Introduction, to 'give appropriate emphasis to literary study of the Old Testament and the history of Israel, two areas which have witnessed remarkable developments since the last volume of essays by members of the Society' (p. xv). What is immediately striking is the focus on the reader, both ancient and modern, with the first of the three sections into which the essays were grouped being headed 'The Old Testament and the Reader'. (The others were 'The Text of the Old Testament' and 'The Old Testament and its Authors'.) In the opening contribution, 'The Reader and the Text', Robert Carroll could perhaps be said to offer a lens through which some of the other essays might be read and stressed the importance of *all* readers, not just those belonging to confessional groups in Judaism and Christianity but also those without any such commitment. The Introduction suggested that 'Reader response criticism has illuminated the complex and dynamic relationship between the reader and the text, and has made evident the significance of the fact that the academic community engaged in Old Testament study is now much more pluralistic than before' (p. xv), but Carroll commented, 'Texts deserve greater distance, more respect and engagement than reader-response approaches would allow' (p. 24).

Some earlier groups of readers were considered by Philip Alexander in his discussion of 'The Bible in Qumran and Early Judaism'. He noted that something which had emerged from recent study of Midrash was that 'early Christians were reading the Old Testament in a manner typical of their time, and in doing so were often taking for granted post-biblical tradition' (p. 36). He highlighted the rich variety of genres of biblical interpretation to be found within the literature of early Judaism, including that of the Dead Sea sect. His concluding comment was that 'Christianity and Judaism as we know them today emerged from the clash of sects and schools of thought within Palestinian Jewish society at the turn of the eras. It was from this intellectual milieu that they derived their essential nature as "religions of the book"' (p. 58).

Two essays in the volume dealt with matters relating to canon, but with very different emphases. Mark Brett discussed ‘Canonical Criticism and Old Testament Theology’ in the section on the Reader, raising some cautionary points about the possibility of doing ‘biblical theology’ and an uncritical tracing of ‘themes’ from diverse traditions. John Barton’s contribution on ‘Canons of the Old Testament’ came in the second section of the volume, which focused on Text. He noted that revival of interest in the various canons had arisen in part because of the emergence of canonical criticism. He made the interesting observation that it is ‘hard to think of any doctrinal difference between churches that is really linked with their adherence to one or other of the canons’ (p. 205). He argued for the necessity to distinguish ‘scripturality’ from ‘canonicity’ and suggested that ‘The status of the books that form the Old Testament was established by use rather than by decree…’ (p. 211).

But to return to the section on the Reader, the two other contributions both stressed a plurality of approaches. Cheryl Exum, writing on ‘Feminist Study of the Old Testament’, commented, ‘Feminist biblical criticism is neither a discipline nor a method, but rather an approach, or, better, a multiplicity of approaches, informed not so much by the biblical texts themselves but rather by the interests and concerns of feminism as a worldview and as a political enterprise’ (p. 86). Her survey raised issues relating not just to the reader, but of authorship or, more importantly, the ‘voice’ to be heard. ‘This methodological move is accompanied by a concentration on authority rather than authorship, on gender positions in the text, and on textual voices as F (feminine/female) or M (masculine/male)’ (p. 101).

Perhaps deliberately juxtaposed with Exum’s essay was John Rogerson’s contribution on ‘Old Testament Ethics’. Towards the end of his essay, he reminded us of the necessity to ‘hear Cheryl Exum’s protest against “prophetic pornography”—prophetic texts in which readers are expected to identify with a male God against an Israel described in female terms as unfaithful wife, harlot and so on, as well as the things that God will do to her to punish or to restore her’ (p. 134). More generally, he argued for ‘as much pluralism as possible in Old Testament ethics’ and concluded, ‘Although often the Cinderella of Old Testament study, its ethics could be said to be its heart; which is why it demands and deserves as many contributions from the most divergent standpoints’ (p. 135). (This was the second topic claimed to be a ‘Cinderella’! Previously it was textual criticism. As has already been mentioned, the only previous essay devoted to Ethics by name was in the 1938 volume).

To return now to the section on Text, the essay on 'Textual Criticism: The Ancient Versions', by Shemaryahu Talmon, interestingly mentioned, in connection with the handing on of oral and written traditions, the significance of 'material aspects' such as the extent of the use of writing, and the writing materials available to someone wishing to make a written record. He also noted how the 'Transmission of the biblical text was profoundly affected by historical events and religious transformations which Judaism experienced at the turn of the era' (p. 151). Later he commented on an increasing tendency to caution over emendation: 'The multiformity of the biblical text in antiquity, evinced by the most ancient witnesses available, namely the Qumran scrolls and fragments, causes scholars to proceed more cautiously with conjectural emendation of seemingly corrupt readings' (p. 163). He noted that this caution had apparently influenced two new critical editions, the Hebrew University Bible and the *Biblia Hebraica Quinta*. John Emerton's essay on 'The Hebrew Language' drew attention to the chicken-and-egg situation (my phrase, not his) which can occur when features of Late Biblical Hebrew are illustrated from late biblical books, and then those books are labelled 'late' because they contain features of Late Biblical Hebrew! He was also able to comment on recent developments in lexicography, including the completion of the third edition of Koehler/Baumgartner (and the publication of the first three volumes of Mervyn Richardson's English translation), the appearance of the 18th edition of Gesenius's *Handwörterbuch*, and the publication of the first four volumes of the *Dictionary of Classical Hebrew*. A feature of the *Dictionary of Classical Hebrew* on whose pros and cons he commented was the policy, subsequently somewhat modified, not to include etymologies or cognates, defending the positive value of evidence from the cognate languages 'provided that due caution is observed' (p. 195).

The 'Text' section also included essays on 'Hebrew Narrative', by David Gunn, and 'Hebrew Poetry', by Wilfred Watson. In the former, the theme of plurality and diversity, already noted in other essays, continued. Narrative criticism was described as a 'broad stream of critical endeavour' (p. 248), and earlier Gunn had commented that 'the attempt by the critic-reader to define so simple a thing as the narrative text is a process fraught with issues that have as much to do with the reader as with the text' (p. 225). Writing on poetry, Watson underlined the fact that 'There is a fundamental difference between *production*, i.e. the creative activity of the poet, and *perception*, the act of comprehension by listener or reader' (p. 255). He then went on to illustrate this by presenting the great variety of features and techniques which can be used by the poet, and their potential impact on the reader or hearer.

The final grouping in this fifth volume focused on ‘The Old Testament and its Authors’. ‘The Pentateuch and the Deuteronomistic History’ were treated together in a single essay by Otto Kaiser. He concentrated on what were recent questionings of, and challenges to, theories propounded by Martin Noth in the 1940s, which had continued to dominate for some decades thereafter. Particular attention was paid to the age and stratification of Deuteronomy, and to whether the development of the Deuteronomistic History was best understood along the lines of a ‘block’ or ‘stages model’ which sought to identify the successive stages of bringing together blocks of material, or in terms of a ‘strata model’ which posited a series of redactional layers. He suggested that, ‘As far as DtrG is concerned, a combination of the stage and strata models emerges, which requires giving up the idea of a single work extending from Deuteronomy 1 to 2 Kings 25 in favour of a more complicated stage and strata model which still needs further working out’ (pp. 314-15).

Writing on ‘Prophecy and the Prophetic Books’, Joseph Blenkinsopp highlighted social-scientific approaches but noted that discussion of the social location and function of the prophets had to confront ‘the problematic nature of the passage from text to prophetic *realia*, including prophetic biography’ (pp. 324-25). With regard to the relationship between prophecy and law, he noted that it was no longer possible to address this in terms of relative priority. Unlike the essay by Baumgartner in the 1951 volume, Katharine Dell’s treatment of ‘Wisdom in Israel’ focused just on texts within the Old Testament itself. She raised issues of the social and historical context of ‘Wisdom’ and, in commenting on the various suggestions regarding the social context of Proverbs, she noted the view that there is no real evidence for the existence of ‘schools’. But in her discussion of Ecclesiastes she was at least willing to consider that Qoheleth was ‘probably a wise man’ and ‘possibly a teacher in a wisdom school’ (p. 365). At the end of her contribution she welcomed the fact that ‘wisdom literature has begun to find its rightful place in an evaluation of Old Testament theology’ (p. 369), noting a tendency to see it as more integral.

There were two essays on ‘The History of Israel’, the first by Keith Whitelam sub-titled ‘Foundations of Israel’, and the second by Lester Grabbe sub-titled ‘The Persian and Hellenistic Periods’. In the former, Whitelam criticised what he referred to as a ‘history of the gaps’ in which ‘the biblical text takes priority and is only supplemented by archaeological data or non-biblical materials’ (p. 379). Here, as he has done elsewhere, he spoke of the ‘emergence’ of Israel, and with regard to the early monarchic period he commented: ‘The idea of a major state, let alone an empire, centred on Jerusalem in the tenth century BCE has been increasingly disputed in recent years as each element of this once interlocking network has been re-examined' (p. 392). He was able to take note of the Tel Dan stele, but suggested that some of the interpretations placed upon it did not stand up to scrutiny. At the end of his contribution he picked up the title of the volume as a whole, but in terms of how the social, political and historical contexts of scholars have influenced what they write. Lester Grabbe also spoke of gaps: 'Our knowledge of the Persian and Ptolemaic periods still has enormous gaps, and a good deal of what is presented in standard histories represents more wishful thinking than carefully documented historical reconstruction' (p. 403). In his essay he was at pains to assess what sources are available for each period before attempting a reconstruction of events and making comments on specific aspects. It is noteworthy that he came to the defence of Antiochus Epiphanes, suggesting that 'Much unsubstantiated calumny has been written about Antiochus IV' (p. 420). Towards the end of the essay he summed up the situation: 'the Persian and Hellenistic periods were very much formative periods in the development of religion, literature, and identity of the Jewish people. Yet this time in the "history of Israel" is also to a large extent enigmatic' (p. 423).

It was in the final essay that we find John Day's treatment of 'The Religion of Israel'. Here an interest in the influence of Canaanite religion on that of Israel was in evidence. He argued that Yahweh was not a Canaanite deity in origin and challenged the suggestion that Yahweh and El were equated, noting that 'in early poetic texts such as Judg. 5: 4–5 Yahweh is associated with the storm, which, though reminiscent of Baal, does not fit El' (p. 429). He drew attention to possible areas of syncretism, and noted that Josiah's reform was not specifically about removing Assyrian cults because the deities removed were Canaanite. Using a very catching phrase he pointed to an 'increased interest in the actual religion of Israel in all its strange otherness' (p. 432). He questioned the belief that the concept of covenant was relatively late, and also suggested that the view that Daniel was the earliest 'full-blown apocalypse' was no longer tenable in view of evidence from Qumran for the earlier dating of the Astronomical Enoch and the Book of the Watchers.

10. *Concluding Observations*

The sub-title to this essay may seem rather corny, but I believe it to be true. The volumes contain not only a wealth of scholarship, but ample evidence that Old Testament study has not been static, and has accepted changes of emphasis—perhaps sometimes rather slowly—and has not been inward-looking insofar as it has attempted to take on board insights from other disciplines. They reflect the Society's ongoing concern to make the fruits of scholarship more widely accessible and available beyond the academy, something further indicated by the willingness of members of the Society to contribute to two series of Study Guides on the books of the Old Testament. The volumes seem to have been well received. Mention has already been made of the popularity of the Peake volume, and in his essay in the present volume Eryl Davies provides evidence relating to the Anderson and Clements volumes.

The volumes reveal changes in the Society as well as changes in scholarship. Trends worth noting include the shift away from the feeling of a necessity to include specific essays on relevance for Judaism and Christianity, and an acknowledgement that commitment to or even interest in the study of the Old Testament is by no means confined to the confessional. The male/female ratio of contributors hitherto is now a matter of history, and in the future the balance is likely to reflect more accurately the much changed gender balance within the Society.

The final volume highlighted the relationship between the reader and the text. This survey has inevitably been somewhat subjective—this reader engaging with, and responding to, these texts. But the reading of these texts has underlined that their production is something of which the Society can be proud as it celebrates its first hundred years. And it is good to know that, even now, the next instalment is in preparation.

A Snapshot of SOTS at 100: Collegiality and Diversity in the Membership of the Society for Old Testament Study*

Katharine J. Dell

1. *Changes in SOTS Membership over the Years*

a. *The First 25 Years*

It took only three people meeting to examine Hebrew at the University of Wales in early summer 1916 to make the suggestion to set up a Society for Old Testament Study. Those three were Professor T. Witton Davies, Principal William H. Bennett and Rev. Prof. Theodore H. Robinson. It was then decided to discuss the idea further at a gathering of teachers in theological colleges held in Cambridge, at Queens' College (on 29th June 1916) at the invitation of Canon R.H. Kennett. Prominent scholars of the time such as A.S. Peake and Dr (then Mr) S.A. Cook were there and a decision was made to form the Society. A circular was sent out inviting all well-known Old Testament scholars to participate and it was signed

* I am grateful to several people for their assistance in the preparation of this chapter: Eryl Davies (SOTS Archivist), for arranging for me to visit the SOTS archive in Bangor, for his hospitality and assistance, and for reading a first draft of the essay; Heather McKay and Vivienne Rowett (past and present Membership Secretaries), for providing me with membership data; Jonathan Stökl (SOTS Information Officer), for his help in setting up Survey Monkey, and helping with the formulation of the questions and with the collation of the results; David Clines (coordinator of the 1994 survey of members), for digging out information about that questionnaire and data from an old computer; John Jarick (editor of the present volume), for useful suggestions and information; and Douglas Hamilton (my husband), for his creation of the charts on Excel and for the time that he has generously given to this work. In Section 1 of the essay, all mentions of the 'Minutes' refer to the minute books of either the General Committee or the Business Meeting.

by six leading men in the field: W.H. Bennett, M.A. Canney, T. Witton Davies, A.S. Peake, T.H. Robinson and J. Skinner. At the first meeting of the Society for Old Testament Study at King's College London on 3rd January 1917 there were fourteen members present of a possible 30, that being the number, after the initial circulation, of the opening membership. These members were the leading Old Testament scholars in Great Britain. Of those fourteen, one was a Jewish scholar—H. Gollancz—while the rest were Christians of various denominations: 3 Congregationalists, 1 Wesleyan, 3 Baptists, 5 Anglicans and 1 Presbyterian. The first President was Principal W.H. Bennett and the first Secretary T.H. Robinson. It seems that only one paper was read in the end at that opening meeting: Rev. Canon R.H. Kennett on 'The Origin of the Book of Deuteronomy'. A committee was set up consisting of four members: W.H. Bennett, G.B. Gray, R.H. Kennett and T.H. Robinson. It was resolved (as recorded in the Minutes) 'That the original members of the Society be those present at this meeting and approving these resolutions and that others who were unable to be present but had signified their approval of the proposed Society should be invited to join it'. Of the 30 members, only five were not ordained and two of those five were female members: Miss G.M. Bevan of London and Mrs Herbert Knowles of London. (It is interesting that the latter was designated by her husband's name, a common practice in society at that time.)

During the First World War there were various letters sent to members, circulars that kept the Society alive—one was to reappoint the officers and committee for 1918 and there started to be records of members' publications, that being an important element of the purpose for which the Society was set up. (This latter activity was later to be subsumed under the auspices of the *Book List*.) There was a 5 shilling subscription to be a member and a record of membership started to be kept. By 20th March 1918 there were 34 members, of whom only six were not ordained. By the second meeting, held two years later on 16th–18th July 1919 at the end of the First World War when it was deemed safe to meet, at Dalton Hall, Manchester, there were 35 members, but only five attended the meeting. It was decided to hold two meetings a year, with members reading papers at each, one during the Christmas vacation in London and one during the summer outside London. This pattern continues today, although the Winter Meeting can no longer be held regularly in London. At the second meeting there was a presidential paper on the first evening from W.H. Bennett and three further papers. It is interesting that the sessions are all described as 'discussions' with a leading presenter, rather than as 'papers' in the formal sense we know today.

The following meeting at King's College Hostel, Vincent Square in 1920 saw 12 in attendance out of a total membership of 40, so numbers attending meetings were low in those early years. The President was Rev. Prof. A.R.S. Kennedy of Edinburgh and the Secretary the same T.H. Robinson, who remained Secretary for many years until 1946. Canon G.H. Box joined the committee. There was an attempt to increase the membership which led to a statement of the aims and methods of the Society. Of the 40 members at that time the first 'Sir' was Sir John McClure of Mill Hill, and another woman joined—Mrs H.W. Sheppard of Cambridge. She exhibited a facsimile page and proofs from a forthcoming edition of an important manuscript of the Old Testament dating from 1419 from the library of Trinity College, Cambridge.

The fourth meeting was held in Edinburgh with 10 members present and a guest—Mr Matthews of Coates Hall, where the meeting was held. Thus began a practice of inviting guests, at first from the local area, but later on some wives and some distinguished foreign scholars. By this time there were 49 members and new members included a few clergy plus four non-clerics, namely Mr I. Abrahams of Cambridge, Major W.J. Thomson of Kidderminster, Mr C.G. Montefiore of London and Miss G.M.I. Blackburne of London. At this point it was decided to appoint a Treasurer, Rev. Principal G.P. Gould of Cambridge. The President for 1921 was announced as Rev. Canon R.H. Kennett of Cambridge. The rule was set up that applications for membership be supported by two existing members of the Society, a rule that still holds today. There was an outing at this meeting to the library to see the *Codex Edinburgensis*. It is a good SOTS tradition to have an outing, although the modern trips are not always as academically sound as a visit to a library!

At the London meeting in 1921, Miss M.S. West of London was proposed as a new member plus five others, all 'Reverends'. The death of Rev. Principal W.H. Bennett was announced. By then there were 59 members but still a concern to increase numbers. It is written in the Minutes that 'There is still room for advance in this direction and we should keep before us the possibility of introducing the younger men. We are not working merely for today or for this year; we hope that the full value of this Society will be manifested in later generations in an increased interest and more complete co-ordination of Old Testament studies in this country' (T.H. Robinson, Secretary's Report, Winter 1921). The Society found its way to Cambridge in July 1921 to Cheshunt College. In the absence of the President due to illness, the chair was taken by Rev. Prof. G.H. Box. There were 17 members present and 8 visitors. There were 10 new members proposed taking the total up to 68. Cheshunt College was warmly thanked in the Minutes, 'for this entertainment'.

In 1922 the President was Dr G.B. Gray and at the January meeting 27 members were present, including two women attending a meeting for the first time. It was reported that there were 20 new members since a year previously, one resignation and one death (Rev. Principal G.P. Gould), making a total membership of 77. Clearly attendance at meetings was improving. In the summer SOTS was at Oxford at Keble College and there were 29 present and 2 visitors. Nine new members were proposed, one of them female—Miss E. Hippisley of London. It was decided that the committee would be enlarged and that there would be a rotated retirement from it. There were by then 85 members. The outing was to look at Hebrew manuscripts in the Bodleian Library.

At the London meeting in January 1923, 25 members were in attendance plus 6 visitors, some foreign: Rev. Prof. A. Mangano of New York; Rev. Prof. A.C. Patterson of Pretoria, South Africa; and Rev. Prof. G.H.C. Angus of Serampore, India. There were 9 new members and the total number had reached 93. Throughout these early years it is noticeable that very few papers were read at meetings—normally only three in total, including the Presidential address, just occasionally four. By July 1923 the number of members just exceeded the magic number of 100, at 101. Held at University House, Birmingham, there were 18 present at the meeting and 3 visitors, including one C.G. Naish from Syria. Ten new members were proposed, two of them women.

At King's College London in 1924, 37 were present, five of them women (all Miss) and six new members were proposed. The total stood at 106. One of the SPCK volumes on *Jonah and Ruth* described as being 'in press' was written by one Mrs Coltman who was also doing *Obadiah*, so women were clearly beginning to be involved on the publication side. There is still no sign of them, though, on the committee. In that year a summer school for Old Testament studies was suggested to be held at King's. This was a part of what was felt to be an important wider mission to schools, teachers and interested lay people. The Summer Meeting that year was at Dalton Hall, Manchester, where 25 were present and 2 visitors. Twelve new members were proposed, including two women, bringing the total membership to 118. At this Meeting, the qualifications for membership were discussed: 'The Society found it necessary to define the qualifications for membership, which had hitherto been somewhat vague' (T.H. Robinson, in *Record and Revelation*,[1] p. 500). This is more clearly defined by this statement: 'The Society has a broad basis of membership, the only necessary qualification being evidence of ability to appreciate the Old Testament in Hebrew. Every shade of religious opinion, Jewish and Christian, is represented, and it has been found in practice that all can meet in happy co-operation on the basis of their common interest' (Robinson, p. 501). Although the Society was set up by academics, it is clear that a broader remit to include any persons who are interested in the subject was adopted early on, crossing borders of faith and nationality. The precise membership qualifications were defined as follows in the Minutes:

> In normal cases candidates for membership should possess at least one of the following qualifications:
>
> a) Have published contributions to the study of the Old Testament.
>
> b) Occupy a recognized teaching post, giving instruction in Old Testament subjects.
>
> c) Have obtained a University degree or similar diploma involving study of the Old Testament in Hebrew.

At this meeting there was discussion of the idea of an international gathering of Old Testament students at 'Leyden' (which actually took place in 1927)—a recognition, perhaps, of the need to involve graduate students, an important mission of SOTS today. The trip was to the Museum of Egyptology. A list of members with their addresses was posted in the back of the first Minute Book, the forerunner of today's membership list well before the days of email!

In 1925 at King's College London, the idea was suggested that a foreign scholar might be invited to read a paper to the Society. It was decided that Professor H. Gressmann of Berlin would be invited for the Winter Meeting 1926. This is an important practice in SOTS today, although the guest speakers from abroad usually come to the Summer Meeting. The membership stood at 127 at the Winter Meeting and 134 by the Summer Meeting which was back at Cheshunt College, Cambridge. The idea of a British delegation to Holland to join Old Testament scholars over there was mooted, but such a visit was not held until 1927. A suggested visit

1. T.H. Robinson, 'Appendix: The Society for Old Testament Study', in H. Wheeler Robinson (ed.), *Record and Revelation: Essays on the Old Testament by Members of the Society for Old Testament Study* (Oxford: Clarendon Press, 1938), pp. 499-503.

to Palestine was also indefinitely postponed. There were three papers at this meeting plus an illustrated address from an American, Rev. Prof. E. Grant of Haverford, Pennsylvania. There was a visit to the Cambridge University library to visit the *Codex Bezae* and *Nash papyrus*.

By January 1926 there were 139 members and H. Gressmann, the first German scholar to visit the Society, gave his paper, which included slides of archaeological discoveries in Byblos. The Summer Meeting was in Glasgow at Queen Margaret Hall. The membership stood at 141, but it was noted that some members were seriously in arrears and it was decided to introduce the rule that after three years of not paying membership dues the membership would lapse so that the person would be deemed to have resigned. There was a visit to the University of Glasgow. It was decided at this meeting to hold the 1927 Summer Meeting in September to facilitate the inclusion of 'foreign Old Testament scholars'.

In December 1926 the Winter Meeting (for 1927) was held—it was quite a regular practice to hold it in December rather than January in these early years. There were 147 members at that stage. It was at this meeting that Honorary Membership was instituted for people from the British Empire, a maximum of 12 in the first instance. The Summer Meeting was indeed held in September at Keble College, Oxford, and it had been decided to have more papers, including short ones rather than all long. Papers were also permitted in English, French and German, and abstracts of the papers were sought for the meeting. There was also going to be a report on the proceedings as this was seen as a special meeting. There were a record 80 present (members and guests) and the papers found their way into a volume of *Old Testament Essays*.[2]

By December 1927 (the 1928 Winter Meeting) there were 152 members. The new Honorary Members numbered seven and were listed as: Prof. K. Budde (Marburg); Prof. B.W. Eerdmans (Leyden); Prof. H. Gunkel (Halle); Prof. J. Hempel (Greifswald); Prof. A. Lods (Paris); Prof. J. Powis Smith (Chicago) and Prof. P. Volz (Tübingen).

By the following summer the number 150 had been reached, although at the Summer Meeting in Cardiff there were only 15 members present with Professor T.H. Robinson as President. Some students of G. Henton Davies and A.R. Johnson are recorded as present at this meeting, although it seems that their teachers were not! The death of Very Rev. F.W. Wordsley's son is recorded, a matter that reflects the 'family feel'

2. *Old Testament Essays: Papers Read before the Society for Old Testament Study at its Eighteenth Meeting, Held at Keble College, Oxford, September 27th to 30th, 1927* [by various contributors, and with a Foreword by D.C. Simpson] (London: Charles Griffin & Co., 1927).

of the Society, which, being small, has always been very supportive of its members. Professor K. Budde was welcomed at this meeting as the senior Honorary Member of the Society and three papers were read, including one from Budde. At this meeting also 'The question of the desirability of electing a lady to serve on the committee was discussed' and it was decided to report back on this topic to the next meeting.

In January 1929 in London the number of members was 152. There was a new Honorary Member—Professor A. Causse of Strasbourg. Item 5 in the Minutes of the meeting states the recommendation regarding female presence on the committee: 'that there is no bar to the election of ladies at present, and that it is undesirable that there should be any such bar. On the other hand it is not desirable that anyone, whether lady or gentleman, such be elected save on grounds of general suitability. Moreover the committee is a small working committee, and additions of members for this or that purpose would not be convenient.' The Summer Meeting was held again at Keble and 159 members are recorded. No women emerged on the committee at this point, despite (or perhaps because of) the recommendation.

At the Winter Meeting in 1930 membership stood at 161 and the election of members outside the British Isles was agreed. Five papers were read. By the summer of 1930 that membership number had gone down to 160, probably due to a death or resignation, or maybe arrears because it is recorded that four members were in arrears and thus deemed to have resigned. The meeting was held at High Leigh, Hoddesdon, Herts and 31 were present with five papers read and four new members proposed. A SOTS representative, Prof. J.M. Powis Smith, was sent to the American SBL which was celebrating 50 years.

In 1931 at the Winter Meeting we have the first paper read by a woman, Miss M.A. Murray on 'Recent Excavations in Southern Palestine', described as a Lantern Lecture. By then there were 9 Honorary Members. Membership was down to 154, perhaps because of those arrears. SOTS was at Rankin Hall, Liverpool in the summer and it was decided to send two members, Dr S.A. Cook and Rev. Prof. T.H. Robinson, to represent SOTS at an Orientalists Congress in Leiden. The idea of the *Book List* was instigated at this meeting and in fact first rolled off the press in 1933. There had been lists of recent publications sent out by the Secretary right from the start but this had grown long and unwieldy. It was time for a proper list such as we enjoy today. Membership was down to 151.

In the Winter of 1932 five papers were read, including one from Miss B.K. Rattey on 'The Teaching of the Old Testament in Schools'. She found her way onto the *Book List* committee and served for a number of years. There was still no woman on the main committee. Another Honorary Member was elected—Prof. J. Pedersen of Copenhagen. The downward trend of membership continued, with only 150 members listed. The Bulletin contained a list of members in that year, including 10 Honorary Members. At the Summer Meeting in 1932 at Handsworth College, Birmingham three papers were read and there was a further talk on the Hebrew vowel system by Dr A. Mingan. A visit was made to the Library of the Selly Oak Colleges. It was at this meeting that a Hebrew Bible was obtained to be used as a Presidential Bible. Membership was down to 148, despite 8 new members that year—non-paying resignations seem to have contributed!

In January 1933 in London it is recorded that there were 147 Ordinary Members and 8 Honorary Members, making a total of 155. In July the meeting was held in Manchester and a New Testament 'visitor', C.H. Dodd, gave a paper in the Old Testament field. There was a fresh drafting of the 'rules' of the Society and membership stood at 158. By January 1934 a full list of members appeared in the Bulletin and the greetings of Honorary Members were starting to be recorded. Five papers were read at the Meeting in London. The Summer Meeting was held in Edinburgh and the membership count was 151. The winter of 1935 saw plans for a gathering of international Old Testament scholars in September, with 14 going from Britain in the end, 12 of whom were SOTS members. The Summer Meeting was held again in Cambridge and overall numbers were up to 157.

The Winter Meeting of 1936 was held at Westminster College, London and 2 Honorary Members were elected. The Summer Meeting was held in Ripon, N. Yorks. Numbers were creeping up, being recorded as 164 at the Winter Meeting and 167 by the summer. The 1937 Winter Meeting saw 57 attendees and plans being made for the Society's 21st birthday in 1938. A new volume of essays was planned under the editorship of H.W. Robinson and the main celebration was going to be in the summer of 1938 at Keble College, Oxford. The 1937 Summer Meeting was held in Richmond, Surrey and records 166 members. At the 1938 Winter Meeting the election of 'overseas persons' to membership was confirmed and the number stood at 170. In the Summer of 1938 congratulations were received from other Societies at home and abroad and a number of visitors from abroad attended the meeting. Membership was up slightly at 182.

The Winter of 1939 saw a meeting at King's College London, but war was starting in Europe. The Summer Meeting in Cambridge records a plea for help to Dr (formerly Professor) P. Kahle of Bonn, a Jewish professor who had his job taken from him by the Nazis and was on his way to

Britain. He was made an Honorary Member of SOTS and a fund was set up by members to offer practical help for his family—again, an example of the kindness and family feel of SOTS that continues to this day. Although a meeting was held in 1940 in the winter there was no Summer Meeting that year and subsequently no meetings for the rest of the war years. As before, the Bulletin kept members informed of any news.

The next Minute book starts up in 1946 with the 22nd Winter Meeting being held at Regent's Park College, Oxford with 183 members on file. T.H. Robinson finally retired, having been Secretary of SOTS for 29 years, and was presented with a *Festschrift*, *Studies in Old Testament Prophecy*.[3] Indeed he was also President that year. An international meeting was planned for September. At this point there were 183 Ordinary Members and 10 Honorary Members. A new rule was introduced: those who were being proposed for membership were permitted to attend the meeting at which the membership application was being considered. In the summer of 1946 in Cardiff, eleven papers were read and the membership fee at last went up from 5 shillings a year, to 10. There was the creation of the category of 'Life Members' who were exempt from paying due to long service and retirement. Attending the meeting were a number of visitors from Holland and wives of UK members were more in evidence. 194 members are listed. The Winter Meeting of 1947 was held in Bristol rather than in London and the membership number went over the 200 mark to 202. It crept up again in the summer to 214. No meeting was held in the Winter of 1948, but the Summer Meeting came to Manchester, with 20 Life Members being recorded at that point. The 24th Winter Meeting at King's saw the number of members rise to 222 and in the summer in Bangor that number was up to 230.

The Silver Jubilee of the Society was celebrated at that 25th Summer Meeting with six papers given, one by G. von Rad on 'The Holy War in Israel', which later appeared as a monograph dedicated to the Society. There were a number of foreign guests, visitors and wives of members. At the 1950 Winter Meeting there was a special dinner held for the Jubilee and a new volume edited by H.H. Rowley. 248 members were recorded, 12 Honorary, 227 Ordinary and 9 Associate Members, and this new way of recording numbers according to these three categories was born. Associate Membership was set up, which was effected from 1950. It was basically the same as Ordinary Membership but Associate Members had no vote at meetings. This distinction was eventually abolished in 1995.

3. H.H. Rowley (ed.), *Studies in Old Testament Prophecy: Presented to Professor Theodore H. Robinson by the Society for Old Testament Study on his Sixty-fifth Birthday, August 9th 1946* (Edinburgh: T. & T. Clark, 1950).

An invitation was received from the Dutch to visit Leiden in 1950, thus cementing an ongoing relationship there. The Archbishop of Canterbury congratulated SOTS on its 25 years and said 'The notable thing about the Society was that within it persons of all denominations could completely co-operate in the study of the Old Testament, their arguments being directed in the ascertaining of the truth, every member helping the other in that quest' (*The Times*, 6th January 1950).

b. *An Overview of the Next Decades*

Space does not allow continued meeting-by-meeting analysis, so I will just pick out some highlights. Membership was fairly quickly on the rise after the 25th Anniversary celebrations, reaching 301 (Honorary 15; Ordinary 256; Associate 30) by the winter of 1953. That year saw the first congress of the International Organization for the Study of the Old Testament (IOSOT) in Copenhagen. In the summer of 1954 a Hospitality Secretary appears to work alongside the Secretary and Miss Beryl Smalley (later FBA) of St Hilda's College, Oxford gave a paper on 'Wyclif and the Old Testament'. This is the first time I can see a woman in an academic job listed as giving a paper. It was not until the summer of 1956, though, that a woman actually made it onto the committee—Miss O.J. Lace, who joined the committee from 1957. By 1961 Baroness E.F. de Ward, the woman who was to become the first female President of SOTS, was on the committee. Another woman joined in 1967—Dr Catherine Alder (note Dr rather than Miss or Mrs). By 1963 there were 393 members and by the time of the Jubilee in 1967 there were 406. As part of those celebrations 60 went on the postponed tour to Jerusalem in September 1966, 35 members with wives and other guests. The numbers rose quite sharply over the next decade or so, with 450 reached in 1970 (Honorary 18; Ordinary 343; Associate 89). By 1973 a list of members was produced, the first for some years, and the membership stood at 461, with 15 Honorary Members included in that number. In 1975 a distinguished Associate Member was His Imperial Highness Professor Prince Takohita Mileasa of Japan and in the following year Baroness de Ward became the first woman President. Membership numbers stayed at around 450 during the 1970s. In 1983 the Minutes record 9 new Ordinary Members and 5 new Associate Members, but do not record the total—but it did include 17 Honorary Members. By 1992, the 75th Anniversary of the Society, when *A Short History of SOTS* was written by Prof. John Rogerson, he records 474 members: 345 Ordinary, 111 Associate, and 18 Honorary. Members come from all kinds of background by this stage—university, church, teaching, freelance—and from sundry religious, and non-religious, backgrounds.

A separate Membership Secretary was appointed in 1998 and this was Dr (now Prof.) Heather McKay of Edgehill University. She set up a database and was able to keep a detailed note of categories of members, their locations, their gender profile and the state of their subscriptions. In July 2004 there were 446 members, of whom 18 were Honorary Members, 134 Life Members (of whom around 50 regularly supported the Society with donations), and 294 Ordinary Members. The distinction between Associate Members and Ordinary Members had been abolished in 1995, as a result of a membership survey, but the category of Life Members seems now to be recorded. Another change introduced as a result of the 1994 questionnaire was that graduate students could be recommended for membership. The location of members in 2004 was as follows:

England 246
Scotland 32
Wales 19
Northern Ireland 4
Republic of Ireland 11
Mainland Europe 40
Israel 8
USA 43
Canada 10
Australia 14
New Zealand 3
Other overseas 16

The gender ratio was 81% male and 19% female (which was recorded as an 'all-time high'). The Membership Report added information about numbers of new members annually which averaged (over 8 years previously) at around 13 per year.

A decade later, in July 2004, the then Membership Secretary, Mrs Vivienne Rowett, reported 513 members (compared to 503 in December 2013), 18 of whom were Honorary Members, 157 Life Members, and 338 Ordinary Members. The male/female ratio was 70%/30% (and by 2015 it was 69.23%/30.77%). The location of members was recorded in a broader way as:

UK 330 (64.3%)
Europe 66 (12.9%) (including Eire & Norway)
North America 73 (14.2%)
Rest of the world 44. (8.6%)

These proportions had remained relatively stable for a while, and they continue to be so at the time of writing.

2. *The Membership Questionnaire of 2015*

In 2015 a membership questionnaire was sent out (electronically and on paper) by Dr Katharine Dell (with the assistance of the Society's Information Officer, Dr Jonathan Stökl) to attempt to gain a picture of the membership and of wider issues to do with the Society, present and future. This had been done before in 1994 (by Prof. D.J.A. Clines with others). The results of the questionnaire are reproduced below with some comment and comparison with 1994. In 1994 the questions were similar, and this 2015 version was based upon it, but the electronic form in which it was sent out (Survey Monkey) did not allow more than 20 questions and so there was some inevitable variation (and updating).

a. *Personal*

The first question asked the rather delicate question of age, but formulated by decade. This chart compares with 1994 and perhaps the most interesting finding here is that we are quite clearly, like the rest of society, an ageing Society.

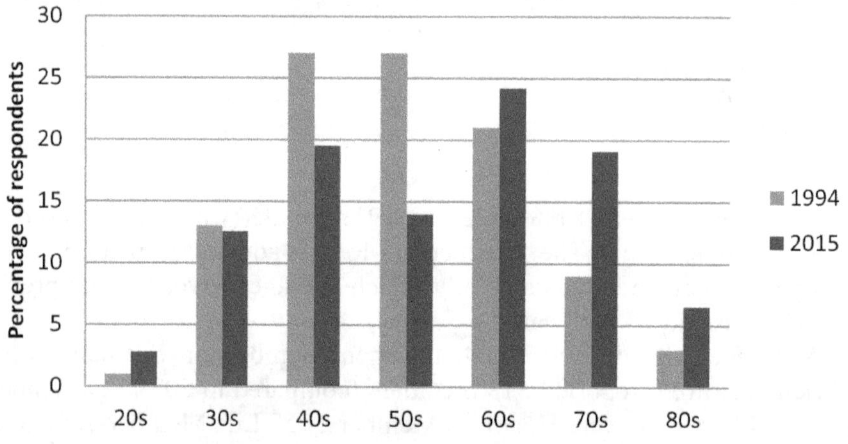

Chart 1. *Age Profile*

The second question was 'What is your gender?' Compared with 1994, there is a much greater female presence in the Society (now at 30%), although there is still room for a more equal gender balance.

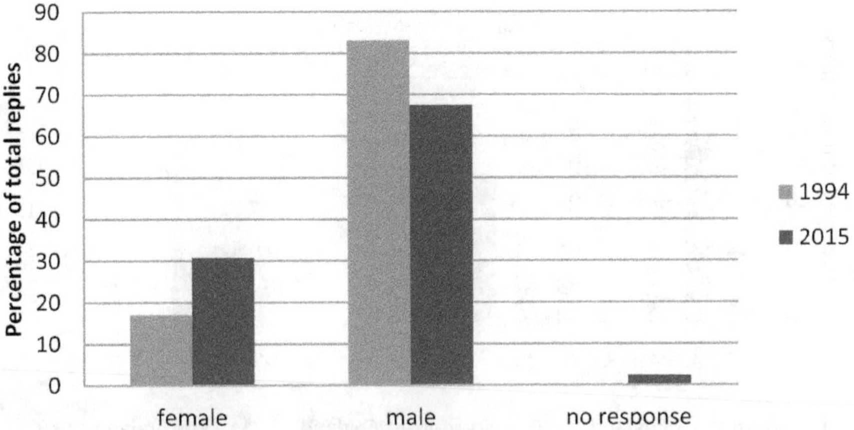

Chart 2. *Gender*

Question 3 asked 'How long have you been a member of SOTS?' This too shows our longevity and is of course partly reflective of the answers to Question 1 about age.

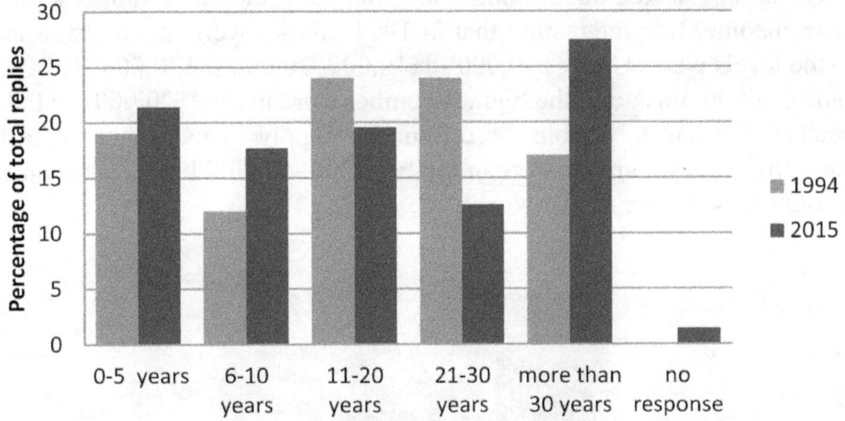

Chart 3. *Length of Membership*

The fourth question asked people where they live, to get an idea of geographical distribution of members. South-East England seems to have had the most dramatic increase in popularity at the expense of the Midlands and North-East England.

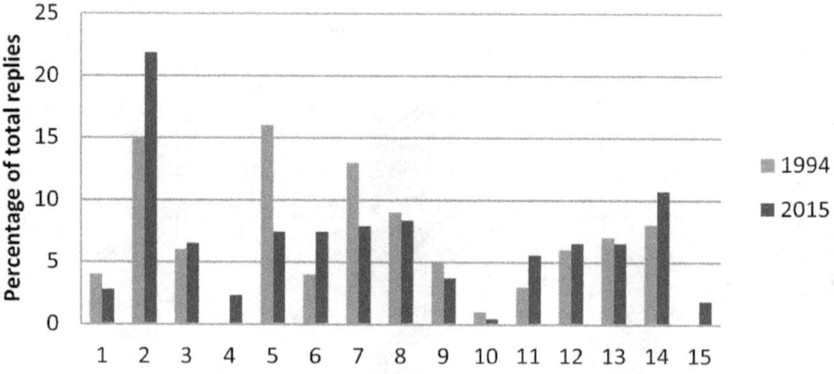

1	South-West England	6	North-West England	11	Eire/Ireland
2	South-East England	7	North-East England	12	Europe
3	London area	8	Scotland	13	USA
4	East Anglia	9	Wales	14	Other Overseas
5	Midlands	10	Northern Ireland	15	No response

Chart 4. *Geographical Distribution of Membership*

Question 5 asked about annual income. Here the chart simply shows 2015 income. It is interesting that in 1994 salaries were much lower and so the levels were 'Under £10,000', '£10,000–20,000', '£20,000–30,000', and '£30,000 plus', and the highest number were in the '£20,000–30,000' bracket. We had to double these figures to apply to today but interestingly the highest number were in the '£20,000–40,000' bracket, not up as substantially as one might expect.

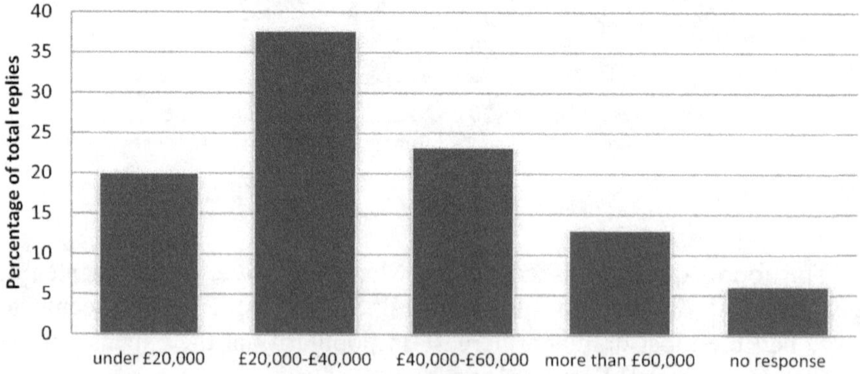

Chart 5. *Annual Income (2015)*

b. *Professional*

The first question in this category was 'To what extent is your present post (or, if you are retired, your most recent post) an Old Testament/Hebrew Bible one?' Here we can compare with 1994 and we see that the number of full-time Old Testament jobs has risen and that the number of part-time jobs has reduced, but not substantially.

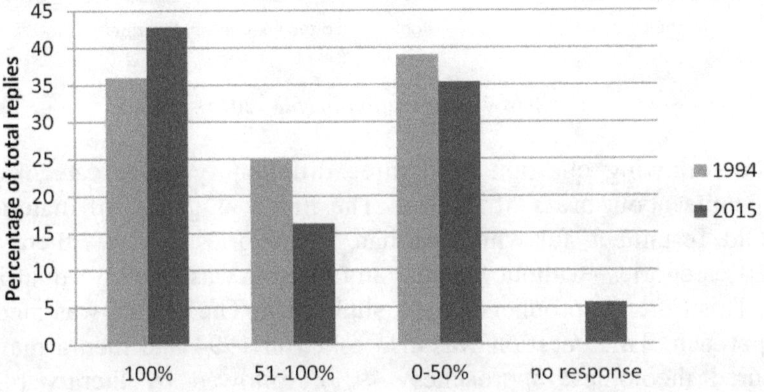

Chart 6. *Old Testament Content of Present Post*

The second question asked people the related question of whether, when they retire from or leave their post, they would expect it to be filled. In 2015, 55% said yes and 27% said no, although 19% did not reply to this question. In 1994, the figures were 86% yes and 14% no. This is quite a dramatic change and perhaps reflects the present academic climate in Universities and in regard to the shrinkage of Theology and Religious Studies generally both in this country and abroad.

The next question asked 'Have you ever published on an Old Testament/Hebrew Bible or related topic?' Very few answered no in 2015 and it is clear that this is what most of us are engaged in at various levels. In 1994 articles were slightly more in the lead at 83% for an article and 66% for a book (formulated as two separate questions in that survey). In the 'other' category here, book reviews were mentioned, as were encyclopaedia entries and editions of maps of biblical times, bible reading notes and booklets, newspaper articles and online articles, dictionaries and learning modules. The commentary genre was also separately mentioned as were monographs and *Festschriften*, but those were understood by the question asked to be included under 'books'.

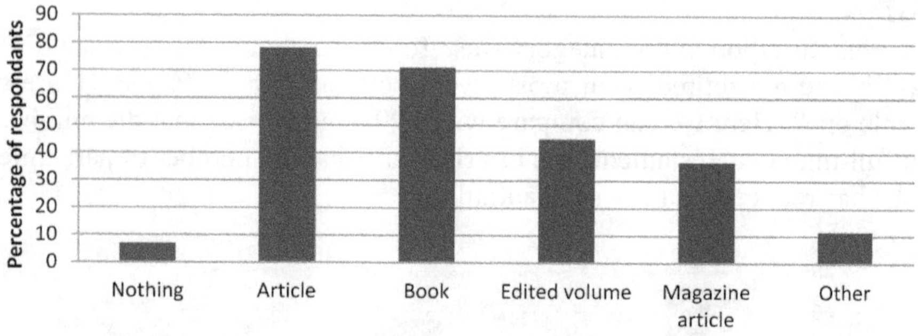

Chart 7. *Publication Profile (2015)*

The following question used three different types of categories to ask people about areas of interest. The first was genres of material in the Old Testament, for which we had 5 categories. In 1994 there were only 4 categories (without Psalms) and interest was roughly equal in all four. This time the prophets have a slight lead. The second was methods of approach. This question was also asked in 1994 and then a majority favoured theological approaches (49%), followed by literary (42%), historical (37%) and linguistic (33%). This time, in 2015, 'literary' is in the lead with 'theological' in second place. The third category, a new one for 2015, is placed under the rough heading of 'historical' interests. A strong interest in reception history is reflective of trends within the subject.

There was an option in this question to include other interests, and answers included: ancient versions; anthropology of religion; apocalyptic texts and apocalypses; apocrypha and pseudepigrapha; archaeo-astronomy and ancient mathematics; bible and ecology; canon; critical methods; ethics; feminist readings and studies; hermeneutics; identity studies; imagery and symbol; intertestamental books; Josephus; law; material culture; monotheism; narrative criticism; Peshitta; postmodern approaches; rabbinics; relationship of the Testaments; Second Temple Judaism; Septuagint; social justice; social-scientific studies; textual criticism; and Ugaritic and Ugaritology.

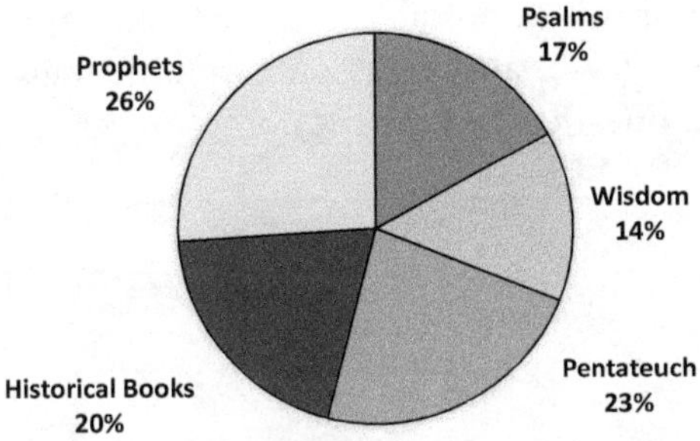

Chart 8. *Old Testament Genres*

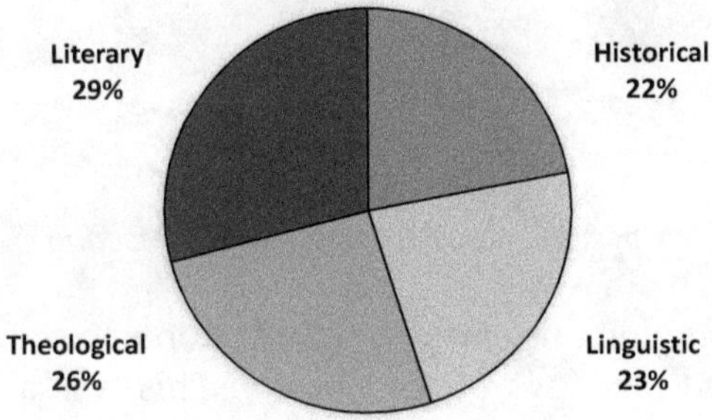

Chart 9. *Method*

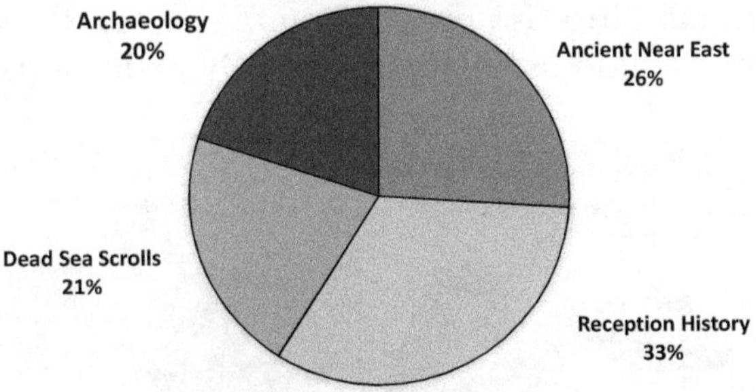

Chart 10. *History*

c. *Society Meetings*

The question 'When did you last attend a SOTS meeting?' was asked both in 1994 and 2015 and so a comparative chart is helpful. Answers remain similar, although perhaps there is a slight trend now for attending less frequently. We did not ask the question this year whether members would prefer one meeting or two (a possible change to one meeting per year was opposed by 68% in 1994), although some commentated on this point in answering the final question (see below).

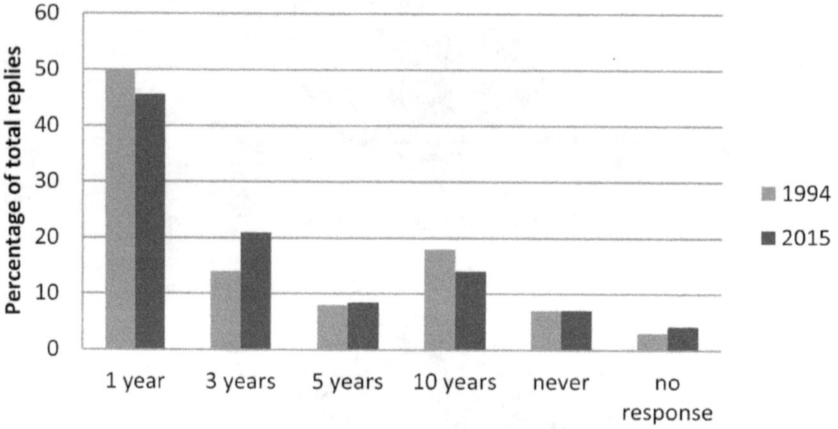

Chart 11. *Last Attended a SOTS Meeting*

The second question in this category asked people to state the purpose for which they attend meetings of the Society. This was asked in 1994 but with six categories rather than five which made comparison difficult, so the chart here just shows the 2015 answers. Then 'catching up with what is going on in Old Testament studies' got the highest vote, a category not used this time as it was felt to overlap with the others. Clearly collegiality is at the top of our 2015 list, but it is comforting that the sharing of our research is important to us, although strangely giving a paper oneself is less so!

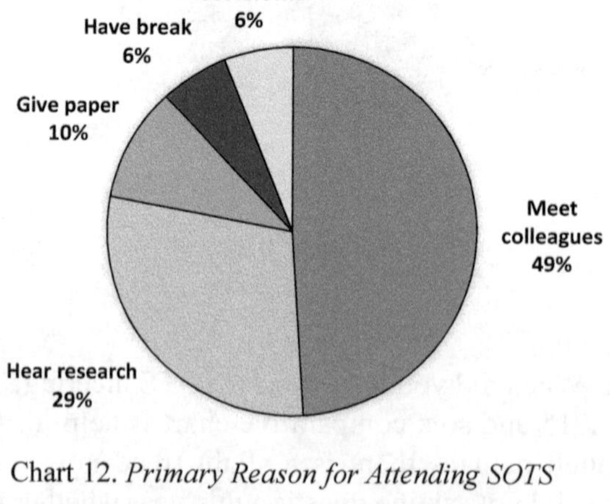

Chart 12. *Primary Reason for Attending SOTS*

The next question asked people to select options that they would like to see more of in the programmes of future meetings. In 1994 this made up a number of shorter questions so comparison is difficult. However, at that time the idea of surveys appealed to 54%; thematic meetings appealed to 69%; and 81% thought that concurrent sessions were a good idea, something that has fallen from favour in the 2015 survey. In the 'Other' category many were satisfied with the way meetings are now, but some interesting suggestions were also made. Some called for more top scholars; some for better quality papers; some for discussion of 'big questions'; and others for a wider range of papers so as to reflect members' interests. Panel discussions on topics and more discussions and debates got some support. More cross-disciplinary and experimental papers were suggested, including on art, music and culture. Some thought that sessions giving an update on research in the field might be helpful—maybe regular overviews of where the discipline is going. Something relating to teaching and course design would help some, and reflection on the profession appealed to others. A possible avenue for some was more emphasis on relating to the modern world theologically.

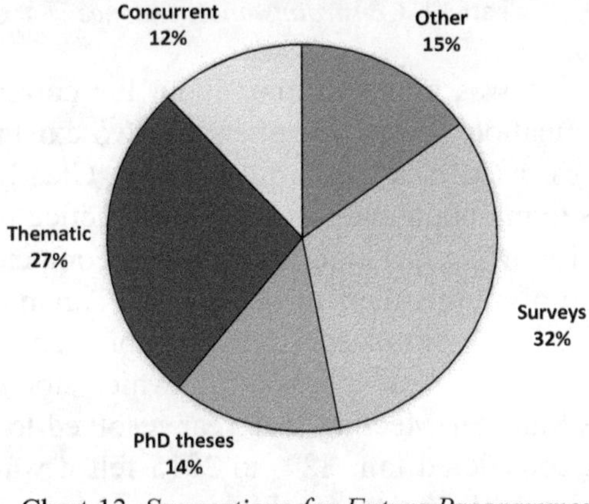

Chart 13. *Suggestions for Future Programmes*

A question followed asking about constraints on attendance. This was also asked in 1994 but with slightly fewer categories. In the 'Other' category some felt that age or health problems were a hindrance to attendance, others all kinds of family demands from grandparenthood to looking after children in the school holidays or ill relatives. Some felt that the programme for a particular meeting hadn't always appealed to them—some papers are too specific for some, while not chiming in with their own research for others. Some said that the opportunity to present a paper would provide a further incentive for buying a plane ticket, whilst others commented on the cost of travel at New Year. Some were constrained by distance, others by the demands of attendance at other conferences. Sometimes the Winter Meeting clashed with term time and the summer with other conferences. It is clear that it is difficult to satisfy everyone!

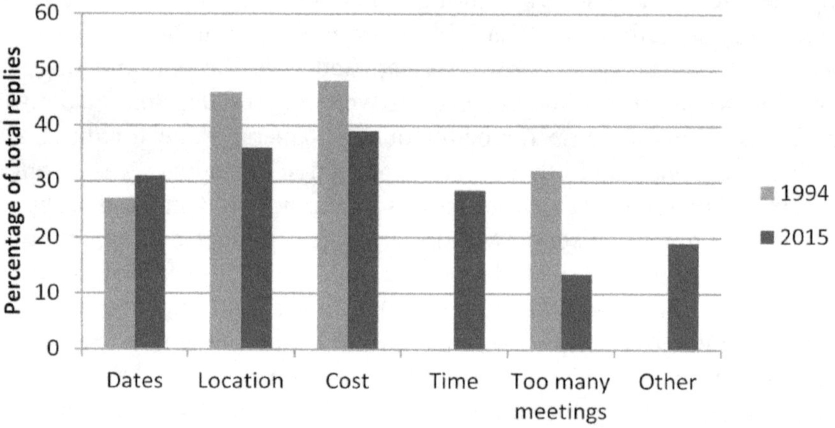

Chart 14. *Constraints on Attendance*

The next question was a simple one, about the current procedure of proposal and nomination of new members by two existing members. A large 85% said yes in 2015, as 92% did in 1994. Clearly this is a good system for SOTS to maintain and has been our practice from early times (see above). The following question was whether competence in Hebrew should be required of all members of the Society. Again 81% said yes in 2015, as 85% did in 1994. This seems uncontentious. The final question in this section asked about the subscription rate which stood at £24 in early 2015 (though the Summer Meeting that year resolved to raise it to £30) and whether it is considered fair. 82% in 2015 felt it was about right (a survey result not available in time for the Summer Meeting!), and in 1994 82% of members thought the then rate of £18 was about right too.

d. *Society Policy*

The first question in the policy section asked 'Do you think the Society should stay an essentially professional society of those employed to teach and research the Old Testament/Hebrew Bible?' In 2015, 83% answered yes, as did 82% in 1994. In the 'Other' section in 2015, some rightly felt that 'Employed' was a misnomer since the Society exists for those with academic interests in the subject area whatever their employment. Independent and freelance scholars are an essential component of the Society, as are those in Church and Synagogue, as others pointed out.

Graduate students looking for employment are also an essential component nowadays. It was also mentioned that having a post specifically in Old Testament/Hebrew Bible is a luxury these days and that many lectureships are in related fields such as history or cultural studies. The second question asked was, 'Do you think the Society should be essentially a research-oriented society?' In 2015, 78% said yes, whilst in 1994 only 55% answered yes. Perhaps more emphasis on research as a result of the Research Excellence Framework and other government policies has led to this change in perspective. The next question asked whether the Society should devote more energy and income to promoting Old Testament/Hebrew Bible studies (in addition to holding meetings for members). 52.5% said yes to this in 2015, as compared to 82% in 1994. This may suggest that we are already doing this quite successfully nowadays. In the 'Other' category on this question suggestions for self-promotion of the Society ranged from laying on day conferences for schoolchildren, particularly targeted at A-level Religious Studies; more outreach to promote biblical studies in schools; more outreach to undergraduates studying theology in universities; more engagement with the church; more TV documentaries, maybe even one about the Society; more ventures such as the SOTS Wiki and 'resources' on the webpage, and maintenance and enhancement of our, already strong, publishing programme.

The final question asked for any comments people might have about the Society in the past or in the present and any views about planning its future. This was an open question and I can only represent a few views here—quite a few answers overlapped with questions already asked about the format of meetings and so on. Comments were made about the vulnerability of the subject in the modern world, and suggestions made for more openness to cross-disciplinary research and widening participation in the light of the shrinkage of the field. More openness to religious communities who use the Old Testament/Hebrew Bible was mentioned, including to Muslims. An effort to raise funds to enable scholars from developing countries to take part was suggested. Some, however, felt that too much breadth would lose the Society its identity and that it should consolidate as it is now. Many commented on the friendliness, collegiality and supportiveness of the Society, although some suggested that new members, especially those not in the mainstream 'profession', sometimes felt daunted by the group. An attempt to reach younger members through the website and electronic media was suggested. The question of how many meetings a year was raised, some suggesting that this issue be revisited by the Society. Whilst some expressed a preference for just one meeting, there was no consensus as to which one this should be. Quite a few said, though, that attending two meetings a year was not viable for them. Some expressed a preference for more parallel sessions, others for the advantage of all being at every session, thus promoting collegiality and learning about topics one would otherwise not have discovered. There was a call for papers being less 'read' and more 'delivered' and a call for 'humility' in the spirit of 'genuine collegial research'. Someone wrote, 'I value just knowing I belong to it'; and another, 'Keep up the excellent work!'—both very good reasons for the existence of a Society like this one.

In conclusion, this survey of the membership has illustrated the way in which the membership of SOTS has changed, diversified and grown over the years, reflecting changes in the subject and in society at large. It has remained a professional Society, collegial and friendly, small and accessible, and yet with a good sense of tradition, of fairness and of fun. The Society exists to promote the quest for real and in-depth understanding of that elusive set of texts that is the Old Testament/Hebrew Bible and of an ever-widening diversity of related fields; and it is its members who have a genuine sense of privilege that they have been drawn to studying these ancient texts and interacting with others who feel the same way.

The Way of the Future? Into Our Second Century

Paul M. Joyce

As the Society reaches its 100th birthday, it is timely to attempt to look ahead and consider the direction in which the Society and the study of the Old Testament may be moving. I begin by reflecting briefly on some features of the Society's past and present.

In January 1993 Richard Coggins delivered his Presidential Address under the title 'The Society in the Remainder of the Century'. The address, characteristically thoughtful and witty, was concerned to identify some of the issues that would confront the subject of Old Testament study in general and the Society in particular in the time up to its centenary in 2017. Six such issues were identified and discussed. These were, in brief, the importance of the SOTS *Book List* as a means of maintaining awareness of developments in the field; the tension between perceptions of the Hebrew Bible as 'word of God' in some authoritative sense, and as a collection of ancient material eminently worthy of study but not to be privileged above other texts; the decline in the number of students of Hebrew; the structure of the Society's programmes; the Society's name; and the likely implications of the continued rise of literary studies as a conversation partner for biblical studies. Several of these issues will be considered in the course of this reflection.[1]

Elsewhere in this volume, Ronald Clements has characterized the Society from its beginnings in terms of its 'broad basis, freedom from confessional restrictions and aloofness from religious prejudice' and also of its being 'exploratory, outward-looking and inclusive'.[2] Fine aspirations,

1. I had the privilege of serving as the Society's Home Secretary during the presidential year of Richard Coggins. I am grateful to him for sending me a copy of his Presidential Address while I was preparing this chapter.

2. See above, p. 23.

but as the Society begins its second century we should ask self-critically how well we have lived up to them. 'Freedom from confessional restrictions and aloofness from religious prejudice': as we shall see, there is reason to believe there are considerable challenges here still. But in our time, it is the phrase 'exploratory, outward-looking and inclusive' that arguably presents even more extensive challenges and forces us to address the extent to which we measure up in terms of today's wide-ranging diversity and inclusion agenda. A range of potential issues arise, including questions of gender and sexuality; Judaism and the Society; religion and the secular; Ireland, the rest of Europe, and the wider world. I propose to reflect on these before then suggesting the main direction in which I see our discipline developing.

1. *Diversity and Inclusion*

a. *Gender and Sexuality*

There has arguably been some progress in relation to gender in the life of the Society, albeit painfully slow. We have had just three women Presidents so far: Eileen de Ward (1975), Margaret Barker (1998), and Cheryl Exum (2010). David Clines, again in the present volume, notes that the growth in numbers of female paper readers has been remarkable.[3] When he suggests (at the end of his chapter) that 'Only in two areas that I can readily identify has SOTS moved on in the last 20 years, intellectually speaking', one of these areas he identifies as 'Feminism (in 6 papers) and gender issues (masculinity in 4 papers)'.[4] One stage in this development was a morning at the Edinburgh Summer Meeting of 1994, when in a rare exception to the SOTS norm that paper sessions are all plenary papers, the Society experimented with parallel programmes of short papers, one strand of which dealt with 'Feminist Criticism' (the other strands being 'Theology of Creation' and 'General Topics'). Of course, the fact that papers were scheduled concurrently with two others at any one time did mean that selection between sessions was possible, and moreover I note that all of the speakers in the Feminist Criticism section were women. Nonetheless, that morning arguably represented a significant step. Moreover, at the same Summer Meeting Athalya Brenner addressed the whole Society on the question 'Who's Afraid of Feminist Criticism?' It should be added too that some men have been among those who have pressed gender issues, among them David Clines, Hugh Pyper and John Goldingay.

3. See above, p. 103.
4. See above, p. 113.

Feminist criticism of the Bible has been with us a very long time, of course, at least as far back as Elizabeth Cady Stanton's *Women's Bible* of 1895.[5] But the story of our adjustment to this revolution has barely begun. Like many others in our field, I was impacted by feminist criticism from the 1970s on, including through the personal influence of Phyllis Trible, who later joined us for the Summer Meeting in Aberdeen in 1990. My first brief published engagement with related issues appeared in that same year.[6] But it is one thing to be influenced intellectually and also indeed to attempt to modify one's behaviour, both individually and institutionally; beyond this the challenges are substantial and run deep, as they do in relation to a number of other issues of diversity. Gender-related questions (in my case, connected with my mother) play a central part in my own deepest personal issues, as acknowledged in my contribution to the Barton *Festschrift* in 2013.[7] And this is the root also of my interest in applying psychological insights to study of the Bible. It is to be hoped that as well as feminist criticism the theme of masculinity (in all its complexity) will receive further attention. I shall be returning to the matter of the personal and the emotional in relation to biblical studies later.

Mention of the name of Phyllis Trible, of course, invites acknowledgment of the vast range of feminist criticism, a more radical dimension of which has been modelled by one of our past Presidents, Cheryl Exum, to whom also I am myself indebted. Exum highlighted not only gender issues but also issues of sexual orientation in the Presidential Address for 2010, which challenged viewers' assumptions about roles and identities in artistic presentations of the book of Ruth. There is much scope in the largely unaddressed area of biblical studies and sexual orientation (or indeed other aspects of the LGBTQ+ agenda, including gender identification and transgender issues), which does not seem to have registered much yet on the Society's programme, Jo Merrygold's presentation in January 2016 being another rare exception.

5. Elizabeth Cady Stanton, *The Woman's Bible* (Edinburgh: Polygon, 1985), originally published in 2 vols., New York: European Publishing Company, 1895–98.

6. P.M. Joyce, 'Feminist Exegesis of the Old Testament: Some Critical Reflections', in J.M. Soskice (ed.), *After Eve: Women, Theology and the Christian Tradition* (London: Collins/Marshall Pickering, 1990), pp. 1-9.

7. P.M. Joyce, 'David Dancing: A Psychological Reading of 2 Samuel 6', in K.J. Dell and P.M. Joyce (eds.), *Biblical Interpretation and Method: Essays in Honour of John Barton* (Oxford: Oxford University Press, 2013), pp. 272-84.

b. *Judaism and the Society*

Another issue of inclusion relates to the place of Jewish members in the Society. Again the picture is a very mixed one. The first Jewish President of the Society was Claude Montefiore in 1930. He was followed by Herbert Loewe in 1939—it is interesting to note that SOTS was led by a Jewish President as the Second World War started. Jacob Weingreen was President in 1961, followed by Edward Ullendorff in 1971 and Raphael Loewe in 1981. Other distinguished Jewish members have included Geza Vermes, Bernard Jackson, Martin Goodman and now Hindy Najman.

The British Association for Jewish Studies (BAJS) was founded in 1975. Geza Vermes, its first President, writes in his memoir that he was inspired by attendance at a meeting of the Association for Jewish Studies in the United States to set up a similar organization in the UK.[8] But in another sense the context of the emergence of the British Association was SOTS. The two societies have continued to relate positively, for example the Summer Meeting in Oxford 2011 included a day's Joint Meeting with BAJS.

There are problematic issues, however. Coggins in 1993 raised forcefully among his key issues the name of the Society: 'The Society's name: at a time when the Christian assumptions underlying the title "Old Testament" are increasingly being scrutinized, is the present name of the Society satisfactory?'[9] When David Clines was President in 1996 there was a thoroughgoing review of many aspects of the Society (including a survey of members), in which the name of the Society was thoroughly explored but left as it stands. It is important not to generalise, but I know that this is an issue that still grates for some members, both Jewish and Gentile. The term 'Old Testament' is of course an entirely proper one within Christian theology; whether it is appropriate for a Society in the public domain is more debatable. That it remains in place is perhaps largely a matter of pragmatism and the recognition of the widely held popular usage.

Arguably more important than the name are issues raised by a distinguished Jewish member, Stefan Reif, in an important paper in 1999 entitled 'Jews, Hebraists and "Old Testament" Studies'. Among other

8. G. Vermes, *Providential Accidents: An Autobiography* (London: SCM Press, 1998), p. 185.

9. I commonly use the term 'Hebrew Bible' in other settings, but in the context of this contribution to the centennial volume I have referred to 'Old Testament' throughout.

questions, Reif asked to what extent it may be argued that there are still to be found in the field approaches to the subject that leave Jews feeling uneasy about full participation. Although he discerned some encouraging signs of more pluralist and ecumenical trends, he traced the continuation of earlier negative attitudes into our own times and pointed out that numerous statements can reveal a high degree of tendenz rather than a commitment to critical analysis: 'Some scholars were presenting what was in effect Christian theology in the guise of critical study, or what amounted to political bias as if it were historical analysis'. Reif concludes: 'It remains to be seen which of these philosophies, the truly liberal or the tendentious, will ultimately triumph in the context of Old Testament studies in the United Kingdom in the new millennium'.[10] Ironically the trend for biblical studies to reengage with the situation of the reader (in general, in my view, a positive development, of which more later) has arguably moved us away from the detached academic mode that could readily accommodate closer collaboration between Christian and Jewish colleagues, or indeed between other groups.

c. *Religion and the Secular*

There are other questions about the Society and religion. Richard Coggins in his Presidential Address of 1993 raised as his second issue: 'The tension, already present and likely to increase, between perceptions of the Hebrew Bible as "word of God" in some authoritative sense, and as a collection of ancient material eminently worthy of study but not to be privileged above other texts'. Coggins continued: 'This tension becomes more acute with the development on the one hand of literary studies of the material with no special religious concerns and on the other of great interest in the Bible in "third world" countries'. It is a matter for celebration that the Society has managed to continue to have both members who are religious (of whatever tradition) and also members who are decidedly secular in their orientation. This is not to say that there have never been tensions on this kind of issue, as anyone present at the Summer Meeting of 1994 may recall, when questions relating to the debate over the historicity of ancient Israel, and divisions between maximalist and minimalist approaches (often connected one way or another with religious attitudes, overtly or

10. Stefan C. Reif, 'Jews, Hebraists and "Old Testament" Studies', in A.G. Hunter and P.R. Davies (eds.), *Sense and Sensitivity: Essays on Reading the Bible in Memory of Robert Carroll* (JSOTSup, 348; Sheffield: Sheffield Academic Press, 2002), pp. 224-45.

implicitly), led to a raising of temperatures that has rarely been seen at a SOTS meeting![11]

There has been a long tradition in the Society of Christian parish clergy attending. Indeed Richard Coggins himself first heard of SOTS when he was a curate over 60 years ago. Such members as Mel Gray and Paul Winchester continue this tradition today. For much of its life the Society featured 'Prayers' in its published programmes. By this was meant in practice Christian prayers, of course. This has been far from uncontroversial. Indeed at one time in the 1990s, it seems to me, there was a danger of the Society fragmenting over issues around its relation to religion. We are indebted to the diplomacy and political nous of a number of colleagues, not least John Rogerson, that the Society managed to navigate some tricky waters and has remained as inclusive an academy as it has. The programme for January 1994 was the last to include prayers; the next programme included on the back the words 'Any individuals or groups seeking assistance in making arrangements for special events or gatherings during the course of the Meeting (e.g. for prayers, editorial meetings, book displays) may contact the Home Secretary'.

d. *Ireland, the Rest of Europe, and the Wider World*

It may surprise some that I should list Ireland in a sequence of issues of inclusion. When the Society met for the first time in 1917 it was just nine months after the Easter Rising, and well before the establishment of an independent Irish Republic. The Society was and remains the guild of Old Testament scholarship of these islands as a whole. But the extent to which we adequately acknowledge this has sometimes disappointed me, as one whose heart is Irish, if not (yet) his passport. Before one of our Dublin Summer Meetings, I recall a senior member saying that we were going to foreign territory! Among Irish Presidents have been Jacob Weingreen, Andrew Mayes and John Bartlett. Other distinguished Irish members have included Kevin Cathcart and Martin McNamara, the latter doing much to foreground the Irish Biblical Apocrypha. And happily we currently have a Secretary based in Dublin, in David Shepherd.[12]

11. Some published reflections of debates around that time include Philip R. Davies, 'Method and Madness: Some Remarks on Doing History with the Bible', *JBL* 114 (1995), pp. 683-705; and Iain Provan, 'Ideologies, Literary and Critical: Reflections on Recent Writing on the History of Israel', *JBL* 114 (1995), pp. 585-606.

12. In addition to important Irish contributions to critical scholarship, both more traditional styles of work and new approaches, I cannot mention Ireland and the Bible without reference to another mode of biblical interpretation at which the Irish

Even before this past year heightened awareness and sensitivity to matters of European identity (with the UK referendum on EU membership of 2016), I have regretted sometimes hearing reviews of SOTS membership statistics that refer to 'Europe' as other, rather than speaking of 'the rest of Europe'! The Society, of course, values highly its many members from other parts of Europe. Many SOTS members are active also in the European Association of Biblical Studies. But obviously there is a whole world beyond Europe. The historical-critical paradigm with which many of us have largely worked was shaped and developed in Europe, reflecting many of the assumptions of this context including its modernism, its positivism and its evolutionary ideas. Indeed, it would not be unreasonable to describe it as a eurocentric approach. Challenges have come from a number of quarters, including Latin American liberationist reading (for example, Jorge Pixley), African perspectives (for example, Madipoane Masenya), and the bringing to biblical studies of the experience of the indigenous peoples of Australia and America (for example, by Mark Brett and Daniel Smith-Christopher). More generally, there is hopefully increased sensitivity to issues of race, postcolonialism, and orientalism. David Clines notes in his contribution to the present volume, speaking of presenters at the Society's meetings, that 'it is noteworthy how many papers have been given by overseas speakers, 22.3%, in fact, or rather more than 1 in 5'.[13] The current refugee crisis in Europe (part of a global phenomenon, of course) might inspire fresh reflections on the contexts out of which the biblical narratives were generated. Casey Strine and others are doing valuable work in this area; of related importance is the sociological analysis of Ezra–Nehemiah by Katherine Southwood.

SOTS has been closely associated in various ways with the International Organization for the Study of the Old Testament (IOSOT), which was established in 1950 as part of reconstruction after the Second World War. It could fairly be said that IOSOT has tended to be markedly eurocentric, both in terms of geography and of methodologies. However, after a first meeting outside Europe in Jerusalem in 1986, it met in Stellenbosch, South Africa, in 2016, and moreover its programming has by degrees become increasingly diverse. Another international body with which many SOTS

excel in our time, namely the Bible in song. I have in mind above all Van Morrison and U2. Here too we have a range, from the theological—even at times evangelistic—in the music of U2 through to the more ambiguous literary allusiveness of Van Morrison.

13. See above, p. 99.

members are involved is the US-based Society of Biblical Literature. We happily seem to have moved beyond some older tensions here: at one time some SOTS colleagues would claim that diary clashes with SBL meetings were a matter of indifference to SOTS members. As we celebrate our Centenary as a society, we should perhaps remember that the SBL was established as early as 1880! In fact the SBL has exercised some influence on SOTS over the years, not only in the steady spread of newer methodologies but also in matters of style. With regard to the way that Presidents are referred to, for example, throughout the twentieth century this was of the 'Revd Professor H.H. Rowley' style, and concomitantly members' name-badges at meetings, when used, generally displayed titles and initials of participants. As of the coordinated gathering with the SBL International Meeting in Cambridge in 2003, however, members' badges have displayed names without titles and moreover since 2004 the SOTS Bulletin has listed Presidents in the same way, both customs adopted from SBL usage in modification of SOTS's former 'formality'. I should say that my own experience of the Society, from the late 1970s on, has always been one of welcome—I think of Norman Whybray dispensing wine to young strangers at the dinner table and of outings at which senior scholars would share wisdom and bibliography with the most junior of aspiring scholars. And then there is the SOTS bar, an important focus of conviviality and networking—the Officers of the Society are aware that organising a bar can sometimes seem as important as arranging the academic programme! The President for 1966, Henton Davies, wrote to me in 1992 (though not thinking of the bar, I suspect): 'Koinonia was always a great feature of SOTS'. But how genuinely inclusive SOTS is may be a different matter—in fact I know personally, as readers perhaps will also, a number of friends who have not discovered a congenial home within SOTS. The Society is at its best when it is functioning as an inclusive community of scholars. The current SOTS Wiki project (envisioned as a centennial contribution) is an excellent example of this, and one that will hopefully bring the advances of modern scholarship to a much wider audience than has been possible in previous generations. It relies on a far greater degree of collaboration, and less concern for individual credit, than biblical scholarship has typically done thus far, and moreover the project may well lead naturally into fruitful discussions of connections between our scholarship and the interests of the wider world.

There are other important questions of diversity and inclusion not addressed here, of course. Disability is an issue that has impacted biblical studies over recent years through the work of Saul Olyan, Jeremy Schipper and others.[14] But this has barely impinged upon the Society's programming, as yet. I think of Hugh Pyper's touching on related questions in his paper in celebration of the 2012 Olympic Games and of a discussion of the exclusion of disabled priests in Deborah Rooke's paper on a feminist reading of the priestly requirements of Leviticus in 2015.

It is time to attempt to look ahead and consider the direction in which the Society and the study of the Old Testament may be moving. In doing so I make a conscious connection with the foregoing discussion of diversity and inclusion. For in one sense or another I see the healthy future of the Society as depending on its increasingly global perspective and on its growing awareness of our shared humanity as scholars and as readers. Important here too is a readiness to bring to the study of the Bible what we have learned in modernity about the nature of the human being, as well as highlighting those aspects of the biblical tradition that focus on related questions. A model here is John Rogerson's Presidential Address of 1989, in which he asked with the psalmist of Ps. 8.5 and with Habermas, 'What does it mean to be human?'[15]

2. *Humanity and the Future of the Society*

A memorable evening thirty years ago highlights the wide gap that can seem to yawn between the Society and the wider experience of humanity. Picture the scene. A golden July evening in Manchester in 1986. At the old Maine Road stadium the rock band Queen comes on stage, at the height of their pomp, to a roar of appreciation from a crowd of tens of thousands of fans, gathered in the open air. Half a mile away, at one of the halls of residence of Manchester University, a mere one hundred SOTS members have gathered to listen to the distinguished German scholar Otto Kaiser read a paper on the second book of Samuel. The sounds of Queen reverberate across the city, and at least a few of the biblical scholars wish they could be at Maine Road. But as Freddie Mercury launches into 'I Want

14. Saul M. Olyan, *Disability in the Hebrew Bible: Interpreting Mental and Physical Differences* (Cambridge: Cambridge University Press, 2008); Jeremy Schipper, *Disability Studies and the Hebrew Bible: Figuring Mephibosheth in the David Story* (LHBOTS, 441; New York: T&T Clark, 2006).

15. John W. Rogerson, 'What Does it Mean to be Human? The Central Question of Old Testament Theology?', in D.J.A. Clines, S.E. Fowl and S.E. Porter (eds.), *The Bible in Three Dimensions: Essays in Celebration of Forty Years of Biblical Studies in the University of Sheffield* (JSOTSup, 87; Sheffield: JSOT Press), pp. 285-98. Cf. John W. Rogerson, *A Theology of the Old Testament: Cultural Memory, Communication and Being Human* (London: SPCK, 2009).

to Break Free', one of the scholars firmly closes the last open window on the music, leaving the windowpanes to rattle to the rhythm of 'We Are the Champions'. As Professor Kaiser comes to discuss the incident of King David dancing before the Ark of the Lord, he has the presence of mind to add '—as well he might dance this evening!' But the overwhelming sense that this episode conveys is of two worlds, with little in common, those who read and study the Bible being a tiny ghetto-like minority separated from the great bulk of humanity and out of touch with the lives and interests of most of their contemporaries.[16]

In a letter to me in 2003 Otto Kaiser recalled this 'humoristic event', as he called it, and commented also on 'the serious problem of the public decline of interest in the Bible in the western world'. He added, 'I have only to remember the days of my former predecessor Karl Budde, who usually every year wrote at least one booklet on an Old Testament subject which became published by our local press and must have found the interest not only of the theologians as professors and priests but also of the educated public'. 'In the present', he continues, 'every biblical scholar has learned that even his best books become absolutely ignored outside a small group of specialists. If we would write on far eastern religion or the Islamic world we could be certain that even the big newspapers would take notice and at least a lot of educated people would read it. Now we are', he concluded, 'in a similar situation as the late Platonists in the fourth and fifth century'. This is a sobering challenge to the relevance of our work—though I rather think that today colleagues including Yvonne Sherwood, Hugh Pyper and Katie Edwards might take issue with Kaiser's pessimistic diagnosis, suggesting that, if we have eyes to see it, the broader public is just as open to being interested as ever they were and that the Bible's cultural impact is pervasive, albeit in often surprising ways.

A major shift in Old Testament studies in the last half-century has been the move to emphasise the role of the reader, in his or her cultural context. It seems to me that this development, and its relationship to the historical focus of much of our work, is the central issue relating to the identity of Old Testament studies in our time—and an indication of its future.

The thoroughgoing recognition of the cultural and ideological location of the reader or interpreter owes much to the seminal work of Hans-Georg Gadamer.[17] Within our own field David Clines has done much to press

16. Cf. Paul M. Joyce, 'Reading the Bible in the Public Domain', in F.M. Young (ed.), *Dare We Speak of God in Public? The Cadbury Lectures for 1994* (London: Mowbray, 1995), pp. 67-79.

17. Hans-Georg Gadamer, *Truth and Method* (London: Bloomsbury Academic, 2014), originally published as *Wahrheit und Methode* (Tübingen: Mohr, 1960).

what he has called 'readerly questions'.[18] Another influence is the liberationist insistence that one has to be poor and marginalised to have any hope of understanding scripture. And there are pre-modern antecedents that have been recovered too: Augustine was emphatic that, once technical skills have been acquired, the scriptural text can only then be understood aright if the reader has the right disposition. These and other very diverse factors have played a part in shaping a profound shift in perspective.

Most of those active in historical criticism of the Bible were brought up on an objectifying paradigm within which the detachment of the reader and the definition of the text as 'other', historically located, were emphasized. And this approach bore rich fruit, contributing massively to our understanding of the Bible over the past several centuries. But as readers we are also subjects, real human beings. Taking this seriously can pose quite a challenge to many of us within the historical-critical guild. Each of us in fact experiences a text in his or her own way. As readers we bring much to the task of interpretation, though paradoxically, the more we can understand about who it is that is doing the reading, the freer we shall be in relation to our own biases.

I have been much influenced by the insights of psychology and psychoanalysis (albeit as an amateur committed to interdisciplinary work) and I am persuaded that there is much here that can enrich our understanding both of the biblical text and of the reading experience. There has been much work over recent times exploring the differences between personality types, much of it springing from Jung's personality typing. Examples include the Myers–Briggs Personality Test and the Enneagram. Among the polar distinctions made between personality traits on the Myers–Briggs Personality Test is that between 'perceivers' and 'judgers'. 'Perceivers' tend to be those who are always aware of possibilities and issues and are typically inclined to negotiate towards truth consensually. 'Judgers' prefer clear-cut distinctions and clarity in discrimination. The historical-critical tradition of biblical studies, in all its strength, has been shaped, I suggest, largely by 'judgers' or at least by the 'judging' instinct. However, it seems to me that biblical studies has been sadly impoverished by a failure to engage with the 'perceiving' side of human nature. There is much to be gained by correcting this deficiency, so that more exploratory and heuristic modes of reading can contribute more. In this we have much to learn from the rabbinic approach to interpretation as an exchange between multiple different perspectives, often left unresolved but valued precisely for the further conversation it will generate. A related issue is the

18. David J.A. Clines, *What Does Eve Do to Help? and Other Readerly Questions to the Old Testament* (JSOTSup, 94; Sheffield: JSOT Press, 1990).

Kethiv–Qere distinction, which deliberately preserves multivalence in the text, as if to encourage further reflection.[19]

My own primary orientation is to be a 'perceiver' and it was a real breakthrough for me when I first realized that this was one reason why a certain amount of the historical-critical approach, and especially its tendency in some cases to attempt to nail down a univocal meaning even within a poetic text, seemed alien to me. However, we can all develop additional aspects of our personality and I have learned to adopt a more 'judging' mode in interpretation, albeit aware that I am often modifying my deepest instincts when functioning in this way. The personality differences between us as interpreters are instructive and can be illustrated briefly by an encounter between two distinguished former presidents of the Society, Wilfred Lambert and David Clines. The encounter went something like this. Professor Lambert had been instructing the Society on a fine point of Mesopotamian usage, and declared, 'You can't be too careful!' Professor Clines retorted characteristically, 'Oh yes you can!' Well, which are you? A David or a Wilfred, a Lambert or a Clines?[20]

I am fully committed to both poles in the reading of the Old Testament, that is to say the more historical and the more readerly, and I am sure that the Society will remain so committed.[21] I believe in the need for patient teasing out of textual and historical probabilities through close work and public conversation. At the same time I remain agnostic about how much we can know for sure about many matters, and also very positive about the value of heuristic modes of exploring reading possibilities, whose legitimacy does not depend upon historical verification. We need both partners in the conversation, the historical and the readerly. Without a proper acknowledgement of the place of both, we are in danger of drifting into either irrelevant antiquarianism or self-absorbed fantasy.[22] That said, I feel that as a Society we have some catching up to do on the readerly side and my hope is this will happen over the years ahead.

19. Conversation seems to me to be such a fruitful notion in this area. It is, of course, an everyday concept, but it is also one theorized by David Tracy and others; for example, David Tracy, *Plurality and Ambiguity: Hermeneutics, Religion, Hope* (London: SCM Press, 1988).

20. Cf. Paul M. Joyce, 'The Prophets and Psychological Interpretation', in J. Day (ed.), *Prophecy and Prophets in Ancient Israel: Proceedings of the Oxford Old Testament Seminar* (LHBOTS, 531; New York/London: T&T Clark International, 2010), pp. 133-48.

21. Cf. Paul M. Joyce, 'King's College London, Samuel Davidson, and the Scope of Biblical Studies', *JTS* 65 (2014), pp. 407-24.

22. On the latter, see Terry Eagleton, *The Illusions of Postmodernism* (Oxford: Blackwell, 1996).

3. *Taking the Humanity of the Reader More Seriously*

By way of illustration, I now present three examples of taking the humanity of the reader more seriously, each of them rather different.

a. *The Anger of God*

I am currently working on a commentary on Amos,[23] and so I am having much cause to think further about the language used about divine judgment in the prophetic books. I am trying to do this through reflection on the nature of religious language and also in the light of what we are learning from the human sciences about anger and reaction to it.

Religious language typically projects human experience onto the transcendent; I do not myself assume that this must have reductionist implications. More specifically, much discourse about the divine employs anthropomorphism, whether constructing the deity as person, parent or simply existent being. Turning to Amos, for the audience addressed by the prophet, troubling events (whether an earthquake or the looming shadow of imperial conquest) demand explanation, which is essential if some structure of meaning is to be sustained. The projection of anger onto the transcendent, in this case onto the national deity, is a strategy that can provide an explanation more satisfactory than the victory of other gods or indeed the advent of meaningless chaos.[24]

Initially this is irrational, unexplained anger, such as a child all too often experiences from a parent or teacher (the proverbial clip behind the ear from out of nowhere, without apparent cause). 'God is bloody angry', the prophet is effectively saying. In an important sense, feelings are just there (whether they are our own or those of another)—they simply have to be acknowledged, rather than explained, excused or judged. Anger is a primal emotion, one that precedes any interpretation. By projecting anger onto the deity, current or impending disaster is related to a framework of meaning, albeit in a way that is disturbing and scary, indeed irrational.[25] A second stage comes when Israel, through its prophets, begins interpreting

23. For the Illuminations series (Eerdmans).

24. Alongside anthropomorphic language, Amos also employs zoomorphic, especially leonine, imagery with reference to the deity. On this, see Aulikki Nahkola, 'Amos Animalizing: Lion, Bear and Snake in Amos 5.19', in A.C. Hagedorn and A. Mein (eds.), *Aspects of Amos: Exegesis and Interpretation* (LHBOTS, 536; New York/London: T&T Clark International, 2011), pp. 83-104.

25. Some of the implications of modelling the deity as an irrationally angry, indeed abusive parent may well call for ethical critique, which will often be informed also by the insights of feminist criticism.

the anger that its powerful deity seems to feel. This is a more rational exercise that typically attempts to connect the apparent anger of the deity with the improper behaviour of Israelites. And it is this that leads on to the articulation of notions of justice and punishment, retribution, and theodicy. The perceived divine anger may now be related to putative causes of that anger, whether social injustice, cultic abuse, or other sins. Traditional notions of right and wrong behaviour may be drawn upon, as may guilt feelings looking for a justification.

It is interesting to consider how the more we learn about the ambiguity and complexity of human emotions, the richer may be the picture we can paint of what is going on in religious language. To some extent that is happening when one separates the primal experience of projected divine anger from the secondary stage of theological interpretation in terms of justice and retribution. Anthropomorphism may be an inevitable feature of such biblical discourse, but the more we learn about the human being, the more we may hope to understand about the rich complexity of that which may be projected onto the deity.

b. *The Biblical Metaphors of Remembering and Forgetting*

More briefly, a second case involves language of remembering as religious following and forgetting as apostasy. These are common metaphors in the Old Testament; for example, 'Remember that you were a slave in Egypt, and diligently observe these statutes' (Deut. 16.12) and 'They forgot God, their saviour, who had done great things in Egypt' (Ps. 106.21). However, in our own time, much has been learned about the physiology of memory and memory loss, and dementia and Alzheimer's Disease have become sadly familiar features of many family groups. Today we realise that remembering is not altogether a function under our control; we may unwittingly and passively be robbed of our memory. And so the capacity of 'forgetting' to function as a metaphor for sin may be qualified or undermined. That is, unless one chooses to pursue it precisely as a model of the complexity of human moral response. Could perhaps inability to remember become a metaphor for the limitations on the freedom of the human will? This could be expressed in more secular terms or in more theological terms—in the language of social or psychological determinism, or in that of biblical and traditional theological notions such as grace and predestination. Not quite a dead metaphor, then, but one into which new life could perhaps be breathed.

c. *Reception: The Solidarity of Human Beings in Extremis*

I mentioned earlier that at the end of his chapter in this volume David Clines highlights two areas in which he could readily identify that SOTS has moved on in the last 20 years, intellectually speaking. The second of these was the study of the reception of the Bible (on which he counted 30 papers).[26] This is an area in which one can discover shared common ground between human beings separated by time and space. In the work that Diana Lipton and I did together on Lamentations,[27] we discovered a striking example of the solidarity between human beings in situations of extremity. The theme of hunger is prominent in Lamentations. Mothers are so hungry that they cook and eat their own children: 'The hands of compassionate women have boiled their own children' (Lam. 4.10; cf. 2.20). The Yiddish poet Abraham Sutzkever wrote more than eighty poems while fighting for survival during the Shoah. In one of these poems, 'To My Child', written in the Vilna ghetto in 1943, Sutzkever writes in the voice of a man who did not merit even the appalling fate of eating his infant son. Perhaps it was of his own dead son that Sutzkever wrote:

> Because of hunger
> or because of great love…
> I wanted to swallow you, child,
> when I felt your tiny body
> cool in my hands
> like a glass
> of warm tea…
> Maybe you will blossom again
> in my veins.
> I'm not worthy of you, though.
> I can't be your grave.[28]

26. See above, p. 113.

27. P.M. Joyce and D. Lipton, *Lamentations through the Centuries* (Blackwell Bible Commentary; Oxford: Blackwell, 2013), pp. 158-60.

28. A. Sutzkever, 'To My Child' (trans. C.K. Williams), as published in D.G. Roskies (ed.), *The Literature of Destruction: Jewish Responses to Catastrophe* (Philadelphia, PA: Jewish Publication Society, 1989), pp. 494-95, and reproduced here by permission of the copyright holder, University of Nebraska Press. For an extensive analysis of the poem, see D.G. Roskies, *Against the Apocalypse: Responses to Catastrophe in Modern Jewish Culture* (Cambridge, MA: Harvard University Press, 1984), pp. 231-37. The original Yiddish poem, 'Zum Kind', was published in A. Sutzkever, *Poetishe Verk* (Tel Aviv: Yoyvl-komitet, 1963), vol. 1, pp. 278-79.

Although the poem does not refer explicitly to the book of Lamentations, it seems likely that Sutzkever recalled its cannibal mothers when he spoke as a father who wanted to swallow his own baby. Intentionally or not, this extraordinary poem suggests a powerful and moving reinterpretation of the Bible. Typically commentators have interpreted Lam. 4.10 to mean that women who should be compassionate are not, or alternatively that women who had been compassionate no longer are. However, if we bring together the Lamentations text and the Sutzkever poem, two products of human beings in extremis, how can we condemn as uncompassionate those Judahite mothers, when confronted by the complex and ambiguous emotions of the compassionate father?

I contend, then, that the healthy future of the Society depends on its increasingly global perspective and on its growing awareness of our shared humanity as scholars and as readers. This will involve us in a range of ways of taking the humanity of the reader more seriously, in his or her cultural context, individually and socially, and also learning from what the human sciences, critically received, might teach us about the nature of the human being. It seems to me that such a development will do much to heal the impoverishment of too much of our work and to complement the important historical-critical dimension of our shared task.

As Abraham fathered a child of promise at the grand old age of a hundred (Gen. 21.5), so perhaps we may hope that after one hundred years of journeying there is much for the Society to look forward to!

STOS

Summer Meeting 2016, at Hulme Hall, University of Manchester.
The Presidents for 2016 (Adrian Curtis) and 2017 (Paul Joyce) are both in the front row, sixth from the right and sixth from the left respectively.

Participants in the above 'Snapshot of SOTS at 99'

(1) David Clark, (2) David Ray, (3) John Day, (4) Karen Kai-Wen Yuan, (5) Rosalie Ní Mhaoldomhnaigh, (6) Paul Joyce, (7) Katharine Dell, (8) Adrian Curtis, (9) David Clines, (10) John Jarick, (11) Ann Jeffers, (12) Alun Thomas, (13) Hedy Hung, (14) Phyllis Brown, (15) Paul Winchester, (16) John Healey, (17) John Bartlett, (18) Joseph Blenkinsopp, (19) Vivienne Rowett, (20) Fleur Houston, (21) James Aitken, (22) Hindy Najman, (23) Stuart Weeks, (24) Alison Gray, (25) Rebecca Watson, (26) Julie Woods, (27) Sandra Jacobs, (28) Janet Tollington, (29) Michael Thompson, (30) Gwen Knight, (31) Cynthia Crewe, (32) John Tudno Williams, (33) Siobhán Dowling Long, (34) Cheryl Exum, (35) Zanne Domoney-Lyttle, (36) Achitha John, (37) Kengo Akiyama, (38) Jennifer Andruska, (39) Cat Quine, (40) Suzanna Millar, (41) Eliza Allen, (42) Katherine Southwood, (43) Irene Jones, (44) Andy Lie, (45) Julianne Burnett, (46) Michele Freyhauf, (47) David Shepherd, (48) Bernard Jackson, (49) William Tooman, (50) Anselm Hagedorn, (51) Casey Strine, (52) Katie Woolstenhulme, (53) Meg Warner, (54) Seth Cole, (55) Holly Thompson, (56) Elaine Reid, (57) Trevor Pomeroy, (58) Walter Houston, (59) Nicolas Wyatt, (60) James Patrick, (61) Hugh Pyper, (62) George Nicol, (63) John Wilks, (64) Margaret Barker, (65) Dwight Swanson, (66) John Sawyer, (67) Alec Gilmore, (68) Penelope Barter, (69) Jessica Keady, (70) Jenni Williams, (71) Karalina Matskevich, (72) Cynthia Chapman, (73) Nancy Nam Hoon Tan, (74) Miriam Cantwell, (75) Philip Jenson, (76) Susan Gillingham, (77) Nathan French, (78) Matthew Lynch, (79) Alastair Hunter, (80) Pekka Pitkänen, (81) Suee Yan Yu, (82) Mervyn Richardson, (83) Alan Millard, (84) Philip Alexander, (85) George Brooke, (86) Martin O'Kane, (87) Nathan MacDonald, (88) Hugh Williamson, (89) James Mulroney, (90) Brian Howell, (91) Matthew Collins, (92) Rosanne Liebermann, (93) Danny Crowther, (94) Gordon McConville, (95) Miriam Hinksman, (96) Janet Fyffe, (97) Lester Grabbe, (98) Kathy White, (99) Heather McKay, (100) Lindsey Askin, (101) Hans Barstad, (102) Hallvard Hagelia, (103) Nathan Eddy, (104) Jonathan Stökl, (105) Carly Crouch.

Index of Names